Contents

KU-493-423

The Film Series

1 Anglo-Saxon attitudes
Multi-cultural teaching in 'all white' areas: among
infants in Cumbria, in primary schools in Leicestershire,
at a comprehensive in Buckinghamshire.

2 A primary response
Ways of getting to know pupils and building on their home
cultural backgrounds in class, filmed in four racially mixed
London primary schools.

3 Your community school
How Tindal Primary School in Birmingham has developed
its contacts with parents and the local community.

4 Languages for life
The case for mother-tongue teaching at primary
and secondary levels.

5 School report
The results of a three-year teachers' working party on
multi-cultural education at Birley High School in Manchester.

6 Teacher, examine thyself!
Bradford teachers review their personal attitudes in the
first 'racism awareness' workshop set up by an LEA.

7 Does school hurt?
Young people of Moroccan, Greek Cypriot, and Asian
cultural backgrounds reflect on their experience of schooling
in London, with observations from a West Indian exchange teacher.

8 Education versus prejudice
Teaching about racial prejudice to fourth and fifth formers
at comprehensives, particularly in 'all white' areas.

These films, each 25 minutes long, are available in many Teachers'
Centres or for hire as video cassettes from Concord Films, see page
211; for group discussion notes see page 11.

A film summary of the above series

Anglo-Saxon attitudes

A 50-minute compilation film of extracts from the series was made
and shown by the BBC in 1982/3; it is available for viewing or
borrowing at most Teachers' Centres. Ask for the *50-minute* version
of *Anglo-Saxon Attitudes* which is a completely different film from
the first in the series above. It is specifically designed as a visual aid
to stimulate discussion in staff rooms, INSET or Initial Training
Courses about the need, within Multi-Cultural Education, for
combating racism in school. Suggestions for effective use of this
film are given on page 166.

4

1 In search of multi-cultural education

Who is the book for?

This is a handbook for teachers who are professionally interested in what their colleagues in other schools are thinking and doing. It is not a book of academic educational theory, nor is it a book whose teaching suggestions all require a great deal of preparatory work for teachers, or the sort of extra resources which it would be unrealistic to hope for in a period of education cut-backs.

The aim is not to tell teachers what to think about multi-cultural education, but to introduce some aspects worth thinking about. The accounts of multi-cultural teaching practice are given less as models to be followed in detail than as suggestive examples to inspire teachers' own ideas and to inform staff room discussions.

In 1980/81, as a producer in the Continuing Education Department BBC TV, I was asked to see if we could make a series of films which would stimulate the interest of teachers who have not previously considered whether they should be bringing a multi-cultural approach to their work, and which would offer ideas to help those who remain uncertain about what a multi-cultural approach means, and how it might be adopted. Almost all teachers' groups advised that what they wanted was less a prescriptive than a descriptive approach – not to add to the discussions of philosophy of multi-cultural education already available, but rather to show through a selection of case studies what multi-cultural education is being taken to mean in terms of actual school practices (seen, as necessary, 'warts and all').

Given that all practice requires a rationale, and given that multi-cultural education is as much a matter of teachers' personal attitudes and of approaches both across the curriculum and within the 'hidden' curriculum as a matter of demonstrable classroom techniques, this was no easy task. Still, the list of films in which we made this approach our starting point appears on page 4; the primary job of this book is to support and extend that series of case studies. There are one or two innovative sections, like 'From school to work' (on careers teaching) and Bhikhu Parekh's thought-provoking ideas on 'sympathetic imagination and multi-cultural education' which do not appear in the films, but otherwise, we follow the film series' general shape and sequence of ideas. Thus the book acts as a forum through which teachers from very different schools, in different parts of the country, share thoughts and teaching suggestions based on their experience of trying to put multi-cultural approaches into practice. From simple beginnings, it is arranged to build cumulatively to a fuller picture of the main aspects and rationale of multi-cultural education.

Although of course certain headings will appear more immediately relevant to their work than others, we hope that teachers – whether at primary or secondary schools and whether or not they teach children from ethnic minority groups – will peruse all the sections, since each sheds light on the others, and the whole adds up to a great deal more than the parts.

What is it about?

To all the contributors, multi-cultural education implies at the very least an attitude that welcomes – indeed celebrates – the cultural, linguistic, and ethnic diversity which exists in British society. In some ways it is only appropriate, therefore, that instead of the conventional linear format, the sections of this book are compiled from reports from a range of sources, from different standpoints and written in a variety of styles. In this respect, the book reflects the wide assortment of ideas, experiences and teaching practices that we found in 1980 when as a project team we set out in search of multi-cultural education through a long series of visits to academic experts, inspectors, advisory teachers, parents' groups and pupils, as well as to teachers in their own schools.

We soon discovered that it would not be possible to offer a tidy and comprehensive overview of multi-cultural education – rather, the films and the book offer glimpses into some of the more interesting ideas and suggestions we came across. Needless to say, the fact that we do not begin by systematically reviewing the arguments about how the term 'multi-cultural education' should be defined does not mean that, in our view, formulating a precise definition is unimportant. It is just that most of its different aspects will emerge clearly enough on reading through the sections; and we were often told that there is a lot to be said for encouraging teachers to decide its possible detailed meanings for themselves in staffroom discussion.

At the same time, I should say that we are well aware that there are different schools of thought in this field. Some teachers assume that 'multi-cultural education' refers only to what needs to be done to meet special needs – especially in language support – that many bi-lingual children have in learning English as a second language. Some amplify this to include ways of getting to know ethnic minority pupils as individuals in terms of their different family and community cultures, both as a basis for supporting their sense of self-esteem and identity, and as a basis for bringing such cultures into what is taught in the classroom. Others take a wider view again, seeing multi-cultural education as something for *all* children in all schools, laying emphasis on ways of revising the curriculum in all subjects to reflect a global perspective broader than traditional Eurocentric assumptions. According to this view, it is the bulk of 'white' British children who are the most educationally deprived, in an increasingly interdependent world, by the mono-cultural and parochial confines of many schools' curricula and the conventionally Anglocentric approach to their subject taken by many teachers. Still others put the emphasis in multi-cultural education on the contribution of schools to good race relations – how teachers can help directly to prepare the next generation to live together in a successfully multi-racial society. Much more is implied by this view than taking an 'anthropological' (and arguably patronising) interest in the cultural background of ethnic minority children, or even than giving an international dimension to subject teaching. The vital first step is for teachers themselves to appreciate that racism is not just a matter of overt colour prejudice and discriminatory attitudes that they don't personally share. The need is for teachers first, to deepen their understanding of the facts of racial disadvantage in our society; second, to acknowledge and identify the unwitting racist attitudes still embedded in our language and culture; and third, to check out ways in which the school itself may embody forms of institutionalised racism.

The book takes no single line on these differences of emphasis. There is material derived from them all, and in reading the sections it should become easier to see how these different perceptions of multi-cultural education are all closely inter-related. Most of the teachers speaking through this book see multi-cultural education as an all-embracing concept, including the celebration of cultural diversity, anti-racist teaching, and a concern about ensuring equal opportunities for children of all ethnic groups. They also see a particular place in a multi-cultural curriculum for world development studies. In no sense do these ideas imply less concern for the acquisition of basic skills and the achievement of academic standards. They would emphasise that a multi-cultural curriculum requires as much rigour as the traditional curriculum.

Who is it about?
One danger from this eclectic approach is that it may not always be clear, in using the generalised term 'ethnic minority children,' exactly who is being referred to. The term is too commonly used simply as a euphemism for 'Black' British children, particularly those whose parents came to Britain from Asia and the Caribbean during the last

twenty-five years. In the particular context of teaching about *racism*, and the causes and effects of racial disadvantage in Britain, that meaning may be apt enough; and in sections 10 and 15, and parts of the section 'From school to work', it may be understood in this way.

In the more general context of education in and for a *multi-cultural* society however, it is inadequate, and a wider meaning is assumed in this book and the associated training films. We take it to include all minority groups whose backgrounds have roots in cultures which originated from abroad – including, for example, all parts of Europe and Africa, as well as Asia and the West Indies or, indeed, from Britain's own Celtic fringes. In this wider meaning it is vital to recognise the differences between the Asian and West Indian cultural backgrounds, and indeed between different Asian countries and regions, and between different West Indian islands. These differences must not be overlooked just because of the common experience of colour discrimination within British society.

It is worth remarking that in referring to 'cultural backgrounds', the contributors are not thinking in terms of frozen stereotypes; they feel it is important to reflect not only the historical traditions and customs, but the modern changing realities of minority communities – the children from which are British, having been born in this country. No less important are the dynamic and evolving forms of such cultural values as minority children experience them in interaction with their peers.

I make these perhaps obvious points to ensure that the recurrent use of the term 'ethnic minority pupils' is understood according to the context, and to ensure that the common euphemistic meaning does not distract attention from the over-arching perspective of this book: that the English language and heritage make up 'just another culture' which is itself enriched by mutual respect and dialogue with the other cultural backgrounds our society includes – be they Welsh, Irish, French-Canadian, Bengali, Greek Cypriot, Caribbean, East European Jewish, Estonian or Black American. It may be worth underlining that all the contributors take it as a matter of course that such 'cultural pluralism' needs recognition equally as much in those schools which do not have children of minority backgrounds as in those which do.

We recognise that some teachers write off the attention being given to multi-cultural education as a temporary fad or trendy fashion. We know, too, that others dismiss concern about minority pupils as a marginal matter, hardly worth worrying about compared with what they see as obvious and widespread forms of disadvantage in our school system – perhaps connected with illiteracy and innumeracy; or the urban/rural divide; or inadequate resources; or sex discrimination; or disadvantages based on some teachers' attitudes to 'working class' children in school. Certainly, these often overlapping problems are very real. Certainly too, there are middle class teachers who have come face to face with questions about how to respond to working class children in school and who will rightly see this book seeking to open up and inform discussion on the analogous question: how can schools better respond to the needs of ethnic minority pupils, to ensure that along with all other children their abilities are fully developed, and that they are equipped to compete for jobs on a basis of equal opportunity? But one of the key messages of this book is that anyone looking, in effect, for forms of compensatory education for ethnic minority pupils, will in fact find a huge range of interesting and innovative educational practices from which *all* children, of whatever class or ethnic origin, can benefit.

Thus there can be no doubt that the arrival of West Indian and Asian and South European workers and their families in the 1950s and 60s did much more for British society than meet the needs of labour-hungry industries and the transport and hospital services. It occasioned the present movement towards multi-cultural education, so making a great contribution to a potentially richer education for all. More than anything else, this book documents how particular concerns with ethnic minority pupils have led to ideas relevant to pupils and teachers in any school; and how multi-cultural education is less a matter of *helping* a minority of pupils, than of *sharing* ideas, information and experiences among all pupils.

How can it help?
So in what ways should this book be helpful to the teacher who has not made any specialist study of the what, why and how of multi-cultural education, but whose interest has been sparked by the films? The aim of the following sections is not only *to offer insights into why* a multi-cultural approach is being more and more widely adopted in schools, but also *to share some practical ideas on how* it can be done, within the area of a teacher's own discretion at school. Teachers of course do not operate in a vacuum; their work takes place within a school structure and policy, and often relies for success on the co-operation of colleagues. So the book can also be regarded as *a compendium of arguments and examples* of what is done in other schools, to be used by teachers seeking to stimulate change in their own school, perhaps through contributing to staffroom meetings or discussions, or more informally, in talking with colleagues and heads of departments.

Just to expand this last point: we have found that within the national picture of a patchy and piecemeal process of change towards multi-cultural practice, the initiative to such change within any particular school will depend on many factors – the Local Education Authority's policy and its political will to implement it; the influence of inspectors and multi-cultural advisers; the content of initial teacher-training and in-service courses; the attitude and leadership of opinion by the head teacher; perhaps the influence of parents' groups, or pressure from a union branch. In some extreme cases, change has come about as a response to crisis – where the obvious alienation of pupils has forced a reconsideration of both staff attitudes and the relevance of the curriculum.

However, in many schools we found that significant changes have resulted from internal staff initiatives. An example is where teachers bring questions of whole-school policy formally onto the staffroom agenda: such policies might concern language across the curriculum, more openness towards parents, or a formally stated position on racism. Usually, these are starting points for exploring the other aspects of multi-cultural education. Other examples are shown in the films, where teachers, feeling the inadequacy of their teacher training in equipping them to take a multi-cultural approach, have not waited for a training course to be offered, but have set about filling the gap for themselves. The film 'School Report' shows the results of an internal teachers' working party on multi-cultural education at Birley High School, Manchester. (Their report, *Multi-cultural education in the 1980's*, a revealing and useful document for all schools, is available from Birley High School, Chichester Road, Manchester, MI5 5FU.) In an interview for the film, one of the Birley teachers advised:

To get multi-cultural change, the first thing to do is to nobble the head. But if you can't do that, then get on and do it for yourselves, because it's so urgent. Get some information, make contact with the National Association for Multi-Racial Education (NAME), or the Commission for Racial Equality (CRE); then share your findings with your colleagues and get them talking, perhaps through showing these films, on videotape or whatever . . .

At a Keighley Primary School we found that the staff had arranged regular evening meetings to discuss questions like:

Why do we still call some of our children 'immigrants' when they are born in this country?

What account do we take of the children's different cultural backgrounds?

How have we explained our schooling methods to all the parents?

What do we feel about children using their own community language in school?

If we accept that educability depends on a child's level of confidence and self-esteem, then we are recognising and valuing in school those aspects of his or her cultural identity on which that self-esteem is built?

Can a school have many 'Black' children of diverse backgrounds, but still be run as a narrowly 'White' institution?

Incidentally, the staff at that school would strongly deny that to ask such questions is a preface to adopting what is called a 'soft' approach. Concern for academic standards, knowledge and skills acquisition is not reduced by recognising that children's own thoughts and activities are central to the learning process and can only be helped by the care a teacher takes to get to know his or her pupils.

We hope that this book and the films will be used to stimulate and inform such staffroom discussions. The films are designed not only to be suggestive and helpful to teachers in thinking about these matters on their own, but also in exchanges with colleagues. These might be informal exchanges about whether the content of the films could have useful application within their own departments; or they might be more formal in-service training sessions structured around the films. Special discussion notes to aid such meetings are available by sending a large stamped (24p first or 18p second class post) self-addressed envelope to:

Multi-Cultural Education
BBC Television
London W12 8QT

Group discussions

Whether used in a staff room, as part of a review of school policies, or on a teacher training course, the notes for discussion group leaders indicate ways of using extracts from the films, together with selected chapters of this book, as resources for examining particular themes or topics in multi-cultural education. Suggestions for using the 50-minute compilation film *Anglo-Saxon attitudes* appear on page 166ff. While of course, any discussion would be built on a better platform of information if each participant knew the whole context of the book, some examples of thematic 'packages' would be:

Community language provision at multi-ethnic secondary schools: chapter 12; and programme 4.

Mother tongues in multi-ethnic primary schools: chapter 12, and programmes 2, 3 and 4.

Relating to parents and local community in multi-ethnic schools: chapters 3 and 11, and programme 3, together with relevant parts of 2, 4 and 6. In addition, for teachers who find cross-cultural communication difficult with some ethnic minority parents, insight and suggestions are offered in 'Crosstalk', a training film on common sources of mutual mis-understanding, available from Concord Films (see page 211). It is accompanied by the 'Crosstalk' booklet, from NCILT, Havelock Centre, Southall, Middx.

What is a relevant curriculum – particularly in a multi-ethnic secondary school? Chapters 1, 7, 8 and 9, and programmes 1, 5 and 7 (also 9 and 10).

Racism awareness among teachers: chapter 6, 10, 14 and 15 and programme 6, along with programme 5 and parts of 7. Agendas of possible discussion questions are outlined on pages 10, 162 and 165 ff. Important additional insights into the nature of racism in Britain are offered in the booklet 'Five Views of Multi-Racial Britain' (see page 211).

Teaching about prejudice – particularly in 'all-white' areas: chapters 6 and 9, and programmes 1 and 8. An additional resource especially useful for groups considering racial prejudice for the first time, and also good for use in class, is the film 'Fred Barker Goes to China', available from Concord Films (see page 211). This is a light comedy of what happens when Fred moves to China to take work as a hospital ancillary worker. It gives insight into the experience of being a first-generation immigrant worker, and it serves as an introduction to questions of prejudice, immigration and emigration, and communication across cultures. A trainer's manual, *Worktalk*, which outlines ways of structuring information and discussion based on the Fred Barker film, is available from The Runnymede Trust (see page 211).

Another resource is the BBC Schools TV film 'Why Prejudice?' from the series *Scene*, also available for hire on VCR from Concord Films.

A note on terms
There is by strict academic standards some imprecision in this book in the use of certain terms. Some contributors, for example, use the words 'multi-cultural', 'multi-racial', and 'multi-ethnic' as loosely interchangeable; others have careful distinctions in mind. However, rather than impose a false consistency, I have left their words unamended.

A very useful short overview of the problems of concepts and terminology in discussions of multi-cultural and anti-racist approaches in schools is given in an article entitled 'Race, prejudice and education: changing approaches' by Professor Michael Banton, available from *New Community*, Vol 10., no 3, published by the C.R.E. (see page 211); or from the pamphlet *Teaching about prejudice*, report number 59, from the Minority Rights Group, 36 Craven Street, London WC2N 5NG (01–930 6659). Note also articles and books detailed on page 210.

John Twitchin,
Continuing Education Department
BBC Television

2 Getting to know each other

The starting point for teaching any new class is to win the confidence of the pupils, to get to know them as individuals, and to encourage them to get to know each other. In ethnically mixed schools, there may be a particularly high premium on handling these initial steps with informed care and thought. An idea of the possible effects on ethnic minority children if teachers overlook such steps, or are not equipped with the sensitivity they require, comes across forcefully in the film 'Does school hurt?', in which pupils reflect back on their experiences. Some examples of a 'multi-cultural' approach to getting to know each other in an ethnically mixed primary school are shown in the film 'A primary response'; other ideas on this theme, as used by primary school teachers in 'all white' areas, feature in 'Anglo-Saxon attitudes'.

Tackling language barriers
Trying to relate to a new class is perhaps most difficult for the teacher who has children who speak little or no English. Such an experience can be very stressful for the children and frustrating for the teacher. Although it is a difficulty which faces only a proportion of teachers in particular parts of the country, we start with this brief account by Rosemary Clarke of some of the ways, shown in 'A primary response', that she set about making contact with the children in such a class. Rosemary, who taught at the school pictured on the front cover, Edith Neville Primary School in North London, found her class included some Bengali-speaking children who spoke no English, and several more who though they could speak some, could not yet write it:

My first step was to contact the ILEA who put me in touch with one of the Bengali-speaking advisers. On my behalf he wrote a letter to the parents inviting them to come into school to help. Nine replied immediately, offering their services.

As some of my children had been making a picture/story book for the younger children, I asked one mother to translate the story into Bengali, so that it could be read in both languages.

Other parents worked through materials I had obtained from a Supplementary Community School with a group of Bengali-speaking children. These were in the form of stories and written exercises in mother-tongue.

My second step was to contact the E2L department at a local comprehensive school, and some of my Bengali-speaking ex-pupils there, inviting them also to assist. They could write stories themselves or translate English ones into their mother-tongue. These were then recorded on tape in both English and mother-tongue – a useful exercise for them, as well as providing resources for use in class.

I also contacted fifth-formers at another local comprehensive who were following a child development course. This was very successful, as speakers of a variety of mother-tongues came forward. Sometimes fifth formers can be assigned to primary schools on work experience schemes – if they are bilingual, this not only helps the teacher and the young ones, it is valuable experience for the students themselves, especially if they are interested in taking up teaching. The older children each read stories and discussed them with one particular pupil. They were able to help with story writing and exercises in mother-tongue, which developed from the stories. They helped us make the multi-lingual signs to post up around school – for example, a 'Welcome to Edith Neville School' for the front doorway. Signs around the school in three or four languages are a good way to reflect the equal status of all languages in the eyes of the children. This is also helped by sharing some of the phrases from the mother-tongue with the children who only speak English. From an early age songs can be learnt together and different calligraphies examined so that other languages will not seem alien.

I visited a nearby Bengali Supplementary School. This I found very valuable as I was able to borrow work-book materials in Bengali and I was also given a list of two hundred words which are the same or similar in Bengali and English. I was surprised to find that these included many useful words like milk, window, aeroplane, mug, Lego, clock, table, chair, bus, train, apple, pencil, class, ice cream, crayon, rubber. The list immediately opened up all sorts of unexpected channels of communication with the children who speak very little English. I was also given a list of typical classroom phrases, written first in Bengali, then phonetically, and thirdly in English. The teachers were very willing to offer help and suggestions, which I found a great morale boost in the many difficulties I was encountering. Parents, supplementary school helpers and other representatives of community organisations are often very willing to help. It is not just that they can help in interpreting for, and in listening to, children speaking and reading in their own particular languages; they can also help translate and explain in Bengali particular concepts I might be teaching of basic mathematics. In this way, those children are less likely to fall behind in other subjects while they are still gaining fluency in English. It is also important to visit the local library and discuss the provision of mother-tongue books with the librarian. Here it is impossible for me to assess the levels of difficulty, so again parents can be asked to help to gauge and record the levels of difficulty of a selection of books for use by everyone.

In class topic work, wherever possible, mother-tongue is used on pictures, posters, maps and notices which are used by everyone, in the hope that everyone can share the knowledge.

Celebrating diversity

The principle of seeking teaching support in mother-tongue from community leaders, from parents, and from secondary school fifth and sixth formers, is clearly very helpful if children who speak little English are not to fall behind and if the teacher is to be able to build a rapport with members of the class. This remains true even when class teachers have assistance from a specialist E2L service. (Questions about helping children with their English within the primary school classroom are picked up in more detail in the later sections 12 and 13.) Most primary teachers have classes where this does not arise, or where problems with basic English are not so severe as to prevent children and teachers getting to know each other, provided positive steps are taken to encourage this. The general principle of building on the children's own experiences and family histories will be familiar to primary teachers, but it may be interesting to note some starting points used in an ethnically mixed class. We asked Barbara Roberts, who taught at Ecclesbourne Primary School in Islington, for her own account of the teaching ideas she is seen using in 'A Primary Response':

When I first came to London from Scotland, I was faced with the challenge of teaching and establishing a satisfactory relationship with a multi-cultural class whose ethnic backgrounds were entirely different from any classroom situation I had ever experienced. I was unsure and unprepared, and I became aware that my attitudes with regard to race and colour were confused and inappropriate.

I realised through some of the questions asked by the children about Scotland that if I could start by talking about my own home background and encourage the children to share similar information with me and the rest of the class, this could be a start towards a positive use of the cultural diversity within the class and really getting to know each other.

The curricular policy within our school is largely child-centred and I base a large proportion of my teaching methods on project work. Alongside the learning skills involved I try to introduce a multi-ethnic perspective which will also involve the linguistic and cultural variety within the classroom.

In a project on 'Ourselves', the class recorded and classified information about themselves, working with a partner or in a small group. The children then compared findings, and we listed differences and similarities. The differences were all superficial and not restricted to race or colour. The class also produced some interesting self-portraits and writing about themselves which we made into a book to share with everyone.

A new Welsh girl joined the class and I encouraged her to talk about Wales and her previous school. This led to a discussion on accent and dialect. I spoke in a Scottish accent and read some poetry in dialect. We also had some examples of other dialects from the children, notably a little piece from two girls of West Indian background. From this we talked about how dialect relates to where we all come from and we should never be ashamed of the way we speak as it is part of ourselves and our personality. The children also agreed that it is wrong to laugh at or make fun of the way we speak.

I am very proud of the bi-lingual children in my class, and we went on from accent and dialect to different languages. Some of the bi-lingual children read out stories in their mother-tongue and translated them for us. It was interesting that a story read in Serbo-Croat was the familiar story of 'The Enormous Turnip' and the Turkish boys read one of Aesop's Fables. The point was made that there are similarities as well as differences in the stories read by children all over the world. We are also making a book on languages which has generated a lot of enthusiasm and interest. I feel this work on languages creates a respect for each other and can foster a feeling of pride in those children who are learning English as a second language rather than leaving them only with a feeling of inadequacy in their reading and writing of English.

When we discussed accent, dialect and language, it brought up the question of 'why we are here?', as well as 'where do we all come from?', and I wanted to explain that migration has not been confined to recent years and that people have been settling in other countries throughout history. I told the class the story of the Highland Clearances and tried to point out some reasons why people migrate (social, economic, political). When we made a list of the countries represented in our classroom through our family backgrounds, there were fourteen countries on the chart. One of the Turkish boys had brought in a picture he cut out of a magazine. It showed crowds of people running in a marathon race in New York. The diversity of race and colour in the picture was another example of people from different countries who had settled in one city.

As an art and craft activity, we did some work on hands. One group made plaster casts of their hands using mod-roc and wire and another group drew outlines of their hands. The children's interest and attitudes to differences in skin colour are very natural. I seldom focus too directly on this. But I did feel it important for them to see for themselves that skin colour differences are only a matter of degree and can be very subtle. I asked the group to place their hands on a piece of white paper and a piece of black paper. We all saw that no one's hands were 'black' or 'white'. They were all different shades between the two. We took great care to blend paints and inks to get the correct skin tones and although our hands all had similar outlines not one person had the same skin colour as another. However, once the context of common bone structures was established, it was agreed by the children that this was only another superficial difference.

I have learned a great deal from the children I have taught since coming to this multi-cultural school. I admire the respect they have for one another's cultural backgrounds once these are drawn out and shared in the class. I hope as a teacher working and living with them that the values and attitudes I see being nurtured within them will be reinforced in their later schooling, so that they become responsible adults, glad to live in a multi-cultural society.

Where are we all from?

It is noticeable that Barbara Roberts gives clear recognition in school to children's actual or potential bi-lingualism. Questions of supporting such bi-lingualism are taken up in more detail in the later section on questions of language. But it is also noticeable that for Barbara, it is important in getting to know each other to have a clear picture of migration and settlement patterns and to share this with the children. Many teachers told us that they found such a picture a vital stepping stone towards understanding children in terms of their family background; it is also something that can be built up collaboratively, by looking at the composition of the class itself. So for teachers of ethnic minority children to whom an idea of recent migration patterns in Britain is not already clear and familiar, Clare Demuth explores this particular point in a little more detail. Clare has taught in schools in England and in Botswana and was for several years Information Officer of The Runnymede Trust. She begins her report by introducing three young people, one of whom, the Moroccan girl Suade, is seen in the film 'Does school hurt?' speaking frankly of her experience of arriving in a British school:

Suade came to North London from Morocco in 1974, aged fourteen: 'I was totally cut off if it hadn't been for my English teacher who spoke French. I was lucky in a way, because the other Moroccan girls couldn't speak any other language than Arabic; but there was no help at all from other teachers. You were put aside – they didn't make you feel at home.'

Raymond moved from Liverpool to South London in 1979, aged eight: 'When I came to school I felt very lonely because I had no friends. In Liverpool people talked different and played different games. They had a Liverpudlian accent. Down here no-one could understand me and I was different than all the rest.'

Ying Rang Choo came with her mother from Hong Kong to East London in 1975, aged eleven: 'When I first came to this school there were no Chinese people here, except in higher classes. I was the only Chinese girl in my year, and I was a bit nervous. I thought it was funny seeing coloured people – Greeks. I thought in this country there were English people. I didn't know there were so many different races. The first day the people in my class were quite friendly to me and they kept asking my name. All I could say was my name. The next day I learnt to say Yes or No.'

These children had had a family experience that is common enough among our school population: they all left familiar territory to come to school. Raymond's family moved from Liverpool to South London at the end of 1979. His father, of Asian origin, came from South America; his mother from Liverpool. At eight years old he was thrown into a class where friendships were already established and he, with his strange accent, was 'different than all the rest'. Suade's family moved from Morocco to North Kensington in 1974, when she was fourteen. At the time she spoke French, Arabic and a bit of Spanish – but no English. Ying Rang Choo came from the New Territories of Hong Kong in 1975 when she was eleven. Her family now live in East London, and while her parents commute weekly to the Chinese restaurant they own in Croydon, Ying is left to look after her two brothers and grandmother at home in Poplar.

Why did these families move from the familiar to the unknown? And as teachers, how can we not only bring our pupils' family histories into our picture of them as individuals, but also enable them to share their experiences with the whole class? These questions arose, for example, in the case of Class 6N, a class of nine to eleven year olds in the South London school in which Raymond found himself at the end of 1979. None of the children in his class were immigrants, though five out of the six who had been born outside London had moved to London from the north, and one girl, although born in Leicester, had spent some time in Zambia where her father was working as a doctor. This class was typical in the sense that there are now very few immigrant children entering British schools. Nowadays it is less frequent for children of secondary school age to arrive in British schools directly from overseas, as Ying Rang Choo and Suade did five or six years ago. This means that the experience of the children now in our primary schools, whose parents or grandparents are of overseas origin, is likely to be different from that of their older brothers and sisters who were born abroad and had part of their schooling there. This change from 'immigrant' to 'settler' can been seen quite clearly by comparing the two maps overleaf. The first shows the moves these children and their families made in order to be together in class 6N in 1980. The second map shows the moves made by their parents before they were born.

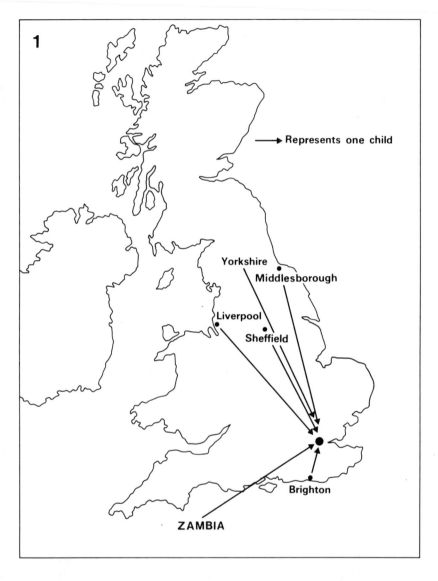

Figure 1

Preparing a wall map to show the countries and regions their families come from is a simple and effective way of showing pupils both the diverse and the common elements of their families' histories. As children are often reticent about themselves, it helps to join in as Barbara Roberts did, by bringing along your own family photographs and marking where you or your family came from. Once the discussion has started, it can lead to further exploration of a particular country or region; a closer look at the varieties of people in the local community;

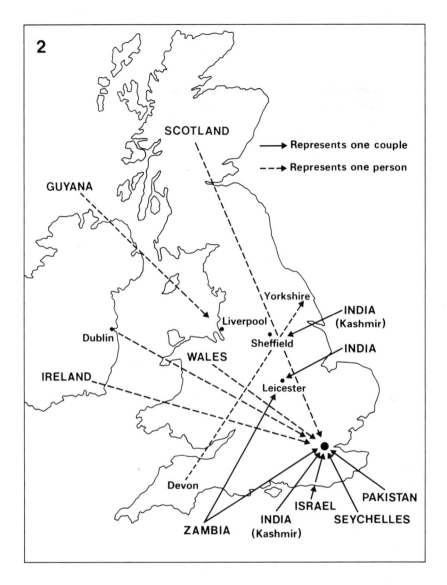

2

SCOTLAND

GUYANA

→ Represents one couple

--→ Represents one person

Liverpool

Yorkshire

INDIA (Kashmir)

Dublin

Sheffield

INDIA

IRELAND

WALES

Leicester

Devon

ZAMBIA

INDIA (Kashmir)

ISRAEL

SEYCHELLES

PAKISTAN

or a search for an answer to the question: 'Why do people move?' Wherever you teach, you are likely to find that the answer turns around a single theme: apart from those families which move in order to escape political persecution, migration from country to city and between regions and states has been largely determined by the search for work.

Asking about the family histories of the children in the class will give an idea of how employment opportunities have attracted people to your locality – or, indeed, how unemployment has driven them away. Where few people have moved into a village or town, you will almost certainly find that many have moved out. Even in class 6N, which is in an area of immigration in the wealthy South East, two of the children had relations who had gone to Australia. And if you have a class in a rural area, or in any area of high unemployment, you are likely to find that some children have relations who have moved – to the cities, to the South East, to Canada, Australia or New Zealand. You have probably done so yourself – very few teachers actually work in the community in which they were born and brought up. In some places, such as Ireland, the West Indies and the Punjab in India, there has for generations been a tradition of people leaving home to find work abroad. England has for centuries been the country where the Irish could find work; however, in the period of economic expansion and high employment in the 1950s, the flow of Irish workers was not enough to fill the needs of England's industries and public services. Along with the governments and employers of western Europe, Britain sought workers from further afield. Like France and Germany, we looked for workers primarily from those countries where there was already some connection, either through a previous colonial rule, or through geographical proximity.

Britain, of course, had colonised widely, instilling ideas of 'the mother country' throughout the British Commonwealth. Thus in Britain the Irish were joined by workers from the Caribbean, from India, Pakistan, Bangladesh, and Hong Kong (all linked to Britain as former or present colonies) and by people from the poorer regions of Europe and North Africa – Southern Italians, Spanish, Portuguese, and Moroccans. Most came to work on the railways and buses, in the hospitals and hotels, in the textile industry and the laundries. They did jobs which, because of bad conditions or low pay, English people were no longer available or prepared to do. Their work served to prop up the unattractive parts of the social infrastructure; in some towns they rescued the small retail trade. Those who came from the West Indies and from Asia received disproportionate press attention: during the 1970s, they in fact together made up only a little over three per cent of Britain's work force, while Irish immigrant workers, for example, still made up more than four per cent. And the combined total of seven and a half per cent was far less than in France and Germany which have eleven per cent of their work force made up of immigrant workers, and tiny in comparison with Switzerland, where thirty per cent of the country's work force is made up of immigrant workers.

The fuller picture that teachers need of the current facts as well as the history of these immigration, emigration and settlement patterns, is available in free handouts from the Commission for Racial Equality (CRE), 10 Allington Street, London SW1E 5EH. It is also covered in Thames TV's 'Our People' films and teachers handbook, details p. 211.

Statistical facts alone are very bare – they come to life through study of how the colonial period influenced not only the post-war immigrants' motives to come here but also the white British response to their arrival. Particularly interesting and important insights on this are set out by Dr Stuart Hall and Dr Bhikhu Parekh in the booklet *Five views of multi-racial Britain*, from the CRE. We particularly draw attention to this booklet since it forms a companion piece to this book. It offers a sociological analysis of race relations in Britain that underlies many of the later sections.

The story of Ying Rang Choo

One way to bring life and meaning to the facts about the immigration and emigration of different groups of workers is to take up individual family histories that teachers can piece together with their pupils. These can prove to be fascinating tales, through which the children build self-confidence while giving both the teacher and the class an exercise in imaginative and emotional understanding. Here, for example, is the story of the family of Ying Rang Choo, the London fifth former mentioned earlier.

Ying Rang Choo's family comes from the New Territories of Hong Kong, an area of mainland China, annexed by the British Government as an overspill area for the burgeoning city of Hong Kong. The people who live there, members of just a few families, had for generations cultivated rice for the markets of Hong Kong. However, in the late 1950s the importation of cheap rice from South East Asia caused the bottom to fall out of the local rice market and forced the villagers to turn to market gardening to make a living. Unfortunately for some of the villagers, climatic changes had made the soil unsuitable for growing flowers and vegetables, so their land was rendered useless.

However, it happened that at the time in Britain, increasing prosperity was enabling more people to eat out, and Chinese food had the attraction of being both novel and relatively cheap. It happened too that Hong Kong was a British colony, and it was easy for someone from the New Territories to get a British passport – not so, it is interesting to note, for people from Hong Kong city itself. (As the British authorities were afraid of giving illegal immigrants from mainland China British passports by mistake, they considered it to be strong evidence of colonial status if applicants bore the name of one of those ancient families who had lived for generations in the New Territories.) Thus, Ying Rang Choo's father left Hong Kong for the streets of Limehouse and Poplar in the East End of London. He went to the London Dockland area, where his family later joined him, because this was where Chinese sailors had first landed, and a Chinese community was already well established.

The story does not end there. Although Ying Rang Choo's family is now established in Poplar, its members are still in transition. Her brother is working in a Chinese restaurant in Germany, while her parents commute weekly to the restaurant they own in Croydon, some thirty miles away in the South London suburbs. Working in a Chinese restaurant, which was for Ying Rang Choo's parents the only way to a new life, is for her the trap which at all costs she wants to avoid. But studying to achieve the necessary languages and qualifications to follow her elder sister into higher education is not proving at all easy as she has to look after her two brothers and her grandmother at home in Poplar while her parents work long hours at the restaurant.

As a story of migration and settlement, this is all typical enough of many families which came to Britain in the 1950s and 60s. Like Ying Rang Choo's family in Poplar, the men moved first, and later when they had established themselves with work and a home, they brought over their wives and children. Five years after her own arrival, Ying's grandmother finally rejoined the family: 'My grandmum only came over here a few months ago. She didn't want to come over at first, but then my sister went back to Hong Kong and persuaded her. We wanted her to come because we love her. My father came over here about ten years ago and then when my mum came over, my granny was in Hong Kong looking after us. She's old now, she's eighty-three.'

Immigration Law
For Ying Rang Choo it was ten years after her father's departure from Hong Kong before the whole family was reunited in Poplar. For others it is even longer, and for some, never. The natural course of family migration over time has often been disrupted by immigration restrictions which have made it an ever more lengthy process for immigrants from certain parts of the world to reunite their family.

Within the overall picture of post-war immigration, the different patterns of movement from each country or region have reflected not only the vagaries of the search for work and the changing requirements of the British economy, but also the restrictions imposed by immigration law. For some teachers it may be important to appreciate the effects of such Laws on the lives of their pupils.

The first legal restriction came with the *Commonwealth Immigrants Act* of 1962, which closed the door to the inflow of male workers to the West Indian, Indian, Pakistani and Bangladesh communities established in Britain in the late 1950s and 1960s. Since then, immigration has been brought under increasingly tight control. Under the *Immigration Act* of 1971, only EEC nationals, people who were born in Britain, or whose parents or grandparents were born here, and those with a work permit, were allowed to come to Britain to work. Until recently the hotel and catering industry was permitted to employ an annual quota of workers who came from countries such as Spain, Morocco and the Philippines. This has now ended and it is very difficult for any but the most highly skilled professional to get a work permit. On the whole it is now only dependants of those already here who are allowed in – and they too have been affected by increasingly tight controls.

Although the British Government accepts in theory the right of people to a settled family life, as enshrined in the European Convention of Human Rights, British immigration law does not recognise those rights in practice. It tends to assume strictly nuclear family structures, for example. Since new immigration rules were introduced in 1980 it has become almost impossible to do as Ying Rang Choo's parents did and bring in aged grandparents. Other relatives such as aunts and uncles have even less chance. As a result, parents who in their countries of origin could have shared the burden of child rearing with the grandparents and other relatives, have in England found they cannot call upon such help. Some chose to leave their children behind under the care of grandparents, often for long periods, on the assumption that when family circumstances changed they would be able to bring their children to England. In the event, many found that when they applied for their children to join them, they faced lengthy administrative procedures with no guarantee of eventual success. The British authorities overseas require documentary evidence that wives and children are the people they claim to be, and in Britain, men who have settled since 1973 may find immigration officials or the police at the door checking on whether they have got accommodation and sufficient funds to support a family. The people hardest hit by the requirements are recent immigrants on low wages, West Indian families where only one parent is in England but the British authorities do not accept that the parent is solely responsible for the child, and Asian families from Pakistan and Bangladesh where the required documentary evidence is often non-existent and processing applications can take a very long time. In Islamabad in Pakistan at the beginning of 1979 many dependant wives and children had been waiting twenty months for a first interview for entry certificates to Britain; after that it could be several months or even years before a decision was reached, all with no guarantee that the application would be accepted.

Some teachers will find that this explains why the families of some pupils are still divided, and why other pupils have arrived in Britain many years after their fathers moved here and at a much later age than is educationally desirable.

Holidays and visits

Many families maintain contact with grandparents or relatives abroad by sending their children for extended visits. Parents with strong religious beliefs may also send their children back in order to give them the sort of religious and moral education they find is not available in England. Visits may last from a few weeks to anything up to two years, although to avoid disruption of their children's English schooling, many parents try to arrange for such visits to coincide with school holidays. Such visits may be the only direct contact that children born in London, or Bradford, or Birmingham, have with their parents' country of origin, so it may be important for teachers to have some idea of what they make of them – not only for their own individual educational development, but also as an experience to share or build on for the benefit of all the children in the class.

Of course some teachers may find that none of the children in the class have ever left the local streets or gone further than a British seaside resort. Others may find that children who have gone abroad are reluctant to talk about their experiences, particularly if they had some fantasy visions about the 'mother country' which were shattered by the realities they saw. But such ambivalent feelings can still be built on, if done sympathetically. In one South London comprehensive school, where the English staff found that some of the children who had been on holiday in Jamaica were finding great difficulty in expressing their feelings about it, they enlisted the help of a West Indian teacher in the school who wrote her own story of a visit to Jamaica in the style of a fourteen year old. This made a model for them to follow, showing as it did both 'good' and 'bad' aspects of the experience. Once the pupils saw similar feelings to their own expressed on paper they were quite prepared to discuss and write about their own experiences.

Sometimes, asking about such trips can produce unexpected enthusiasm. An infant teacher found herself at break-time with a normally shy five year old of Ghanaian origin who had stayed inside with a cold: 'I didn't realize that he had been to Ghana for his holidays. Then, as we were talking, suddenly it was like a torrent unleashed. He just couldn't stop talking about it. I would like to have taped him, but I was afraid to stop the flow. I grabbed an exercise book and wrote a few notes so that the essence of it wouldn't be lost. Ever since, he has been writing up his story. We talk it through, he draws a picture and tells me what he wants to say, and I write down the sentences for him to copy.'

Focus on family background
It is obvious that holidays lend themselves to a variety of follow up work: further exploration of particular countries, displays of things children have brought back, or raising the question of why people move. What is perhaps more important is that holiday discussions can provide an indicator of how ethnic minority children perceive their own connection with their parents' countries of origin, and of how much they know about them. For teachers seeking to get to know such children,

and to help them share their experiences, this is vital information – so staff believe at Wilberforce Junior School, another London school shown in 'A Primary Response'. Teachers there use some simple but effective ideas in addition to holiday reports. For example, one teacher divided the class into groups based on their parents' countries of birth and each group prepared a graphic montage cut from posters and other materials taken from a nearby tourist agency. The pupils were encouraged to write about their own communities, and in one exercise were interviewed, as if for a radio programme, playing the part of their own parents: Why had they come to Britain? What were their first impressions on arrival? Another most animated session about their cultural backgrounds resulted when a teacher played the class six different styles of music as a guessing quiz – a calypso, an Indian raga, a Portuguese folk song, etc.

To teachers who already do such projects these ideas may seem very obvious, but for those who don't, the Wilberforce staff are asking – do you not need to work out similar projects to draw out what ethnic minority children bring to school in terms of their family histories? Doing this gives some affirmation of their sense of cultural identity, indicating that the teacher values rather than ignores the culture of their families. It not only helps the teacher in getting to know them; it enriches the knowledge and imagination of all in the class.

Minority communities
So far, I have drawn attention to the importance for teachers of recognising that ethnic minority children come from families with cultural roots in other parts of the world. It is time to draw equal attention to the fact that most ethnic minority children now entering British schools were born in the UK. Teachers are often surprised to find that many of them have little knowledge of their parents' countries of origin other than what they have overheard from adult conversations or have found from occasional visits. This can mean that in trying to understand such childrens' lives, the question is less, say, of Pakistan or Cyprus than of what it means to live in the Pakistani community of Balsall Heath, Birmingham, or to belong to Haringey's Cypriot community in London. Before we look in detail at how one school related to such a community, it may help to ask why those communities became established in only certain inner-city areas; and why in the twenty odd years since they arrived there more people have not moved out of them.

On the whole, for the post-war immigrants arriving in Britain the only housing they could find was in the privately rented sector in the rundown inner-city areas. Once a number of people were established in a particular area, as the Chinese were in Limehouse, then it was natural, if there was work available, for others from the same town or village in the home country to move to that locality. Although over time many of these people have moved into council houses or bought their own homes, they have rarely moved far from the streets where they first settled. The main reasons for this are detailed in *Race and the Inner-City* by Professor John Rex, one of the public talks reproduced in the booklet '*Five views of multi-racial Britain*' (see page 211). One reason, of course, is that those of Asian or West Indian origin were faced with discrimination on the housing market and by the prejudices and sometimes straight hostility of new and unwelcoming neighbours.

So communities have grown up in particular streets and housing estates, where the older members still identify with a village or region overseas. It means, for example, that if you go to Dominica (one of the small islands of the Caribbean), you will find people there who will ask you whether you know their relations in the Harrow Road or Trellick Towers – the tower block standing above London's Great West Road. Just across from Trellick Towers is another block of flats, where Suad – the girl we met at the start of this report – and her family live. Although Suad comes from eastern Morocco, on the Algerian borders, a high proportion of the local Moroccan community are from Laichi in the north west of the country. Most of these people live in North Kensington and work in hotels and restaurants of London's West End. It may be difficult to imagine their perception of the world. For members of a family which has moved from a village in Morocco to an extension of the same village in North Kensington, who do not speak English, and where both husband and wife work shifts in hotels, their map of the world could well consist of only those three places. For the children of such families, school may need to provide an opening into new worlds, new possibilities.

3 Contact with parents and community

Clare Demuth's report ended with the observation that children work from a map of the world which is narrowly confined to the streets they know, important places, family and friends. Their families and their communities have such unseen maps. Part of understanding the children better is finding out and appreciating the places and happenings they think are important. This would need to be followed up by 'tuning into' other aspects of the community life of which the children are part. This certainly requires good communication skills and a willingness to listen and learn-skills which are now professional necessities for teachers. It is only through acquiring an appreciation of the values, the perceptions, and the expectations of parents from ethnic minority communities that a teacher can fully develop the essential skills of diagnosing educational needs and learning characteristics. And at secondary school level such understanding can be decisive in terms of subject option and careers advice – a point reviewed more fully in the later section 'From school to work'.

The parent/teacher gap
The parent/teacher divide remains wide in many schools. Given the endless pressures on time, it is all too easy to regard parents more as a nuisance to be tolerated than as a source of help. This is an attitude formally condemned in the Taylor report:

It is the individual parent who is in law responsible for his child's education and whose support in this task is vital. There should therefore be at the individual level also a partnership between home and school. The individual parent will want the school to be an open and welcoming place. He will expect it to provide a framework within which he can communicate with his own child's teacher, in a spirit of partnership, about the child's welfare and progress. We believe that such aspirations

are wholly responsible and that every parent has a right to expect a
school's teachers to recognise his status in the education of his child by
the practical arrangements they make to communicate with him and the
spirit in which they accept his interest.
DES *A new partnership for our schools* 1977

Seen in those terms, the question is what particular 'practical arrangements' and 'spirit' may be needed in schools which serve communities
with ethnic minority groups, where cultural and linguistic differences
can act as further disincentives to trying to close the traditional
gap between parents and teachers? Is it especially important for the
successful education of children at such schools that teacher/parent
barriers be overcome? Adrian Smith, Head of Cabot Primary School
in Bristol, has no doubts. In an article on 'The multi-racial primary
school' he puts it briefly:

A good school is responsive to its community. However efficient teaching might be, skill and time must also be given to this. It is part of the
Head's job to respond to the needs of the community as they see it. The
Head may lose in dictatorial powers but he will gain in educational significance. Beyond the Head teacher there are six basic requirements:

1 The presence of minority groups as staff;

2 Visible value placed on minority cultures and languages;

3 Books of good quality/quantity and of relevant context;

4 Music and games reflecting different cultures;

5 Meal provision, catering for each ethnic group;

6 Availability of school to all parents.

One school which has worked to such principles – especially the last – is
Tindal Primary School, in Balsall Heath, Birmingham. The film 'Your
Community School' is devoted to showing the effects of opening up
this school to parents and community. For six years it was part of an
experiment in community schooling organised by the Birmingham LEA
with the benefit of special funding assistance from the Bernard Van Leer
Foundation (a Dutch charitable trust). Community rooms at the school
were designated both for adult and community uses – pre-school
groups, dress-making classes, keep fit, E2L classes for adults, meetings
of self help organisations, etc – and as an informal centre for parents to
drop in if only for coffee and a chat. Systematic home visiting was
undertaken, and regular meetings set up between the home/school

liaison staff and the rest of the teachers. Headteacher Rob Hughes summarises some of the results of their experience:

We do not make any great claims about having established a multi-cultural curriculum in the school, or that we have a clear and coherent strategy as to where exactly we are going in these terms. But our children and their needs are making us look very carefully at what we are trying to do. There has been a lot of head-scratching and a lot of pencil-chewing over what is relevant and what is not.

Obviously, so far as the curriculum is concerned, content, style and the language within which it is couched are all of paramount importance. If we have any useful experience, it is probably in the way that we try to relate to the children and their parents, and how we see our role within the neighbourhood and the community that the school serves. Tindal was one of several Birmingham schools included in an Educational Priority Programme and it became the base for a successful home-school liaison teacher placement. The school was chosen for this work because it exhibited all the criteria drawn up to identify the so-called EPA school. It is an old Victorian building set in what was once a thriving part of industrial Birmingham, but which had long ago become a gaunt and run-down area of crumbling back-to-back houses and nineteenth century factory workshops. The last ten years have seen an upsurge in the building of new houses, the overhaul of older properties, and the gradual implementation of a comprehensive housing action area plan under a city sponsored urban renewal programme. For many of the same reasons in other cities, Balsall Heath became from the mid 1960s onwards, the home, at least initially, for many immigrant families from the West Indies, Pakistan and India.

The school was seen increasingly as one of the few remaining stable institutions in an area undergoing considerable change. (It was also the time, of course, when labels like 'educationally deprived' and 'disadvantaged' were being tagged onto schools of this sort.) It was against this general background that the school became involved in 1974 in the Birmingham Experiment in Community Education sponsored jointly by the Van Leer Foundation and the Birmingham Education Committee, which continued formally until 1980.

The project had many aims, but the overall idea was described at the time as 'to develop closer functional links between school and neighbourhood . . . with a view to strengthening the role of the school in the educational and social development of its neighbourhood'. What this came to mean is illustrated in the film. Now that the project is over I really do think that we have managed to weave the school, at least to some extent, into the fabric of Balsall Heath. In the process, of course, we have had to look quite closely at our own values and organisation. The last thing that we have been able to do is assume that the school is at the centre of community activity. Nor have we been able to shield ourselves behind the professional mystique that we as teachers are so often expected to do. We have also had to modify our own styles of management because of the many contacts and leads both into and out from the school. It is no good relying on the more traditionally head-teacher-centred way of doing things when as well as being constantly involved with voluntary and statutory organisations and individuals on the 'outside', we are at the same time attempting to establish groups 'within' that are genuinely able to offer advice, and in some cases help us to redirect the policy-making of the school. I would guess that the fundamental point for us has been that we have had no option but to review how we see our own role as we come into contact with other groups in the locality. The crunch has to come too, in that we have found ourselves, on more than one occasion, in a position where we have been asked by the parents and the community to do certain things, or to re-adjust our priorities in a particular way, when for one reason or another we have been unable to do any of these things. We have also had to cope with the dilemma of moving into areas of possible conflict with the Local Authority itself when we have been linked with other groups in the voluntary sector, or when we have been asked to support individuals who have come face-to-face with bureaucarcy.

There are two organisations in particular, I think, that illustrate the direction we are moving in at the moment. One is our Mother-Tongue Support Group, and the other is the Tindal Association for School and Community (TASC for short). The Support Group was set up when a cross-section of people, but particularly those representing the Asian Community, were invited to discuss how the school might respond more sensitively and effectively to the needs of children from Asian homes. It was quite obvious that the overwhelming concern was for the provision of mother-tongue teaching as an extra-curricular activity, or even that it might be included within the school day. After consultation with the LEA, it was agreed that classes could be established, but that they should be for mother-tongue teaching only. It was also agreed that they should be designed to generally assist and enhance the school curriculum, that we should concentrate, at least initially, on the nine to eleven age range and that they should take place after the end of the school day. We were also granted enough money to appoint a co-ordinator on a part-time basis, whose job it was to recruit a group of volunteers who would assist him with the teaching. In no time at all we had classes in Urdu and Punjabi for fifty children. We arranged for them to meet straight after school for an hour twice a week, and although various alternatives have been thought about, this is still the way they are organised. They are extremely popular, and it is clear that we have touched on something that is seen by our parents, and by people in the community generally, as being of vital importance. The Support Group continued to meet regularly and to monitor the progress of the classes. At first it was concerned merely to ensure their continuation. More recently it was agreed to press the LEA for a qualified teacher to be appointed to the school on a full-time basis, who would be primarily concerned with the development of mother-tongue work with very young children. Obviously, it is not exactly the best time to be making a bid for extra staffing, but it was made and a detailed request was submitted on the Support Group's behalf. In January 1981, we are still hoping that something may come of it.

TASC has a much wider brief. It came about because we wanted to protect and nurture all the various non-statutory activities that had been developed within the school during the six years of the project. But it was also an attempt to hold onto the whole breadth of discussion and support that had also been established during that period.

Setting up the machinery, preparing a constitution and calling the initial meetings was an ardous job, but somehow that was all managed and we now have an independent organisation (in the sense that it has charitable status) based on the school and with a cross-section of elected members including parents, residents, school staff, and representatives from voluntary and statutory organisations. Initially it has concentrated on maintaining the various activities already taking place at the school, the playgroup/drop-in centre, the holiday playschemes, the clubs for old people, the various adult activities and the creation of a community play-area alongside the school. Obviously these are all seen to be of continuing importance, but TASC is still looking for ways in which it can develop and grow. What will eventually emerge is still very much in the melting pot.

Fundamentally, the idea is that the school should be seen increasingly as a base and not merely as a focus. Programmes should extend outward into the community and through TASC we hope to do this. Only from this sort of springboard can we truly develop as a school.

The lesson from Tindal School, and from other schools where close relations with parents, including many ethnic minority parents, have been established, seems to be that a catalyst is required, at least initially – someone on the staff or from the community to act as liaison between teachers who have little time for home visiting, and parents to whom conventional PTA meetings or parents' evenings may seem intimidating. Someone who understands their language and expectations of education may be needed to help articulate parents' views to the school. While it is obviously helpful if a member of staff has this role, this is not the only way: in a South London infants school a project worker from the Centre of Urban and Educational Studies set up a book borrowing scheme for the parents. This had something of the same effect as the Community Room at Tindal. The scheme was subsequently taken over by the parents' group themselves who, from a base in the grounds, now act as a link between the school, new parents and working mothers. At this same school the children now have clubs every Wednesday afternoon, when parents come in and take groups of children for an activity of their choice.

Earlier we saw Rosemary Clarke using parents in language support work in the classroom; Tindal School also arranges for parents to read stories to children in their own language, and to write them down. But apart from language, parents may have expertise in crafts, cookery, or music, for example, which they would like to demonstrate and share with the children. The club system is one way of capitalising on this.

4 Some projects and materials

For many primary teachers there is a general issue underlying their efforts to develop multi-cultural education: do they successfully move beyond *tokenist* recognition that ethnic minority children have parents who come from abroad, or have different home cultures? The point has been made that recognition of such cultures in school is important for underpinning the children's self respect and pride in their own cultural identity. But if such recognition is made only through one or two projects, or a few assemblies celebrating the festivals of other religions, together perhaps with some language support, is this not to overlook the power of the curriculum as a whole? The argument is that in terms of all children's equal right to be *educated*, it is throughout the curriculum that cultural pluralism needs to be reflected. This section includes some ideas and sources of help. We also include some checklists which have been found useful by teachers in identifying subtle as well as unsubtle racism in books and materials used at school.

We start with a glimpse of some projects which illustrate ways of developing the ideas of travel introduced earlier. They are used by a teacher of a middle class at an Infants School in North London. It has been said that 'the acid test of a multi-cultural primary school is that you can enter it at night and tell immediately from the wall displays that there are children of different backgrounds at the school'. With the Chinese calender that Mai Lee had brought from home, the Hindu writing which Tina's father had helped to write, the photos from family albums, and the accounts of visits to relatives in distant places, it is a test passed easily by this school, whose children were all born locally in and around Tottenham in North London. Seventy per cent have at least one parent born overseas – from Cyprus, the Caribbean, Spain and Italy, China, India, and Pakistan:

We started with being a travel agent – all the ways you can travel. Then we did posters to entice people on holiday, and quizzes on countries we've visited or would like to visit. The children brought in things from home from different countries visited by their families and friends, which were displayed as the basis for a school assembly. As part of this assembly the children counted from one to ten in their own languages. At first they had been very shy about the languages they could speak, then gradually they had got more excited – 'I can count too' – until we ended up with thirteen different languages, including one to ten spoken with a strong Scottish accent, which Scott insisted was a foreign language too! Suranjan could speak in three different languages. Our discussions about language were interesting as I found that many of the children hadn't realised that they spoke two languages. As far as they were concerned they could communicate at home and school and that was what mattered.

In the summer term I changed the emphasis and decided to spend time on a specific geographical area, or if possible two, and then run a comparison for similarities and difference. I chose India because I felt that I had in the past put a lot of emphasis on West Indian and African cultures. As three children have definite links with India and had expressed interest in finding out more about it and sharing their knowledge and experience with us, I opted to start with that and possibly follow up with Cyprus.

For many of the children their only idea of India was of starving people and lots of sun. The aim was to make them aware of both similarities and differences, and particularly to become familiar with the fascinations of other cultures. This is something you can't preach – it's got to arise implicitly from the project, and become clear as much from the teacher's attitude and actions, as much as from words.

We started with a collection of items from India – a dish, a sari, some sandals, a calendar and various fabrics. Then we had a general discussion with Arnand, Tina and Suranjan about life at home, food, customs, dress, and we read the book *Pavan is a Sikh* by Sean Lyle (Black, 1977). I brought a sari into school and dressed in it. Then Tina came with hers from home, together with her jewellery and sandals. The children liked Tina in her sari and one boy who often makes prejudiced remarks said how beautiful she was. Her father helped her to write 'Good morning, children' for us in Hindi. The focal point of the work was the bazaar we made out of the Wendy house.

Two books were particularly useful: *The story of Hanuman* by A. Ramachandran (Black, 1979) – the children really liked this story and asked to hear it again and again, and the illustrations sparked off work on mosaics – and *India, the land and its people* by N. Talyarkhan (Macdonald, 1975). We backed this up with photographs of India which the children brought from home as a basis for doing a comparison between the day in the life of a child in Tottenham, London, and of Ramu and Lakshimi in an Indian village. They drew pictures to illustrate the things they did during the night and day and the things the Indian children did. Off and on the work spread over two terms.

Book materials for the primary classroom

Throughout that school, teachers make a special effort to include objects in the 'home corner' which the children would also be familiar with at home, eg lengths of cloth for making saris, saucepans for making tea, black and white dolls, etc. The principle of building on their home experience, including bringing things into school, informs the approach in all classes.

In one of the top infant classes, the focus for one term was on Africa, which had already come up in stories. Several mothers were from West Africa. The assumptions that the children had about Africa were based on films they had seen: of Tarzan, the jungle and animals. The teachers wanted the children to examine these ideas and move beyond them to consider the diversities of African society.

The focus for the work was a blank wall map of Africa which the children filled in with their pictures, amplified with captions. The end product was a collage of information: mountains and rivers, cities and inevitably many kinds of wild animal. Inspiration came particularly from a book of photographs, *In Africa* by Marc and Evelyne Bernheim, (Lutterworth Press, 1974) which illustrates beautifully life in Africa.

More teaching practice from that school is described in the section on English as a second language (E2L) in the later section on language. At this point we pick up the importance in multi-cultural learning of finding the right materials.

David Moore, Head of Religious Studies at the comprehensive Tulse Hill School, in South London, himself British-born black, has set out some of his own observations on the pictorial images that children constantly meet both in and out of school. This extract is from his helpful introductory pamphlet *Multi-cultural Britain*, (1980) available from: Save The Children Fund, 157 Clapham Road, London SW9 OPT.

How negative images can harm children

What effect do negative images have on children? I would suggest that they have a damaging effect. It certainly affects children from minority groups, when they see themselves and the values that their parents hold made to look ridiculous. A number of studies have shown that children from minority groups can go through a period of rejecting what they are. This decreases when minority groups learn to feel pride in themselves and their heritage. Again it diminishes in areas where there is a sizeable community whose members can support one another. However, there is a temptation for the child from a minority culture living in isolation to seek to become absorbed by the majority culture, until such time as it rejects him. In her study of black children fostered by white families, Rachel Jenkins found several cases where the children had scrubbed themselves raw in an attempt to make their skin the same colour as their family and friends.

Another disturbing effect is seen among children who do not come into close contact with children from minority groups and are more likely to accept the negative images.

These attitudes have a detrimental effect on the self-image of children of minorities, and can become a self-fulfilling prophecy. If you tell someone often enough that they are no good, that they are different and strange, they can eventually come to believe it, and then you find that the illusion becomes a reality. To talk of a 'black' or 'colour' problem, is to assume that the people of the minority constitute the problem. In fact, it is basically a *white* problem of learning to accept, understand, and tolerate. The Asian, Cypriot and Afro-Caribbean communities do not have a problem of identity. The majority culture has the problem, in coming to terms with itself, as its role in the world changes from dominant major power towards union with other nations.

It is difficult to assess how the attitudes and beliefs of children – particularly young children – are influenced by what they see and read in school. It has been something of an article of faith among those who practise multi-cultural education, to believe that introducing materials with positive images of children of Asian and West Indian origin into our classrooms can help such children develop a more positive self-image while at the same time breaking down the negative stereotypes held by white children.

It was to establish whether there is any real evidence for this belief that David Milner, author of *Children and race* (Penguin, 1975) carried out a pilot research project on the effect of materials on children's attitudes over one year among five to eight year olds of English, West Indian and Asian origin. (A revised edition was published in 1981 entitled *Children and race – 10 years on* Ward Lock Educational.) Here is part of an article in which David Milner summarised the research in *Issues*, the journal of London NAME (No. 23, November/December 1979):

The study consisted of a year-long classroom intervention programme designed to influence positively the children's racial attitudes by the introduction of first, Multi-racial, multi-cultural curricula and materials; and second, Minority group teachers.

The children's attitudes were assessed before and after the programme using the conventional doll and picture tests employed by most researchers in this area in the last forty years. The study was conducted in schools in three London boroughs and one provincial city, and involved two hundred and seventy-four children of English, West Indian and Asian parentage. In order to compare simultaneously the effects of multi-racial materials with conventional materials, and of minority group teachers with white English teachers, a rather complex 'design' for the study was set up.

The classrooms using conventional materials had been selected as representative of the typical (ie essentially white) English classroom, uninfluenced by the multi-racial nature of its constituency. It has to be said that at the time of the study such classrooms were not hard to find, though they are hopefully now a dying breed. No input was made into these classrooms whatsoever. However, the 'multi-racial materials' classrooms received a very substantial input of materials, principally in the form of books, posters, wall-charts, and, for the infant class-rooms, word-games, number charts, alphabets, etc. (all of which were thoroughly multi-racial, and were produced specifically for the project). The selection of suitable books was the result of a long process of reviewing titles from all over the world, with the assistance of the published bibliographies in this area, and of a number of teachers in multi-racial schools who helped to assess more recently published material. The criteria for selection were simply that the books should portray West Indian and Asian people, in both text and illustration, in a positive non-stereotyped way, either in the context of their cultural backgrounds or in their contemporary urban situation in Britain. In addition there were a number of books portraying black Americans or dealing with race-related themes which embodied the same principles. The books used were Janet Hill's *Books for children: the homelands of immigrants in Britain* (IRR, 1971) and Judith Elkin's *Books for the multi-racial classroom* (Library Association, 1976).

Over the course of the programme the teachers involved were encouraged to develop further work from the materials, and ideas for these projects were fed from classroom to classroom on the project. Inevitably there was wide variation in the enthusiasm with which the various teachers put these into practice, or indeed utilised the basic materials. In some cases the materials were simply 'there' for the children to use if they wished, in others they became the central focus of classroom activities, and produced some encouraging 'spin-off' that had not always been anticipated. One teacher reported how the display of these materials on an Open Evening had delighted a number of black parents who had previously shown little enthusiasm for what the school had been doing. Others related how the materials had seduced the interest of a number of reluctant readers in their classes, by virtue of themes and characters with which they could identify.

At the end of the programme, the reassessment of the children's attitudes produced a mixed, though basically optimistic picture. The least change in attitudes took place amongst the white English children;

while these changes did not quite attain *statistical* significance, it is perhaps significant in the wider sense that any attitude change took place at all given the relatively short duration of the programme and the strength of pressures towards prejudice in the world outside the school. It is worth noting that every instance of attitude change was in the desired direction, that is, towards greater acceptance of the minorities, and there was no single instance of more negative attitudes developing (which might have been expected through simple random variation if nothing else). Turning to the West Indian and Asian children, it was clear that there were very significant effects of the programme in both cases. Of the children who had shown ambivalence about their racial identity before the intervention programme, between a half and two-thirds had become thoroughly identified with their own racial group by the end of it, as evidenced by their responses to the doll and picture test.

It was also possible to determine what aspects of the programme had caused these changes via a series of comparisons. These showed that part of the attitude change achieved could be attributed to the effects of the minority group teachers *per se*, but that by far the largest contribution was made by the multi-racial materials. This conclusion was reinforced by the fact that the greatest attitude change took place in those classrooms where the materials had been most utilised.

Assessing books
In the light of those findings, we give two examples of published guidelines that teachers have found useful, the first American, the second British:

Ten Quick Ways to Analyze Children's Books for Racism
published by the Council on Inter-racial Books for Children, 1841 Broadway, New York, NY 10023.

I **Check the illustrations** Look for stereotypes. A stereotype is an over-simplified generalisation about a particular group, race or sex, which usually carries derogatory implications. Some infamous (overt) stereotypes of Blacks are the happy-go-lucky water-melon eating Sambo and the fat, eye-rolling 'mammy'; of Chichanos, the sombrero-wearing peon or fiesta-loving, macho bandit; of Asian Americans, the inscrutable, slant-eyed 'Oriental'; of Native Americans, the naked savage or 'primitive' craftsman and his squaw; of Puerto Ricans, the switchblade-toting teenage gang member. While you may not always find stereotypes in the blatant forms described, look for variations which in any way demean or ridicule characters because of their race.

Look for tokenism. If there are non-white characters in the illustrations, do they look just like whites except for being tinted or coloured in? Do all minority faces look stereo-typically alike; or are they depicted as genuine individuals with distinctive features?

Who's doing what? Do the illustrations depict minorities in subservient and passive roles or in leadership and action roles?

2 Check the story line The Civil Rights Movement has led publishers to weed out many insulting passages, particularly from stories with Black themes, but the attitudes still find expression in less obvious ways. Some of the subtle (covert) forms of bias to watch for:

Standard for success Does it take 'white' behaviour standards for an minority person to 'get ahead'? Is 'making it' in the dominant white society projected as the only ideal? To gain acceptance and approval, do non-white persons have to exhibit extraordinary qualities – excel in sports, get A's etc.? In friendships between white and non-white children, is it the non-white who does most of the understanding?

Resolution of problems How are problems presented, conceived and resolved in the story? Are minority people considered to be 'the problem?' Are the oppressions faced by minorities and women represented as causally related to an unjust society? Are the reasons for poverty and oppression explained, or are they accepted as inevitable? Does the story line encourage passive acceptance or active resistance? Is a particular problem that is faced by a minority person resolved through the benevolent intervention of a white person?

3 Look at the lifestyles Are minority persons and their setting depicted in such a way that they contrast unfavourably with the unstated norm of white middle-class suburbia? If the minority group in question is depicted as 'different', are negative value judgments implied? Are minorities depicted exclusively in ghettoes, barrios or migrant camps? If the illustrations and text attempt to depict another culture, do they go beyond over-simplifications and offer genuine insights into another lifestyle? Look for inaccuracy and inappropriateness in the depiction of other cultures. Watch for instance of the 'quaint-natives-in-costume' syndrome (most noticeable in areas like costume and custom, but extending to behaviour and personality traits as well).

4 Weigh the relationships between people Do the whites in the story possess the power, take the leadership, and make the important decisions? Do non-whites and females function in essentially supporting roles? How are family relationships depicted? In Black families, is the mother always dominant? In Hispanic families, are there always lots and lots of children? If the family is separated, are societal conditions – unemployment, poverty – cited among the reasons for the separation?

5 Note the heroes and heroines When minority heroes and heroines do appear, are they admired for the same qualities that have made white heroes and heroines famous or because what they have done has benefited white people? Ask this question: Whose interest is a particular figure serving?

6 **Consider the effects on a child's self-image** Are norms established which limit the child's aspirations and self-concepts? What effect can it have on Black children to be continuously bombarded with images of the colour white as the ultimate in beauty, cleanliness, virtue etc., and the colour black as evil, dirty, menacing, etc.? Does the book counteract or reinforce this positive association with the colour white and negative association with black?

What happens to a girl's self-image when she reads that boys perform all of the brave and important deeds? What about a girl's self-esteem if she is not 'fair' of skin and slim of body?

In a particular story, is there one or more persons with whom a minority child can readily identify to a positive and constructive end?

7 **Consider the author's or illustrator's background** Analyse the biographical material on the jacket flap or the back of the book. If a story deals with a minority theme, what qualifies the author or illustrator to deal with the subject? If the author and illustrator are not members of the minority being written about, is there anything in their background that would specifically recommend them as the creators of this book?

8 **Check out the author's perspective** No author can be wholly objective. All authors write out of a cultural as well as a personal context. Children's books in the past have traditionally come from authors who are white and who are members of the middle class with one result being that a single ethnocentric perspective has dominated American children's literature. With the book in question, look carefully to determine whether the direction of the author's perspective substantially weakens or strengthens the value of his/her written work. Are omissions and distortions central to the overall character or 'message' of the book?

9 **Watch for loaded words** A word is loaded when it has insulting overtones. Examples of loaded adjectives (usually racist) are: savage, primitive, conniving, lazy, superstitious, treacherous, wily, crafty, inscrutable, docile, and backward.

10 **Look at the copyright date** Books on minority themes – usually hastily conceived – suddenly began appearing in the mid-1960s. There followed a growing number of 'minority experience' books to meet the new market demand, but most of these were still written by white authors, edited by white editors and published by white publishers. They therefore reflect a white point of view. Only very recently, in the late 1960s and early 1970s, has the children's book world begun even remotely to reflect the realities of a multi-racial society.

The Centre for World Development Education has published a pamphlet, *The changing world and the primary school*, with suggestions for introducing development education in primary school (for CWDE see page 99). It includes this checklist of points about books to promote understanding between people:

1 Choose books which give a sensitive, sympathetic portrayal of people with an emphasis on the fact that they are real people. Avoid stereotypes.

2 Books should recognise that other cultures have their own values; they should not be judged exclusively through British eyes against British norms. Wherever possible, people from other cultures should be given the opportunity to speak for themselves.

3 Information should be as up to date as possible taking into account that societies everywhere are changing and that to dwell on quaint exotic traditions is not presenting a true picture of life in that society.

4 Characters from non-European origins should not always be represented as the underdogs, or in need of help; they should also be shown in positions of authority and responsibility.

5 Any book which in some way portrays a society, whether in fiction, history or the contemporary world, should present fairly the cultural and social mix of that society. This is equally important whether portraying life in Liverpool, Nairobi or the Outer Hebrides.

6 Where issues of poverty or struggle are touched on, recognition should be given to the fact that the wealth of some countries is due to the maintenance of poverty in others and that this poverty cannot be dismissed as due simply to incompetence of the poor. (A similar relationship exists within countries as between them.)

7 Where issues of conflict arise they should be handled openly and not glossed over as if no problems existed.

8 Books should make clear the interdependence between people and nations and the influence that actions by one have on others.

9 Books should encourage a sense of the individual's ability to influence events.

10 Books should be attractive and clear to use so that children can readily find the information they require.

Other guidelines for the evaluation of books
Centre for Urban Educational Studies, 34 Aberdeen Park, London N5 2BL, *Assessing children's books for a multi-ethnic society* 1980 (includes examples of 'good' and 'bad' books).
1978 World Council of Churches, International Working Party reprinted in *Children's Book Bulletin* No. 1, June 1979, *Criteria for the evaluation of Racism in text books and children's literature.*

National Union of Teachers, Hamilton House, Mabledon Place, London WC1H 9BD, *In Black and White-guidelines on racial stereotyping in textbooks and learning materials* December 1979.

These checklists and guidelines are not being offered in support of censorship; some bias after all may be unavoidable. The aim is simply to draw attention to materials that least risk re-inforcing racist assumptions, and to help teachers assess what they use in class.

Since children can't be protected from coming across racist materials outside school, the important task is to find ways of teaching the checklists to children, to equip them to spot negative images in books and the news media for themselves. Some schools have put books into a 'racist museum' section of the library; others glue copies of checklists to the inside covers; others have used *Racism: the 4th R* (see page 56). Also useful is *Reading into Racism – bias in children's literature,* by Gillian Klein, Routledge, 1985. This includes strategies for combating racism in books and materials.

Finding advice and resources

First check your Multi-Cultural Support Service or Teachers' Centre. Below is a list with the primary teacher in mind. It should be taken together with the further sources listed on page 71.

Central Library, 2 Fieldway Crescent, London N5, *Books for under-fives in a multi-cultural society* by Maureen Taylor and Kay Hurwitz (1979).

Commission for Racial Equality, 10 Allington Street, London SW1E 5EH (01-828 7022). *Books for under-fives in multi-racial Britain.*

Centre for Urban Educational Studies (CUES), 34 Aberdeen Park, London N5 (01-226 5437). Stories, songs and picture books for infants and lower juniors in the multi-racial society, and *Information booklet on resources for multi-cultural education.* Visits are welcomed at the multi-cultural reference collection at CUES of over one thousand children's story books. Staff also offer individual advice on book selection or project ideas by appointment.

A very useful list of books and publishers can be found in a survey by Gillian Klein, under the title 'Multi-cultural imagination', in the *Times Educational Supplement* of 9 Jan 1981.

Afro-Caribbean Education Resources Project (ACER), 275 Kennington Lane, London SE11 5QZ (01-582 2771). This independent educational charity has a collection of books and welcomes visits by arrangement. It offers in-service courses on using materials.

Several publishing houses, including Heinemann, Oxford University Press, and Penguin, issue catalogues on 'multi-ethnic' education. Penguin Books' *A multi-ethnic book list for children of all ages*, is annotated by Rosemary Stones, of the Children's Rights Workshop.

The Children's Rights Workshop has a termly journal, *Children's Book Bulletin*, useful for keeping up to date with new publishers (see page 71).

Harmony, 42 Beech Drive, Borehamwood, Herts: annotated booklist *Multi-cultural books for children.*

5 Bringing dialect into children's work

It is a prime job to give all pupils a good command of standard English. Parents, employers, examiners and pupils all expect this; it is a handicap in our society to lack such skill. But learning standard English does not have to be at the expense of other linguistic skills children may have – including dialects. In fact, some teachers find that learning SE can be helped by a sympathetic understanding of dialect.

Many teachers have seen the dialects of British black, and of white English working-class children, as a 'language deficiency' – 'illogical' or 'incomplete' forms of language which hinder the pupils in developing cognitive powers. The work of William Labov in the United States helped to put this view into perspective. He showed that the non-standard English of American blacks was perfectly capable of performing the same functions as the standard form of the language. In linguistic terms it was neither illogical nor incomplete. The problem was the status of those who spoke it (*The logic of non-standard English* by W. Labov, in *Tinker tailor* edited by N. Keddie, Penguin Books, 1975).

Non-linguists often express preferences based less on rational evaluation than on the social value attributed to different dialects. The form used by the powerful section of society is perceived as 'pleasing'; those associated with the poor or less powerful are perceived as 'harsh', 'ugly', 'bad language'.

It can be very difficult for the teacher to relish the living language when under pressure to get his or her pupils to use 'good English'. The pressure on the pupils, however, is greater still. For the young child, his dialect is his first and natural language, spoken by the important people around him, and up until his entry into school is regarded as perfectly adequate. If he is to master a new dialect which will give him access to greater communication, his existing skills need to be built upon and recognised rather than ignored and devalued. A teacher who understands the structure of the children's dialect is in a better position to give constructive help with any difficulties in reading or writing the standard forms. Experienced teachers have found that both the childrens' command of language, and their competence in its various sub-skills, are strengthened by exploring overtly the variety of linguistic and dialectical forms the children either use or know about.

In the film 'School Report', English teacher Sharon Godard at Birley High School in Manchester is shown joining in the reading of a story written in both standard English and a Caribbean dialect. This was her way to initiate a discussion about the children's own experience of dialect usage, and the occasions most appropriate for it. The same approach is taken in some primary schools – and not only as a basis for reading and discussion. For a glimpse of how one primary school teacher builds on pupils' experience of different ways of speaking, as a basis for writing and drama, we asked Graham Jameson, a South London teacher, to describe some work he did with a group of fourth year juniors, children of Caribbean parentage, in the summer of 1980:

The aim was to make ethnicity visible in the curriculum – not through 'black studies', nor by teaching geography and history of the Caribbean, but through reflecting and capitalising on the everyday experience of living 'now, here, and in England'.

I knew the children well: they had been part of my class for the previous two years. We had the kind of relationship of trust between child and teacher that is vital when building on their experience of 'living here and now'. Dialect is close to the heart of the ethnicity which is part of this experience. It can be a very sensitive part, and as teachers we are sometimes asking much of a child to expose his or her *self* in this way. Many of their ideas and feeling belong to a private world not reflected in a wider 'culture' and not legitimated in school textbooks or procedures.

We agreed that in making up and writing down stories about 'ourselves' or 'people like us' we would encounter difficulty in the matter of dialogue. This is obviously very difficult since it is necessary to invent spelling, syntax, grammar etc., and there is no formal written form. However, we had already looked at the work of the Jamaican poet Louise Bennett in her *Jamaican Labrishe* (Jamaica: Sangster's Book Stores, 1966) a short extract from her 'Baus O' killing' gives a flavour of her work:

So yah a de man me hear bout!
Ah yuh dem say dah-teck
Whole heap O' English out sey dat
Yuh givine kill dialect!

I'd experienced difficulties myself in the writing of dialect for a children's story. What I'd constructed on the page looked wrong and I'd asked the children why. We decided that although it was difficult, it was very necessary to acknowledge the varieties of spoken English in the stories. Equally it was important to keep the narrative text in standard written English of as high a formal quality as we could manage. *There is no such thing as standard spoken English; there is such a thing as standard written English.*

Once thought out, each story was read by its author onto a tape-recorder – child and tape-recorder disappeared into a cupboard to ensure privacy. The stories really gained by being thus performed and the way they are performed shows empathy with the created characters. In some ways they are quite surprising; Peggy, for instance, is ordinarily quite shy and undemonstrative, but changes completely when playing the part of 'Monica' in her story.

To give an idea of the results of this way of teaching, a story about 'Charlie' began with his mother speaking:

Charlie sid down. Ah warn chat dis ya ting out properly.
You know since you farder die, me have to cope pan me
own, so no come tell me bout you warn tarn rasta. Me warn
you fe be something big, someting better dan me.

Any Jamaican listening to this read as it is written, will recognise its authentic flavour. Later in the story Charlie goes to the technical college in Dazure Street:

When he got to the college he went in and asked the lady
who was at the desk where he could find the office . . . as
Charlie went through the door he saw the office and he
hesitated. Then he knocked on the door. A voice said
'Come in', and a stern-faced gentleman told him to sit down.

Here we have detailed social observation expressed in very adequate standard English. In another of the stories we get the verbal immediacy of the dialogue:

'Speak up bwoy and doan kiss you teet', Monica shouted
at Eddy, 'Wha you mean you get involved in fight –
Me gwarn bux you tonight you see', Monica continued.

This is coupled with a depth of perception in the narrative:

Monica wanted him to have a better schooling, at least
a better one than hers. He had to understand. Things had
to become clear to him so he could have a nice life and have
a good education – so he could have a better future, and hope.

We also did quite a lot of drama work with an emphasis on role-play. The situation outlined in the drama was given or 'arose', but the script was always continuously created and recreated by the children. It was never written down. Although the value of role-play lies in the op- portunity it gives for the creative understanding of other people and their place in the scheme of things, it also provides a way into writing in character. So from a role-play which revolved around a child arriving late for school, each child was first interviewed 'in character' about what had happened, and then went on to write down what had happened from the point of view of the character she and he had played. What each one wrote reflected the language – Creole, cockney or 'teacherese' – they had used when speaking the part. I found that as long as they were en- couraged to express opinions, verbalise their own ideas and feelings, and listen to and respect other people's, the children came up with their own suggestions for role-plays. We did this specifically in 'question time', several half hour sessions in which the children asked questions on any subject which then formed the basis for discussion and for deciding role-play situations.

Some resources

Those black British children could speak a dialect derived from the Caribbean, as well as their own 'native South London'. Caribbean dialects, or Creoles, vary considerably from island to island. In Britain, most, but by no means all, children of Caribbean background can speak a dialect which has its roots in Jamaican Creole. Two useful introductory books about Caribbean dialects, which both concentrate on dialects of Jamaican origin, are listed below:

Edwards, V. K. *The West Indian language issue in British schools* Routledge and Kegan Paul, cased and paperback 1979.

Harris, R. *Caribbean English and adult literacy* Adult Literacy Unit, 52–54 High Holborn, London WC1V 6RL. July 1979.

Ways of teaching standard English are outlined in the appropriate pack in *Concept Seven-Nine* which was produced for the Schools Council project in 1979. The ILEA have issued curriculum guidelines on *Language in the primary schools;* and the *Reading through understanding* project has produced three sets of books – *Make-a-story* (Holmes McDougall), *Share-a-story, Explore-a-story* (Collins) – which incorporate elements of dialect in the story wherever ap- propriate and has some very useful teachers' notes. These are obtainable from the ILEA Learning Materials Service, Highbury Station Road, London N1 1SB.

6 Race in children's experience

We conclude the section on primary schooling with brief reflections from five teachers on the need to review attitudes to race, together with some 'snapshots' of practice through which they share their perceptions in class. The aim of all these teachers is to help equip pupils to interpret and handle their awareness of both the personal prejudices among adults, and the forces of institutionalised racism, in the society they meet outside school.

First, some observations from Maggie Speed, a teacher at the multi-racial Haselrigge Junior School in South London, a school advised in its multi-cultural approach by the Lambeth Whole School Project:

Whatever I am 'discovering' about learning and teaching by way of the Lambeth Whole School Project suggests a glaring inadequacy in my college of education curriculum, for I have been unable to recall any references to multi-cultural or multi-ethnic education during my three years of training.

I can now admit openly to being mesmerised when I was first confronted by a class of children with whom I had very little in common. I was ignorant of their culture, habits, customs, ways of life and language differences. Even more traumatic, I didn't know how to begin to correct this deficency.

I was born and educated in the West Country and never had the opportunity to mix with and learn from other ethnic groups – there were none in that rural part of England. I had seen one or two black toddlers from a children's home, but my recollections are feelings of kindness, sympathy and pity for them.

I still believe that when the project team started work in our school in September 1978 I was doing my best as a teacher. However I was not happy to have my techniques, provision and presentation scrutinised by the project team.

After several informal discussions with some of them I started questioning myself about attitudes to language and culture, child, teacher and parental expectations, curriculum content and the relevance of what I was teaching. I believe that I will have to assess myself and my work continuously in order to gain the full reward of what I am now thinking and doing. No longer can I accept 'average' performances from myself or the children I may teach, since kindness and sympathy alone do not make for a satisfactory education.

Perhaps such attitudes underpin social injustice.

I am now aware of the pain that some of our children can suffer through lack of sensitivity or sheer ignorance in well-meaning adults; my books and teaching materials need to be free from hurtful things and any bias needs to be handled in an anti-racist way.

I know that there is much more to learn and do, and that there are vital questions to which I must address my thoughts. One such question is the elusive, yet devastating 'covert racism' – a question my college of education should have posed, but which it saw either as irrelevant or unimportant. Alas, how very, very sad for some of us.

In filming her work as a nursery teacher in Cumbria, for the film 'Anglo-Saxon Attitudes', Jean Adams made these observations in interview:

My aim for the curriculum of the pre-school children, who are at the moment totally white in this remote area of North Cumbria, is not only to use the rich natural environment as a basis for stories, language development and creative activities, but to widen horizons and experiences as much as possible. It's very unusual for children to see someone of different race or colour in our district. We occasionally see Chinese, Japanese and possibly Ugandan Asians in Carlisle but not very often. Since some children are often left at home during shopping trips into town, the chances of them seeing a black face, except on the television screen, are virtually nil.

For this reason we have both black and white dolls in our home play equipment and a selection of story books such as Ezra Jack Keats *Whistle for Willie* and *Snowy day* (Bodley Head 1966–67). Great favourites at the moment are Joan Solomon's books about Berron and Montrice, and Kate Leah's about children in a mixed racial community.

But stories and pictures are not the same as seeing and mixing with adults and children of different cultures. So we welcome visitors of different race or colour to come to see us. The first reaction of the children to the visitor, any visitor, is to stare. Some even shrink away and won't sit next to the visitor for a while. One mother said 'he really thinks the colour will wash off like make-up'. This is partly because we live in a very isolated community; it is people contact that children need, as well as the story books and dolls we provide. Over the past few years, we've been fortunate in being able to encourage a number of adult visitors from a variety of ethnic groups. Teachers have been able to visit and work with the project – three from Japan, others from the New Hebrides, Zululand, Netherlands, America, Kenya – so that our children have not been totally dependent on television and book representation of people from other cultures.

During the past nine years of teaching I'd had only two coloured children in my classes. One who is a little Indian girl, adopted by white parents, who was treated like a doll by the other children and fussed over all the time. And later I had a three year old boy of black and white parentage, highly intelligent, who immediately identified himself with a black doll in the house corner. He was very imaginative and kept the other children and us entertained with his stories and songs and poems.

In twenty years or less, our nursery children of today will be parents themselves. Some will carry on the traditions of farming in the same place as their ancestors before them. Some will undoubtedly travel further afield into different social and educational spheres. But whether they remain or go, I feel that even before they reach the age of five, it is important that the foundations be laid for future attitudes and relationships with people of other cultures.

It was in agreement with the view that there is no substitute for 'direct people contact' that two primary schools, one 'all-white' suburban, the other racially mixed inter-city, arranged a series of reciprocal visits, as illustrated in the film 'Anglo-Saxon Attitudes'. Here is an extract from an account by Leicestershire Headteacher, David Houlton, describing why he and a colleague first set up such an exchange:

Some time prior to the project, we had become aware within our own schools of two major sources of concern for teachers. These were firstly the attitude of indigenous children towards minority group children and adults (particularly British Asian). The second source of concern was the attitude of minority group children towards themselves and their own culture. We were concerned at the incidence of self-rejection among these children. This seemed to manifest itself in various ways in the classroom such as embarrassment at being reminded of their families' origins and reluctance to discuss aspects of their culture in the presence of children from outside their immediate culture.

We concluded that since our two schools were so different from each other – one of all White British and one predominantly of British Asians – a project based on a series of reciprocal visits between the two might provide opportunities for approaching these questions with children.

Many teachers believe that by simply attempting to create a 'happy' atmosphere in their schools and classrooms, they would be able to prevent any difficulties of the sort we have outlined, from arising. Harmonious relations would emerge naturally if children were merely allowed to interact within the school. It seemed that many of these teachers believed that children were 'colour blind'.

Possibly the most significant results on this point have emerged from the work of Dr David Milner at the University of Bristol. Milner interviewed some four hundred children between the ages of five and eight of West Indian, Indian, Pakistani and English parentage in their schools. His results showed that the majority of the children (black and white) had a sound grasp of the lowly position which immigrant people occupy in the British social system. This resulted in the majority of the children showing marked preferences for white figures, frequently attributing positive and 'good' characteristics to them and negative or 'bad' characteristics to black figures. In the minds of the majority of the children, white people were preferred as friends in the playground, as classmates and for sharing sweets with. Black people were frequently regarded as 'bad' or 'ugly'. Also, when asked about their possible preferences in adulthood, the children expressed desires to have white people as neighbours, as best friends, and as shopping companions.

We realised these findings showed that the problems which we hoped to tackle during the course of our project were certainly not peculiar to our schools or to Leicester. Rather we felt that they were central to the whole question of education for a multi-racial society, and that consequently our experience with the project might prove valuable for others who, although convinced of the need for intervention with children, had not yet taken any steps in this direction.

After five visits and many projects (some involving black parents), the all-white school children were asked to write down their reactions.

My mum and dad keep on saying lots of things about Indian people. My dad calls them golliwogs. But I say, 'you don't know them because you have never met them. They are ordinary people like us but they are coloured'.

Before I went to East Park I felt a bit frightened ... After I had met them I felt different because I knew they were friendly and I wished we could have stayed a bit longer.

At first I thought they would be wearing saris all the time and they would speak in Indian languages but I was wrong. They only wear saris on special occasions. They were human just like us. Because their skins are a different colour doesn't mean to say they are different all together.

My mam said she don't like them and I said 'how do you know, you haven't even met them. I have made a friend there and his name is Dilip'. When my mam says all those nasty words I thought that it was cruel because they are only human beings like us, only they eat different food.

Clearly one can easily make the mistake of over-emphasising the importance of children's ideas as expressed through their writings, by interpreting these as indicators of significant attitude changes. This is tantamount to self-deception. Nevertheless, we feel that this writing, for many of the children, marks a step forward from the views expressed prior to the project, in the direction of developing greater respect for other people and their way of life.

As for the British Asian children in the other school, it would be foolish to over-emphasise the significance of observations alone, but we have become aware of some encouraging developments. The most important of these, and this has been commented upon by many members of staff, is a greater willingness on the part of the children to discuss themselves, their backgrounds and elements of Indian religious and cultural life with which they are familiar. They are more likely to talk freely about their festivals, their visits to the temple and the weddings which they attend. The shyness which overcame them in the past whenever such matters were raised is no longer in evidence. Perhaps we have made a modest move towards achieving the objects which we outlined at the outset of the project.

The full account of that exchange project is given in *Getting Together*, available from Shaftesbury Junior School, Latimer Street, Leicester.

In his pamphlet *Multi-cultural Britain* (see page 37) David Moore of Tulse Hill School in South London, includes an account of a play scheme for eight to eleven year olds organised in Cambridge. One of the aims was to do something to counteract the prejudices, based on negative group stereotypes, that children pick up from adults in or out of school or from the media:

One of the rooms was turned into an exhibition room and quickly acquired, on loan from the children's families and friends, a large, impressive selection of articles that the children could use and handle. This was very important as one of the aims was to encourage first hand experience of unfamiliar lifestyles in order to break down stereotypes. There were clothes they could wear, cooking utensils they could use, toys they could play with, and musical instruments they could play.

The first day was spent entirely on 'getting-to-know' games. The children were split into four groups, so each child belonged to a small multi-cultural unit, which made it easier for them to make friends. We played name games, leading to a drama we called the 'stereotype game'.

Each small group was given a 'stereotype' to look at: Red Indian, policeman, teacher and tourist. We first asked the children to show us in mime what immediately came to mind. Inevitably the Red Indian group did a fearsome war dance, tying cowboys to a totem pole and scalping them. The leaders then began injecting a few questions and ideas: 'Who lived in America before the cowboys? . . . how did the Indians live, what sort of houses did they build, what food did they live off? . . . how did they feel when the white men began shooting their buffaloes? . . . are there Indians in America nowadays? . . . what sort of lives do they lead?' and so on, all the time encouraging the children to act out their answer or feelings in mime.

In this way, they began to experience for themselves what it felt like to be a Red Indian, and they began to talk about their initial 'stereotyped' images, about how television and comics put across the wrong idea of unfamiliar groups of people, often because it is more entertaining to portray them as stupid, comical, or violent.

Finally, this is the full interview given for the film by Martin Francis, the teacher from Normand Park School in Fulham, seen discussing racial questions with a class of ten year olds in 'A Primary Response':

What do you say to people who accuse you of foisting political issues on young minds?

Well I'm only following the ILEA policy – it's called a multi-ethnic policy – which fully recognises the dangers of racism and what it does to school children. At this moment in our borough the young National Front has been leafletting schools and claims they are getting very good support from white youth. There are marches, racist graffiti, and news of violence. So it is an issue for the children anyway. What I'm doing is lifting the lid off it so that through discussion they can discover what racism is and what has resulted from it before. I think it would be a 'political' act to ignore racism – to pretend that everything's fine when, as the children themselves have already realised, it's not.

But aren't these children a bit young to discuss such an issue properly?

Because racism is part of their daily experience they can never be too young. I know a nursery school teacher who takes up racial issues with parents who've told their children not to play with black children, for example. It has come through from nursery to primary school, and if we

54

leave these questions to secondary school, during the adolescent phase, when they may have fears about not getting jobs and so on, this can leave them ready prey for those racist groups leafletting outside the school.

If we tackle this in primary school, it perhaps won't be set aside later in just a special social studies class, for example. As a primary teacher, I have the children all day, and if an incident occurs, I can stop the lesson, get the children around, and talk about it on the basis of a relationship built up over a whole year. With mutual confidence, they talk about the way name calling really affects them, for example. This is not so easy in secondary school where it's harder to have a special relationship with one teacher. The vital thing is to respect their feelings, because all the time I'm encouraging them to reflect that what they say counts.

What then do you say to a child who has apparently
very racist feeling?

If a child makes racist comments, or gets involved in a fight with a racist undertone to it, we talk it over in a discussion circle. I get the whole class to talk about it – and that way it's often the other children who deal with the racism. When they talk about their own experience, this can get through to the child better than me. After all, the peer group live in the same streets and experience the same sorts of things. But the difference, between what a black child experiences in terms of harrassment, and a white one, is important. And it's important that the white children learn what this difference can mean. I think in our discussion this is what comes out. Similarly, I stimulate their understanding of what it feels like to be in a group that is scapegoated, through study with the children of *The Diary of Anne Frank*. The children can identify with the emotion of someone who was herself a child at the time of writing; and to show that oppression can be resisted, we talk through the revolt of the black students in Soweto, who are attempting to get a better education system.

So what do you see as multi-cultural education?

I think multi-cultural education can easily become just the treatment of exotic topics, exotic foreign food, dress and countries. I think it should be more than that. I think it should recognise the black people who are here and look at the reasons why they're here. It should look at the daily experience of black people. It should also look at the kind of views that the white people have inherited from days of the past, from Colonialism and Imperialism. We have to tackle this head on. We could begin from consideration of things like food and then develop that into something which is more anti-racist teaching. I think that would be something aimed at the white working class kids as well as the black kids. It's not black studies, it's something much more than that. There is a group of teachers that I belong to, ALTARF – All London Teachers against Racism and Fascism – which has published two handbooks. One on the secondary and one on primary education (*Race in the classroom – teaching against racism in the primary school*. We organise workshops on them. I certainly think any school should have a policy about racism and treat racist abuse very seriously.

In a word, multi-cultural education should develop an awareness in all children of the dangers of racism and of the value of living in a multi-cultured society.

All London Teachers Against Racism and Fascism,
Room 216, Panther House,
38 Mount Pleasant,
London WC1X 0AP
(01–278 7856).

ALTARF Publications

Challenging Racism ISBN 0 950 96730 0. Aimed at teachers and school students, this book outlines strategies to implement anti-racist teaching and policies at all age levels. Topics include the Irish in Britain, language and mother-tongue teaching, social studies, police in schools, the position of black teachers and anti-racist policies.

Race in the Classroom The primary workshop on anti-racist teaching strategies.

Divide and Rule – Never! Pupils' booklet based on the film by Newsreel Collective, for use in secondary schools and colleges.

ALTARF Newsletter Up to date news, info, reviews and campaigns – bi-termly.

Racism: the 4th R (BBC 2 *Open Door* film on VHS video) Useful 30-minute film for showing at meetings, in-service training etc. Black and white pupils, teachers and parents relate their experience of racism and the way schools have either ignored it or fought it. Examples of anti-racist teaching. No charge for hire but donation welcome.

Teaching and Racism A discussion document suggesting anti-racist teaching strategies in various secondary subject areas. Now out of print, but available at many Teacher's Centres.

7 Examples of curriculum development

Through the primary school case studies we have begun to build a picture of what multi-cultural education means. We now fill out that picture with some 'snapshots' of curriculum developments at particular comprehensive schools. They serve to show how multi-cultural education is about more than simply making school 'comfortable' for ethnic minority pupils, in the sense of reducing any split they might experience between home culture and school culture. We look at some syllabuses in history, English literature and home economics – with glances at science, religious education, and the arts – which illustrate some general points taken for granted at the schools that contributed them: for example, that cultural 'pluralism' is relevant to all subjects (not just to history and religious education) and that it requires inter-department collaboration across the whole curriculum if it is to be effective. We include an account of a staff working party on multi-cultural curriculum and development education at Stantonbury Campus in Milton Keynes, which makes this case – a case re-inforced by the working party at Birley High School in Manchester shown in the film 'School Report'. Since the school in Milton Keynes has very few ethnic minority students, their report serves also to underline the general point that multi-cultural curriculum development is seen to be as much for 'all white' schools as for those which have ethnic minority pupils. This point comes through again in some extracts we give from thoughts Dr Bhikhu Parekh contributed to the debate on multi-cultural education in 1980, about the place of imagination among our educational objectives. A further general point has already been made: that *tokenist* changes of content – simply substituting some sections of traditional courses by some 'third world' examples, for example sugar growing in the West Indies, to replace coal mining in Wales – do not make for true multi-cultural teaching. This is clear from the start of these introductory observations by the Head of Humanities at an all-boys comprehensive in East London which provides an integrated studies course for the first three years, combining the study of English, Drama, History, Geography and RE:

Changing the content – substituting a study of Indian history for the study of medieval English history – does not in itself constitute a multi-cultural curriculum. Even if such substitutions do take place, they may not counterbalance the hidden nature of standard texts, which often perpetuate bias towards, say, male interpretations of history or towards certain class attitudes. Neither do such substitutions necessarily alter the style of the classroom, or the understanding of what learning and knowing are.

Multi-cultural education, for me, redefines not only the scope of curriculum content, but also the nature of education itself – the pedagogy, the attitudes and activities within the institution, in corridors as well as classrooms. Although I have not the space to expand this statement, I must assert that what follows is not written in the spirit of hot tips and handy hints, but in deep seriousness about the underlying principle of my profession. Whatever the examples, they have occurred in classrooms where the individuals learn to understand and respect themselves and each other, where their language and background is seen as a positive resource, where attitudes are as important as information and skills.

Above all, I would focus on the role of language in learning, the language resources everybody undoubtedly has and uses in expressing, comprehending, negotiating and communicating. Pupil talk – spoken language skills – are not the sole preserve of the English teacher. Many research studies confirm this. Collaborative work, group work, mixed ability classes – all these are part of it. Children learn by talking about themselves, their ideas and experiences, and they learn from each other as much as from the teacher. It is my intention that the pupils in my classes also learn to see *how* they are learning, and to value the activity.

Only within this context does it make sense to me to introduce language not only as the medium but also the subject. In the security of a positive attitude towards one's own language resources, one can discuss differences and their implications. Language is power, but certain dialects – such as Standard English – also have prestige. Although many of my pupils come to me bi-lingual or multi-dialectual or multi-lingual, received pronunciation and the grammar of the 'standard' English dialect may not be part of their language resources yet. It is important to me, not that they master standard English for its 'inherent superiority', but that they understand its role in our society and are able to choose whether or not to use it, without demeaning their current language resources.

Sometimes, with younger pupils, we play a simulation game called 'The Word House' (adapted from one of a pack of three simulations

58

called *The People* GRID produced by the Cockpit Theatre, Gateforth Street, London NW8 8EH). Basically it is a trading game, a trade in individual words and in sentences using them, in which the words are grouped in families according to their origin. These 'families' are peoples or places with whom the English have had encounters, and from whom all the words have been adopted so that most people simply think of them as ordinary English words. The families are Latin, Greek, Celtic, Scandinavian, Dutch, French, Italian, and Indian; the words are generally simple like: circus, museum, button, outlaw, luck, garage, piano, pyjamas. The game structure obviously helps it to be an enjoyable, participatory activity, but the fascination of etymology and how the English language could be termed a patois is the subject of much intense discussion for long after the game is over. It also raises the concept of what language is, and points to the absurdity of terms like 'pure English' (language or people) – since even the language is revealed to be multi-cultural.

In altogether a different kind of lesson structure, groups may read poems like Louise Bennett's 'Noh Lickle Twang' (*New ships* edited by D. G. Wilson, Oxford University Press, 1975) and discuss attitudes to accent and dialect – that of the mother in the poem, that of their own mothers and peers. Poems like Sam Greenlee's 'Immigrants' (*Ammunition*, Bogle-L'Ouverture Publications, 141 Coldershaw Road, London W13, 1975) are more than just fun to read; they raise real questions about attitudes, and the discussions are both literary and political. I admit I am still learning about literatures in English and know least about that from the Indian sub-continent, but African, black American and Caribbean literature has greatly enriched my own reading experience (singularly lacking in my own 'higher education') and opened up valuable resources for my teaching. I find that this literature is essential reading, joyfully received throughout the age range of secondary school. Apart from counteracting racist notions that non-Europeans have no literary culture, these works are a joy in themselves and also serve to give a deeper understanding to the themes of – say – exile and identity. I find the power of story, play or poem, is far greater (as it captures the imagination and the feelings as well as the rational part of the mind) than informational writing.

Certain topics and themes like, for example, 'People on the Move' can provide scope for information and the examination of attitudes. If we look around our classroom and think out across a generation or two, we have among ourselves many examples. If the classroom is one in which individuals can feel secure in discussing things which are personal to them, the talk ranges from examples of people who move from oppression, people who move to find work, people who move against their will and people who will move on yet again. The history, geography and sociology are not abstract but significantly concrete.

I find among other things that pupils will think comparatively, make connections and analogies. Migration and immigration are not only black activities. Cypriots and the Irish, among others, figure largely in our investigation, and the attitudes which have come to regard 'nigger' jokes and gibes as unacceptable extend to Irish and Jewish jokes as well.

Flexibility and negotiation between teacher and class on the lesson content is also, for me, part of multi-cultural education. If our principles say that each one of us, as well as the things which matter to us, is important, then the events in the local community and the mass media which pupils are involved in, or interested in, become equally as important as preplanned lessons on, say, the emergence of Ghana as the first modern independent African state. The autumn term for us begins in the aftermath of the Notting Hill Carnival; I would be wise to photocopy some newspapers and if possible, videotape some news coverage. Hurricane Allen destroyed the homes and livelihoods of family and friends in the Carribbean. Such events are not just trendy ways for teachers to get pupils to discern bias in language and image, they are part of their world and their world should have its place in our classroom. I feel I should be ready and willing to use current events, and be able to collaborate with my pupils and learn along with them – for on many matters they are actually better informed than I. For me, the multi-cultural approach requires a constant, and sincere, care not to slip into tokenism or being patronising; it also fits ill with an 'omniscient' teacher role.

Multi-cultural history

As a result of a staff conference in 1973 at Tulse Hill School, a South London all boys comprehensive, each department was asked to evaluate its curriculum according to relevance to the pupils (many of whom are of West Indian background) and to its multi-cultural content.

As a result, the history department decided to replace the traditional British and European history syllabus with a two year world history course which would be taken by all second and third year pupils following an integrated first year.

Although the department obviously kept in mind the ethnic origin of their pupils, and took their views into account when deciding what material to teach, what is interesting about this syllabus is the framework they use and the way in which they have systematically tried to eliminate Anglocentric bias. So far as possible each civilisation studied is given equal weight in both its positive and negative aspects, and the actions of people and nations are considered in relation to their own stated intentions and to the effects those actions had on others.

The course begins with two terms on the people who came to Britain and incorporates some groups commonly ignored. It is a blend of topics for which commonly available sources can be used, albeit critically, together with materials which the department had to provide:

Second year course

Terms 1 and 2(a)
The people who came to Britain

1.1 Anglo-Saxons. Revision from First Year Humanities using School's Council Tollumd Man Mystery and the Sutton Hoo material. Visit and follow up on Sutton Hoo British Museum exhibits.

1.2 The Viking contribution to Britain. Project style approach. Core booklet with details on Viking settlement in Britain and some general sheets for poor readers. Topic cards on aspects of Viking life and exploration.

1.3 The Norman contribution to Britain. Core information on the Norman background and settlement. Story telling on Conquest. Emphasis on language and survivals. Visit and follow up on White Tower, Tower of London.

2.1 Use of Westminster Abbey showing materials as survivals, eg Richard II's memorial – what was his relationship with fellow Britons – Peasant's Revolt, etc (to be developed further).

2.2 The Jewish contribution to Britain. Core booklet only (no other source available). Background to the Jews in history, Jewish settlement in Britain, position of Jews in British society, money lending and credit, special laws on Jews and their expatriation. Special examination of points dealing with images of Jews.

2.3 European craftsmen, settlers in Medieval Britain. Examination of documentary evidence on work and attitudes to newcomers.

2.4 Black settlers in Britain. Examination of how black people have settled in Britain over two hundred years based on a book by N. File and C. Power, *Black Settlers in Britain 1555–1958* Heinemann, 1981.

Term 2(b)
Modern social history through museums and local studies

In contrast with previous work, a skills approach to make sense of and evoke a sense of the past through material objects. Visit to London Museum and follow up. Walkabouts in the locality – post-war pre-fabs; Brixton windmill; the railway network, tunnel entrances, station and bridge architecture; Brixton's markets, cinemas, theatres, shops, Brockwell Park.

There then follows a two and a half term course on the world in 1400, during which the pupils study Incas in South America, North American Indians, Hindu societies and the Mughal empire of India, Europe (mainly Britain) and the Caribbean Arawak and Carib societies. Although the material used does not keep strictly to the 15th century, the year 1400 was chosen because it is the last date at which the different civilisations of the world can be studied in isolation from each other. The work is based almost exclusively on work books prepared and printed in the department. The books include extracts from contemporary writers, maps, illustrations, narrative, and comprehension questions related to the themes. The aim is to show that many parts of the world had valid cultures and highly developed life styles, at least for the minority, and to give a rudimentary explanation of the basic political and economic organisation and show how this is related to material resources, leadership, trade, law and order, and religion.

According to Nigel File, the Head of Department, the main difficulty is to put positive achievement into a realistic framework, *and* to make the books interesting without relying on the exotic. Given the paucity of materials on world studies, making one's own is the best and cheapest option, and provides the teacher with absolute control over language and content. Uniformity of approach for the different civilisations prevents the course from becoming inadvertently Eurocentric, and the contemporary illustrations used make it clear that 'civilisation' as a concept is a complex, world-wide phenomenon.

Finally there is a term in which pupils study themes of contact, using examples from different parts of the world between 1400 and 1900. These include:

Theme	Examples
Co-operation	Portugal and Congo (early)
Exploitation	Portugal and Congo (later)
Rejection	China and Japan Cudjoe and Maroons

Theme	Examples
Settlement	British in the Caribbean
	Black British
Mission	Christians and North American-Indians
	Muslims and Fulani
Forced Movement	West African Slave Trade
	Convicts from Britain
Voluntary Movement	Gold rushes
	Travellers
Refuge	Huguenots, Jews,
	slave and apprentice runaways
Resistance	Ndongo and the Portuguese
	Nanny of the Maroons and the British

Which themes are chosen in this section depend on the interests of the individual teacher and pupils. The advantage of looking at contacts after studying the different civilisations in their own right is that subjects such as the slave trade can be seen in their proper context, in relation to an African and Caribbean as well as to a European past, and people who have already been shown in action creating their own civilisations cannot so easily be dismissed as helpless victims. The previous work also makes it possible to look at contact between people where there is no European involvement. In this way we can show historically how a particular intention and the will and resources to fulfil it is not the prerogative of any one race or group of people.

A second approach to World History
World studies is not necessarily the prerogative of the history department. At John Bunyan, a 13–18 mixed comprehensive school in Bedford, it forms one four week unit of work within an integrated humanities course which brings together history, geography and re-ligious education for pupils in their first year at the school. Whereas Tulse Hill offered a largely thematic course, the scheme at John Bunyan aims to draw out comparisons between India, China and the Afro-Caribbean world at different points in time. David Grief explains:

Our humanities department had long been considering the possibility of a unit which related directly to the school's cultural make-up. The inhibiting factor had been the absence of any good material, especially in view of the possible sensitivity of too direct an approach. But the Schools Council material on Imperial China and the ILEA material on India and the Caribbean gave us our chance to experiment.

There are five aims behind the development of our world history unit:

1 To provide pupils with a better understanding of some of the countries of immigrant origin. It is perhaps one small contribution towards tackling prejudice;

2 To balance local studies which tend to dominate Humanities work at present by introducing a world dimension;

3 To allow pupils of Asian and Caribbean origin to identify with something directly within the curriculum;

4 To provide an opportunity for individual study. The third year Humanities course involves a lot of direct teaching; pupils need to learn to study independently for fourth and fifth year courses;

5 To lay a foundation for fourth and fifth year work in geography and history as case studies would frequently be drawn from these areas.

Pupils were allowed to choose which country they studied. The only constraints were the number of available worksheets and the necessity of those doing history in the fourth year to study China.

Content and resources

Introduction
(approximately 2 periods)

Location of study areas: Caribbean, China, India. Reasons for study. An overview of the changing world through two thousand years, with three main comparative timelines – Pre-European civilisation, European influence, Securing independence of foreign rule.
Pupils choose one area of study for themselves.

The physical background
(approximately 2 periods)

Location, size, diversity of landscape, climate, population. Teacher lecture with slides; pupils read, take notes, complete map and watch television.

Pre-European civilisations
(approximately 8 periods)

Main question: 'What were some of the achievements of the people in your study area before the arrival of the Europeans?'

Area of enquiry available:

	India	China	Caribbean	West Africa
Village life	✓	✓	✓	✓
Town life	✓	✓	—	✓
Art and architecture	✓	✓	—	✓
Government	—	✓	—	✓
Education	—	✓	—	—
Technology	—	✓	—	—

Resources: videos, 'Traditional India', 'Islands and People', 'Traditional China' all ILEA. Tape/slide sequence, 'The West African Background'.

European influence and colonization
(approximately 8 periods)

Main question: 'What changes were brought about by the entry of Europeans into your study area? Did the Europeans improve or exploit the area?'

Area of enquiry:

	India	China	Caribbean
Reasons why they went	✓	✓	✓
Rivalry between the European powers	✓	✓	✓
Opinions of the people	—	✓	✓
Changes brought by the Europeans	✓	✓	✓
Reaction of the people	✓	✓	✓
	eg Indian Mutiny	eg Boxer Rebellion	eg Slave revolts

Resources: videos, 'Europeans in China', 'British in India', 'Sugar and spice, tobacco and rum', ILEA.
Tape/slide sequence, 'The Plantation system'.
Tape-recording, BBC 'Clive in India', Schools Broadcast.

*Movement towards independence
and freedom from foreign influence*
(approximately 8 periods)

Main question: 'How did the countries free themselves from foreign influence in the nineteenth and twentieth centuries?'

Areas of enquiry

	India	China	Caribbean
Leaders of the struggle, a brief biography	Gandhi	Sun Yat Sen Mao Tse Tung	Toussaint in Haiti
The major events, protests and demonstrations leading to freedom from foreign influence	Swaraj, Indian National Congress, Independence and Partition	Long March War v Japan Civil War	in Jamaica

Resources: videos, 'Modern China', 'India, Pakistan and Bangladesh'. 'India – The Brightest Jewel', and 'One Man's Revolution' (Mao Tse Tung), both from BBC Schools series '20th Century History'.
Tape/slide, 'The Modern Caribbean Society'.

Modern life
(approximately 3 periods)
A brief look at life today in the three areas.
Resources: Those above, plus video 'A Changing Caribbean'.

Evaluation and pupil evaluation
Exploration of the pupils' own ideas and opinions through discussion is crucial throughout the course. We find that such discussion is the key to full involvement in this kind of study.

Major pupil resources
World History Outlines
1 The Caribbean
2 India
Both from ILEA Learning Materials Service, Highbury Station Road, London NI 15B. (Their catalogue of videos has a section on world history.)

Imperial China Schools Council Integrated Studies Project, published by Oxford University Press, 1974, op.

Caribbean studies, from Concordia Filmstrips, Viking Way, Bar Hill Village, Cambridge CB3 8EL.

Multi-cultural literature

Within the first three years of secondary education there is considerable latitude for teachers' choice and experiment. In the fourth and fifth year the search for multi-cultural relevance, depth, and breadth of curriculum content tends to become obscured under the looming shadow of public examinations. One way of maintaining a multi-cultural direction under this pressure is to adopt a mode III syllabus which can then be designed with one's own pupils in mind to explore themes and relationships which are not taken up in the conventional syllabus.

An example of Mode III CSE syllabus in English Literature was outlined in *The English Magazine*, no. 3, Spring 1980 – an important issue devoted to Language, Childhood and Race. This report by Scilla Alvarado shows how the Literature of Africa, Asia and the Caribbean can be brought quite naturally into the centre of an English literature examination course:

The following Mode III CSE syllabus is one of the examination option courses offered in the fourth and fifth year in the school where I teach. All pupils have a small 'taster' of the subject in the third year and it attracts a broad range of pupils. The syllabus was constructed through the recognition that the study of literature in schools has been predominantly Euro-centric in approach and so by selection and omission has continued to perpetuate the myth of European supremacy and cultural superiority.

Over the past decade some African or Caribbean books have crept into some English syllabuses. These can either be studied in their singularity or ignored if the teacher so wishes, thereby maintaining the subordinate position this body of literature still holds, within compulsory English literature. This raises questions about how to introduce a body of knowledge that will have a genuine effect on the ideological bias of the school curriculum. This syllabus was an attempt to create a greater space for the study of a formerly ignored literature and culture. In addition it represents an attempt to 'place' this literature within a cultural and social framework and also to raise questions in the areas of race, sex, work, age, etc while at the same time teaching those basic intellectual skills which black and working class children need if *they* are to challenge the structures of society which have placed them where they are.

The other major section of the syllabus – the social background – has been included to extend the ideas raised by the literature and to encourage an analytic reflection upon one's own experience and society.

Autobiographical writing has become a common activity, particularly in working class urban schools, to encourage pupils to value their own experience as important. Clearly, to extend this beyond a therapeutic exercise, the pupils need to be guided within a framework to

67

enable them to reflect upon their development in the society within which they live. By 'making strange' their own lives, or maybe that of their parents, they may recognise common experiences and pressures and proceed to analyse them in terms of the society and how social practices affect their group.

An investigation of the media has been included as an integral part of the course as it has a significant role in transmitting attitudes and beliefs. Teachers are responsible not only for extending the pupils' view of the world, but also for challenging their perceptions of it as it has been constructed for them. This section of the course concentrates on the images of race as presented in the media.

Literature and society syllabus

Core of syllabus
The students study at least four of the following books in depth plus their social, cultural and historical context. The teacher chooses at least one book from four different sections to ensure as wide a range of cultures as possible and these are studied by the class as a whole. One book from the European section is compulsory. Students are encouraged to read complete novels (as recommended by the Bullock Report) and not just a collection of extracts. The sections are as follows in alphabetical order.

African literature
Things Fall Apart: Chinua Achebe, Heinemann, 1971.
No Sweetness Here: Aidoo Ata Ama, Longman, 1979.
Second Class Citizen: Buchi Emecheta, Fontana, 1977.
Roots of Time: Jefferson & Skinner
Nine African Stories: Doris Lessing, Longman, 1978.
The Study of Literature: ed. H. L. B. Moody, Allen and Unwin, 1972.
Weep Not Child: James Ngugi, Heinemann, 1967.
Young and Black in Africa: A. Ikion Ojigbo, Random, New York, 1971.
The Fisherman: Tom Okoyo, Heinemann, 1971.
Tribal Scars: Sembene Ousmane, Heinemann, 1974

Afro-American literature
Young and Black in America: Alexander and Lester, NY: Random, 1977.
To Be A Slave: Julius Lester, Kestrel, 1970.
Long Journey Home: Julius Lester, Longman 1978, Puffin Books 1977.
The Journey: Murray and Thomas
The Scene: Murray and Thomas
The Search: Murray and Thomas
Major Black Writers: Murray and Thomas
Black Perspectives: Murray and Thomas
Three Against Slavery: Philip Spencer, Scholastic Book Service, 1972 op.

Black-Eyed Susans: ed. Mary Helen Washington, Doubleday, Garden City, 1975.
Black Boy: Richard Wright, Longman, 1970.

Asian Literature
Untouchable: Mulk Raj Anand, Chicago: Inter Culture, 1974.
I Take This Woman: Rajinder Singh Bedi, Chicago: Inter Culture, 1967.
East End At Your Feet: Farrukh Dhondy, Macmillan, 1976 op.
The Whispering Earth: K. S. Karanth, Delhi: Vikas Publishing House, 1977.
From Citizen to Refugee: Mahmood Mamdani, F. Pinter, 1973.
My Village, My Life: Mehanti Prafulla, Davis-Poynter, 1973.
The World of Premchand: Premchand, Allen and Unwin, 1969.
A Mentor Book of Modern Asian Literature: Dorothy Blair Shimer NY New
American Library, 1973.
A Bride For The Sahib: Khushwant Singh, Chicago: Inter Culture, 1967.
Contemporary Indian Short Stories: Ka Naa Subramanyam, NY Advent Books,
1978.

Caribbean literature
Bluefoot Traveller: ed. James Berry, Limestone Publications, 1976 op.
Backfire: ed. N. and U. Guiseppi, Macmillan, 1973 op.
Out Of The Stars: ed. N. and U. Guiseppi, Macmillan, 1975 op.
Moon On a Rainbow Shawl: Errol John, Faber, 1963.
Miguel Street: V. S. Naipaul, various editions.
Joey Tyson: Andrew Salkey, Bogle L'Ouverture, 1974.
A Brighter Sun: Samuel Selvon, Longman, 1974.
Ways of Sunlight: Samuel Selvon, Longman, 1979.
The Sun's Eye: ed. Ann Walmsey, Longman, 1968.

European literature
The Jewish Wife and Other Plays: Bertolt Brecht, NY, Grove 1965.
The Diary of Anne Frank: Anne Frank, various editions.
Andorra: Max Frisch, Eyre Methuen, 1968.
A Scot's Quair: Lewis Grassie Gibbon, Pan, 1973.
Childhood: Maxim Gorky, Central Books, 1974.
An Irish Navvy: Donall MacAmhlaigh, Routledge, 1964.
Hal: Jean MacGibbon, Penguin Books, 1978.
Portrait of the Artist as a Young Dog: Dylan Thomas, Dent, 1965.

Social background
Book, film & TV programme reviews
Written or taped reviews are submitted over the five terms. These should be
concerned with aspects of culture and race. A variety of books is provided by the
school to encourage voluntary, independent reading. Where necessary the
teacher guides the student's reading to cover a variety of areas as recommended
in the core syllabus.

The presentation of race in the media

This section is based mainly on the study of the British Film Institute's Course, 'Images of Blacks' which includes slides, film extracts and full length films.

Autobiographies/Biographies of projects on various aspects of culture and race

The students are encouraged to compile small booklets about themselves or someone else, preferably a person who has come from another culture, and so produce some original research into a person's history and culture.

Extracts are used from some of the following biographies, autobiographies and books about culture in British society:

Lifetimes: Group Autobiographies
(Manchester Polytechnic)

1 A Mancunian couple

2 A Russian and a Mancunian

3 A Couple from Runcorn and the Isle of Man

4 A Barbadian

5 An Irish Couple

6 A Couple from Durham

7 A Mancunian

Small Accidents: Sabir Bandali
Memories: Paul George, Common place Workshop, 1977 op.
Millfield Memories: Doris Knight, Centreprise, 1976 op.
Daddy Burtt's For Dinner: Rose Lowe
A Hoxton Childhood: Carl Jasper, Centreprise, 1972.
Poverty: The Forgotten Englishmen: Ken Coates and Richard Silburn, Penguin Books, 1973.
Into Unknown England: ed. Peter Keating, various editions.

Projects

The students are required to demonstrate a detailed knowledge of a chosen area which is closely supervised by the teacher. This project may include written work/tapes and illustrations and may, where possible, involve contact with the local community.

Most of the books mentioned in that syllabus are available from Walter Rodney Bookshop (see opposite page).

Some sources on literature

Fiction for secondary schools in the multi-racial society (July 1980) from CUES, 34 Aberdeen Park, London N5 2BL.

Children's Book Bulletin termly journal from Children's Rights Workshop, 4 Aldebert Terrace, London SW8.

Dragon's Teeth the bulletin of the National Committee on Racism in Children's Books, 240 Lancaster Road, London W11.

A wider heritage 1980, The National Book League, 45 East Hill, London SW18 2HZ.

English in Education: the issue for Spring 1977 is devoted to multi-cultural approaches, including Ranjana Ash's *Introducing South Asian literature* and a booklist of West Indian writing for secondary schools.

The English Magazine published termly by ILEA, English Centre, Sutherland Street, London SW1.

Association for the Teaching of Caribbean and African Literature (ATCAL) c/o The Africa Centre, 38 King Street, London WC2. ATCAL aims to assist knowledge and understanding of works by African and Caribbean authors. It publishes a newsletter, and has regional groups in London, Leeds, Sheffield, Birmingham, Edinburgh, Exeter and in Kent.

Short stories from India, Pakistan and Bangladesh edited by Ranjana Ash, Harrap, 1980.

Bogle-L'Ouverture Publications, 141 Coldershaw Road, London W13 (01–579 4920) issue an annoted catalogue.

Soma Books, 38 Kennington Lane, London, SE11 4SL – for literature in English and Southern Asian languages.

Walter Rodney Bookshop, 5 Chignall Place, London, W13 0TJ. For catalogue, send large s.a.e.

Exploring dialect in English

Some ideas about the place of dialect, as part of building on the home and social experience of children, were offered by primary teacher Graham Jameson on pages 46 to 48. And the film 'School report' illustrated the sort of interest and rapport built up in her English lessons at secondary level by Sharon Godard in Manchester. For teachers who have not, like Sharon, expanded their English syllabuses to include dialects, we offer some remarks by Caroline Griffin on her work in a South London comprehensive. While they don't tackle the detailed questions involved in using dialects, they point to the value in English classes of exploring different ways of speaking and writing English:

I set out with a mixed ability third year group to explore their own language differences. I began by handing each boy a copy of the story 'Summat queer on Batch'. It's in the Penguin book *Story* and it's in Somerset dialect. I chose that specifically because I was convinced that nobody in the class came from Somerset, and we could all admit to being ignorant of this dialect. So we all started at the same point, finding the clues to the meaning and the accent.

It's a funny story with a good pace and joke ending, all of which is quite important for thirteen year olds. Some of the vocabulary was completely strange and encouraged a close look at context clues before we could find any sort of tentative meaning.

The language was quite difficult. Job Ash went up in the morning, when there was an 'unket' wind blowing, and we all wondered what it meant. The next line was 'He buttoned up his jacket and walked fast' and of course everyone suggested that it might mean 'cold'. We even came to the decision that it might mean 'unkind' which was quite a sophisticated conclusion and possibly correct.

After that discussion I asked for a volunteer to retell the story in his own words. Then I asked them to tell it in any accent or dialect they chose, recording it on tape.

The first volunteer was a British born Jamaican boy who told it in what he thought was a Scottish accent. He was followed by a boy who told it in a strong South London accent, and then one South African Asian boy said he would tell it in a strong South African accent if he could manage it. His cousin, also from South Africa, then gave us his version of Jamaican dialect. The whole class applauded. He was followed by a British born Jamaican boy who must have felt 'I'll show him what it's really like' and did so. Then we had somebody who tried two lines in a Birmingham accent.

The next lesson they demanded that the tape was played. They were very proud of it. Then I decided we would move on and look at Cockney dialect poems from 'Billy the Kid: an anthology of tough verse'. I chose 'A muvver was barfin' 'er biby one night' and 'Framed in a first storey winder of a burnin' building'. We followed the same procedure.

Up to this point we had done no writing, but we had a taped record we could refer back to. The first piece of writing was for each boy to choose the Cockney poem he preferred, to copy it, and to retell it as a story in standard English. He then had to answer two questions:

1 What are the differences between your story and the original poem?

2 Does the poem gain any interest by being written in dialect?

One boy, writing about this difference, wrote:

'My story has been you might say standardised from the raw easy slang of Cockney. I think the poem gains something in the way of interest in its raw state, rather than standardised English, which kind of stamps out the actual meaning of the poem, or the fun of it. When a poem is written in any slang its meaning and humour is in the slang, but when it's written in standardised English the fun and meaning is distorted.'

When I was marking this work at home I discovered that a South
African Asian boy had written out the Cockney poem in his version of
Jamaican dialect. I was unable to assess whether he had done this
accurately so the next lesson I read it to the class and the experts in
Jamaican dialect gave their corrections.

Down Die Plug 'Ole
A mudder was barting (inna bearding) er bieby one night,
The yungest of (er) ten and as smaal as a mite.
The mudder was pore and die bieby was tin,
Ownly a skeleton covered pon (in) skin
The mudder turned round far die soap pon die rack
She wasn't a moment, but when she turn back,
The bieby was gone down and in anguish she a cry (bawl):
Where's ma bieby – and de Angels reply
Your bieby long gone (drop) down die plug-'ole,
Your bieby a (gone) down die plug;
The pore damn ting was to skinny and tin,
'E should 'have it a bath (beard) in a jug;
Ya baby is perfectly 'appy,
'E won't need a bath animore,
Ya bieby 'as gone (drop) down da plug-'ole,
Na last, but a gone befo.

We had a long discussion about the conventions of sound
representation, for example, 'inna' or 'ina'. My only role in this
discussion was to go to other poems written in Jamaican dialect and
show that there were really no particular conventions.

Again it was something I had not expected and I was very pleased to
see that the class had got into the habit of *saying aloud* strange words
that they did not immediately understand, and *then look for context*
clues. They had shown a willingness to experiment with accent and
dialect and they seemed to be enjoying it.

I now decided to introduce some Jamaican dialect to them. I didn't
want to give them the idea that dialect was only printed or studied if it
was funny, or featured people talking, or if it described 'the oppression
of Babylon'. They could all use dialect for a wider range of purposes
than this. I decided to use the poem 'Double Scank' and the first half of
'Yout Scene'. I chose these because they were written by Linton Kwesi
Johnson, who comes from Jamaica and had been at Tulse Hill School
for about two years. In the introduction to his anthology *Dread, Beat
and Blood* (Bogle-L'Ouverture Publications, 1975), he says:

The kind of thing I write, and the way I say it, is as a result
of the tension between Jamaican Creole and Jamaican English
and between those and English English. And all that, really,

is the consequence of having been brought up in a colonial
society and then coming over here to live and go to school in
England, soon afterwards. The tension builds up. You can see it
in the writing. You can hear it. And something else: my poems
may look sort of flat on the page. Well, that is because they're
actually oral poems, as such. They were definitely written to
be read aloud, in the community.

I had asked him to come to school a few weeks before to speak to any
boys who were interested. When he reads he has a great presence and
dignity so the boys were very excited when they knew he had written
these poems. They felt that he spoke about things that they understood
and places that they had explored in Brixton.

After discussion I asked for two volunteers to read the poems on to
tape and these turned out to be two white boys. When they'd recorded
them I asked the rest of the class to make up questions which they would
ask these boys first, to check if they understood what they'd been reading; and secondly, to see what the poems gained from being written in
dialect.

A British born Jamaican boy put the questions which pressed home
in a much more confident way than I could the importance and value of
becoming aware of other peoples' dialects and the nuances of meaning
and subtleties that are involved in them:

I think if it would have been translated into spoken English,
I don't think it would have made much sense, because the type
of dialect which is used makes it sound sense, you know.

I asked them again to put the poem into their own words, but in order to
do this they had to get help, advice and encouragement from the experts
in Jamaican dialect. In the course of this exchange the white boys asked
the Jamaican boys how they felt about coming to school and having to
speak standard English.

Of course, when you first bring a dialect poem into the classroom,
some really like it, others feel uneasy. But the English department has
been using dialect resources for several years now and so working in
dialect has lost its place as 'special'. When I use a *Black Ink Book* (Black
Ink Collective, 1 Gresham Road, Brixton, London sw9) with the third
year, they go straight into it because they have used it, for example, in
the first year. The white boys will volunteer to read parts in dialect, and
the others help with the mistakes. It shows the trust within the group.

I think that the students had become more relaxed about
approaching any language which was strange to them – even if it was the
strange words which belong to the dialect of standard English. They

became more aware of their phonic skills, realising that it helps to say difficult words aloud or to somebody else. They developed the habit of looking at the context in which words appeared in order to find their meaning. They discovered that they had these skills through working with different dialects, and that they could be used in approaching any other material that they came to. It seemed to me that by acknowledging the dialects which existed in the classroom, within the broader context of dialect variation, it made it less easy for them to put somebody down by saying that what was different was impossible to understand.

We also looked at an article Louise Bennett had written in a little pamphlet produced by the Jamaican Tourist Board, celebrating the arts and culture of Jamaica where she talked a little about Jamaican dialect:

So any time we hear anyone call our Jamaican dialect 'corruption' of the English language we just laugh after them and say that if that be the case the English language must be a corruption of Norman French and Latin and all the other languages that the English say English is derived from. What a joke!

That really had a great effect on the group, and it meant that we had a conversation about how language changed, and about how different groups who came to a country brought their own languages with them, and how these gradually became part of the language of the country. I think this may have given them some idea that language is a changing thing, it isn't standard, it isn't a fixed mode of expression, but a changing mode of expression.

These remarks are extracted from a talk by Caroline Griffin, printed in *Issues* of March 1977 (see page 211). Her work is featured in Viv Edwards' book *The West Indian language issue in British schools* Routledge and Kegan Paul, 1979. This outlines the structure of Jamaican dialect and gives many examples and suggestions for encouraging use of dialect in poetry, drama, and creative writing.

Home economics
A multi-cultural curriculum which is confined to the humanities may be unconvincing to pupils. For many, science and practical subjects may seem more closely related to their awareness of growing adulthood and future employment. Unless the curriculum in home economics, crafts and science also reflect the pupils' own community experience, together with a more global perspective, it is possible that teachers of humanities and literature will be seen simply as purveyors of idealistic messages which fall little short of propaganda.

Many teachers have pointed to home economics as having a high potential for multi-cultural approaches – as long as the equally great dangers of tokenism are avoided. An assumption often made is that giving children the opportunity to appreciate the food of different cultures will help in building their respect for the people who made it. While the potential for looking at different cultural traditions within the modern home economics curriculum is far wider than just the practical aspects of cooking, we asked for her personal view on this assumption from Christine Traxon, Head of HE at Holyhead School in Birmingham:

When I first came to this racially mixed school, I had a missionary type of approach. I thought that I would be teaching about things like hygiene – in effect teaching middle class values. If I'd kept that attitude, I'd have been sunk! I soon found that the children already had a good range of knowledge and experience, though different from my own. Some turned out to be carrying fantastic responsibilities at home in terms of shopping and feeding the family; to seek to teach such children how to make something like baked beans on toast would be just an insult.

I try to build an environment where they feel perfectly secure in sharing information about how things are done in their own homes. If I'm aiming to teach about fish, for example, I want it to come up quite naturally what fish they eat at home and how it is prepared. It is so important not to make children feel 'scrutinised', by asking insensitively direct questions like, 'What do you eat at home?'. Understandably, they won't want to be exposed in this way and will probably reply 'We eat the same as you', and never reveal the information they already have, on which a teacher needs to build. So instead of announcing, 'Next week we're going to do Jamaican food', I find it better to introduce one basic food element as a theme and then discuss the different forms it can appear in. If we're taking beans, for example, I'd mention black-eyed beans, and seeing my familiarity with something they know, the children pour in examples of other varieties they know about. If we take wheat as the basis of a perfectly normal lesson, we are soon unselfconsciously talking about pumpernickel, croissants or chapattis. It is a case of building on the similarities to introduce the differences; starting with just the basics of flour and water can lead into discussing unleavened bread, dumplings, Spanish arepas, Jamaican ardough, etc. It is an approach which helps the different ethnic groups to respect each other – particularly in the first year. They'll try chapattis and although they may say 'ugh' to start with, they'll then come to appreciate that it's just flour and water. It's a process which may take time, but its much more exciting to tackle the food aspect of home economics this way.

If I'm not familiar with some children's home customs, I can unwittingly cause offence – and the children will clam up. For example, West Indian children are usually accustomed at home to lay out plates upside down. There are very sensible reasons for this, but it needs care not to imply that this way is somehow wrong, instead of simply different, from what I'm used to. Once we were playing a game where they had to name vegetables, using different letters of the alphabet. It came to B and they said 'bananas'. If one doesn't know, or forgets, that bananas *are* a vegetable for some West Indians, it's very easy to say, 'Of course they're not vegetables'. It's a matter of how you phrase the questions so that you find out from them. 'What made you say bananas?' could lead to a discussion about the differences between vegetables and fruit. After four years teaching I'm still finding out new things – for example, that it is against the religion of some to eat certain things at certain times.

Children will not share their own experience if they are put down – and a tactless remark can so easily pre-empt feedback. In some of the other areas we cover in our syllabus, such as laundry, entertaining, and especially child care, it's vital to bear in mind that some children come from one-parent families. My point is that a 'multi-cultural' approach in home economics is as much to do with the sensitivity in how you speak with the children, as in what you teach.

Some brief observations concerning Home Economics teaching in secondary school are made in the later section on English as a second language, page 151.

Maths and science

In the film 'School Report', Frank Chennell, science teacher at Birley High School, Manchester, was asked if membership of a staff working party on multi-cultural education had led to any changes in his teaching:

It's difficult to bring in a multi-cultural aspect to science teaching, but when I came to this school I noticed that in the lower school science, teachers were using the old combined science scheme which has only white, middle-class imagery. The Inner London Education Authority has produced a scheme called 'Insight into Science' which was developed in schools very similar to ours. On the work cards there are pictures of children – many of them black. That alone, having a black hand, for example, holding a test tube, is something that we have not had before in science materials. In the 3rd-year classes we test foods, in a section on energy, and we encourage children to bring in their own food, so that not only do we test bread and cereals but we have a chapati or some paw-paw or sweet potato as well. I'd like to do a lot more – a visitor once asked me for example, why haven't I got pictures and posters of Arab mathematicians and scientists, or Chinese or Japanese scientists in the lab, such as the man who invented clocks. While the skills and the concepts we are teaching in maths and science are abstract, we find we can be multi-cultural in the context of the examples we choose for exercising those skills. It may be that in maths the only 'multi-cultural' element could be to remember, in giving examples at the board or in written questions, to use names and activities which reflect the ethnic minority communities' place in our society. It may be slight, but no less important for that. We can also see whether our maths and science classes relate to what other departments are doing. Examples of maths problems could be drawn from projects about other countries the pupils might be involved in their humanities classes, for instance.

Multi-ethnic mathematics, an article by Ray Hemmings, appears in the magazine *Multi-Racial Education* Autumn 1980. Copies from F. J Harper, E.L.C., Tile Kiln Lane, London NW13 6BY.

Religions

Most schools now offer some idea of non-Christian religions as part of their religious education syllabus. For teachers of subjects other than religion, it is part of a successful course in history, geography, literature or science, to make room for the religious and customary experiences of their pupils, as well as to help them appreciate the often vital importance of religious traditions in explaining current affairs. A source of information such as *World religions: a handbook for teachers* (edited by W. Owen Cole 1977, published by the CRE, 10 Allington Street, London SW1) is not therefore something for RE staff alone. It also offers insights into the values and perceptions of many of the parents of ethnic minority children in school.

It goes without saying that one way to help become familiar with world religions is to arrange visits to mosques and temples, or to invite into school a Rabbi, an Imam, a Hindu priest, etc, to speak for themselves about their beliefs. Those schools where this is done find that the children are quick to sense the attitude of staff towards such a visitor. In a way, it is an indicator of a successful multi-cultural school that such visitors feel fully 'at home' in the school environment, and are seen by the pupils to be accepted and treated as such.

In 1980, the ILEA published a forty page booklet *Religious education in primary schools in a multi-cultural society*. Prepared in the light of advice from a multi-faith Advisory Council, including the participation of the British Humanist Association, it gives examples of inter-faith work in ILEA schools, and reviews frankly some of the areas of sensitivity within different religious traditions that teachers need to be aware of. Apart from suggested activities and resources for class use, it includes useful addresses for both advice and materials. It is available from ILEA Learning Materials Service, Highbury Station Road, London N1 1SB.

No school need be without the annual *Calendar of religious festivals* issued by the CRE, 10 Allington Street, London SW1. This gives a brief account of the major events in six religions as they occur in the year – and it is free! Also useful is *Believers – Worship in a Multi-Faith Community*, by Collinson and Miller (Edward Arnold 1981).

The Arts

The point was made often enough by contributors in the first part of this book, that we owe it to all children to reinforce the sources of their cultural identity, rather than to ignore them. Teachers' experience tends to confirm that only young people who are confident and proud of their own cultural roots can properly respond to and appreciate other cultures. This gives an extra reason why schools with ethnic minority children in particular, in addition to fully recognising their religions, languages, or dialects, need also to reflect the drama, dance, literature, music, crafts and visual arts that express children's various home or community cultures. Even if it is only activities such as school bands, Asian dance groups, or fashion and hair-dressing clubs, new interests and experiences can be opened up which are rewarding and fun for both pupils and staff.

For teachers wondering how to start such ventures, the basic information can be found in two booklets by Naseem Khan: *The arts Britain ignores* (1976), CRE, 10 Allington Street, London SW1E 5EH and *Britain's new arts*, from Minority Arts Advisory Service, available from CRE. Advice and resources are offered by MAAS (which can supply its *Ethnic arts directory of performing artists and groups* Reprinting, due out summer 1981); by the CRE Ethnic Arts Advisory Committee; and by the Education Department of the Commonwealth Institute, Kensington High Street, London W8 6NQ. The Arts Department of the Commonwealth Institute can also organise workshops for teachers.

Most schools with thriving 'ethnic' arts have found that the first step is to locate the people with the skills and experience in their local community. Often these can be found among the parents – otherwise local churches, mosques, temples and youth organisations will know of dancers, musicians and artists who could be invited into the school to demonstrate or instruct. Local Authorities have details of peripatetic music teachers and artists. MAAS keeps regional registers of arts groups and of ethnic artists; the National Association of Asian Youth (NAAY, 46 High Street, Southall, Middlesex) can also suggest Asian groups and artists. A full list of sources of help is given in Naseem Khan's booklets.

Once launched, a key point of such activities is to try to involve the parents of all children in the school in concerts or demonstrations. In a truly multi-cultural school, of course, such activities would not run only as out-of-school optional extras, they would be linked in with all relevant parts of the curriculum, and staff would liaise on relating them, wherever possible, to projects being done in any subject.

Here is a glimpse of one teacher's experience in aiming for a multi-cultural approach to music teaching within the curriculum. Jill Scarfe teaches at Mount View High School, a comprehensive in Harrow which includes a high proportion of British Asian children, as well as a smaller number of children of West Indian background:

When I arrived in Harrow from Scotland some years ago, I had actually never seen black or brown children before.

Early on, I read an article about a school which had a steel band, and felt it was unfair that that school had something which we had not. We had our first set of pans delivered, generously bought by the school. Then our problems started. All children, even now, who have not played before, approach the pan with the preconceived idea that it is easy to play. This attitude inevitably leads to disappointment when it is discovered that hard work and attention is required. Particularly worrying was the way that children with a West Indian background gave up their steel band work early. The result was that the first time we played at the Commonwealth Institute we had an all white band, several of whom were studying for 'O' level music. But a bus full of children came to this concert, where they watched all the other bands and saw the tremendous potential that these instruments have. This information permeated the rest of the school and now our main school band has a very equal proportion of ethnic groups.

I was shocked by the sarcasm of an 'O' level board examiner when I first suggested that pan playing was as worthy of examination as any percussion instrument. Another examiner however responded with enthusiasm when he heard one of our pupils rehearsing the solo part of Mozart's Horn Concerto on the tenor pan. It was a shame that he needed to hear it used outside its own cultural style to accept it. It happened that our leading pan player has a Beethoven scherzo in his repertoire – which shows that while steel pans are principally a way to appreciate the culture of the Caribbean there are interesting extensions to be experimented with.

While setting up our steel band music, the move to introduce Asian music took place. The music staff were fortunate to have a short but intense in-service course in the complicated study of Asian music. Mr Mishra was a teacher found and supported for us by the NAAY. He came to the school and gave a superb musical impression of a train, on the tabla, which related this unusual instrument to something the pupils understood. We then gave pupils the option of learning sitar, tabla and harmonium and were again faced with the same problems of motivation that we had met when we introduced steel pans.

Very early on, we discovered that Asian children would not stand up and volunteer to learn to play instruments associated with their family background. It appeared, sadly, that they were ashamed and embarrassed. As the project has progressed, this attitude has been reversed. Asian children are now asking for them.

Teenage children are basically influenced by the so-called music of their peer group. It is not always easy to inspire them with other ideas. Respect for any culture has to be won, it cannot be enforced.

We began by giving pupils the choice, as with European instruments, of whether they wanted to play or not. This produced remarks like 'I don't want to do that sitar', and so I now take the line followed in most other subjects – that the instruments are simply an automatic part of the music course.

Every class is divided into four groups and each group spends half a term studying one subject, either an Asian instrument, steel pan, recorder or guitar. After the half term, they all change to another instrument and eventually have studied all four. There is no choice, no fuss, and it is working beautifully. I find that children like firm guidance and pupils who would not have considered playing a sitar last year now happily take their shoes off and settle on the floor to learn. If pupils see that staff presume they will happily accept something, they usually do. It also helps that we make some study of the interesting similarities, as well as differences, for example, between guitar and sitar.

When using staff from another continent there may be an obvious language problem. We are most fortunate in working with somebody like Mr Mishra whose sincerity reaches all his pupils although his English is limited. Like other visiting teachers, Mr Mishra has adapted to the constraints of the thirty-five minutes school period, whereas a normal ethnic music lesson might last three hours. It is natural for both steel pan concerts and Asian prias to last a whole evening.

The situation we have in introducing ethnic minority culture to young children is no different from the difficulties that any twentieth century music teacher has in introducing the works of Bach and Mozart. Our overall aim is to provide these lessons within the curriculum. We have established a CSE Mode III in steel pan, and a four week course in Asian music takes its place alongside the courses in Baroque music and pop music, etc., in the lower school music syllabus. But we have yet to establish with an examining board a way of developing these beginnings into full 'O' level courses. It is of course 'O' levels which many parents, particularly our Asian parents, would rightly like to see.

It is my view that music is simply part of the teaching of skills in communication. Animosity between different racial groups, both in school and in society generally, feeds on lack of understanding, which in turn leads to fear and lack of mutual respect. While life is too short to learn more than a few languages, it is important that we show how music has long been accepted as a form of international language. The Far Eastern countries admire Tchaikovsky; the Russians revere Beethoven; the Germans go into raptures about Elgar. Likewise I maintain that children who pass through the first two years of our school will learn respect for each other's cultures. Those who before rejected their own cultures are benefiting from new self-awareness. As in all music teaching, we cannot expect to see the results of these changing attitudes while they are young. Teenage peer attitudes are vitally important to them, but I am confident that pupils who have spent many interesting hours sitting cross-legged on the floor with a Brahmin priest will be less inclined to see other cultures as a threat, and likewise those pupils who see their steel pan taught in an atmosphere of respect will gain in confidence.

8 Exercising the imagination

This is perhaps a good point to pause for thought. There are many assumptions and implications between the lines of these examples of curriculum development which in a more theoretical book would have to be unravelled in closer detail. There is a good deal of discussion already available – in the writings for example of Alan James and of Robert Jeffcoate – on multi-cultural education in general, and on the curriculum in particular. Details of articles, journals, books and organisations which offer help in clarifying that debate appear in most Teachers' Centres. Here we offer some observations by Dr Bhikhu Parekh which serve to extend the theoretical debate, in the sense that they draw new attention to aspects not covered elsewhere. Dr Parekh has a special perspective on questions of multi-cultural curriculum. Born in India, he came to Britain in 1959. He was a member of the Convocation of the Schools Council, and a member of the Rampton Committee inquiring into the educational problems of ethnic minority children. Apart from his academic work as Professor of Political Philosophy at Hull University, he has kept in close touch with the British-Asian community – not least as a Member of the Commission for Racial Equality. We have already recommended to teachers the insights he gave in the public talk *Asians in Britain* (see page 23). Here he offers ideas to give new inspiration to thinking about the multi-cultural curriculum:

Sympathetic imagination and the multi-cultural curriculum
I submit that our educational system suffers from a serious defect, namely that while it develops pupils' powers of expression, analysis and criticism better than many other educational systems, it fails to develop their powers of imagination. I call this a serious defect because, in my view, imagination is one of man's fundamental capacities, and vitalises all the others.

A discussion of imagination is bedevilled by a basic difficulty. Of all human capacities imagination has been the least adequately theorised. Its nature, role, structure, modes of operation and relations to other human capacities still remain an enigma. If we excluded Kant's somewhat sketchy discussion, no great philosopher has taken imagination seriously and analysed its nature and structure.

There are many reasons for this neglect. Our philosophical tradition has a strong rationalist bias – reason is seen as man's highest capacity, as the sole source of knowledge and the *sine qua non* of moral conduct. Not surprisingly the tradition finds it difficult to accommodate imagination in its theories of knowledge, morality and education. Further, the rationalist philosophers associated imagination with the senses, largely on the ground that like the latter, imagination deals in images: they did not include it among the faculties capable of yielding or assisting the pursuit of knowledge. Indeed they thought that it led men to evade or distort reality, and was therefore a source of error and a force for evil. Accordingly they urged that nothing should be done to encourage it, and everything to curtail its power. This rationalist view of imagination was shared by many a Christian writer. Whether they were rationalists or fideists, the Christian writers on education equated imagination with 'fancy', feared its power, distrusted its influence and proposed ways to curb and even repress it.

While the empiricist philosophers showed better appreciation of the nature and role of imagination, nearly all of them associated it with the senses and thought that it only dealt in sensuous images. Like the rationalists, the empiricist philosopher feared the power of imagination and proposed that it be curbed. As Hume put it, 'Nothing is more dangerous to reason than flights of the imagination, and nothing has been the occasion of more mistakes among philosophers'.

These views were challenged in the second half of the eighteenth century. Predictably, the challenge was mounted by those areas of human endeavour such as poetry, literature and the arts in which imagination plays a crucial role. Shelley, Keats, Wordsworth, Coleridge, Schelling, Schiller and others emphasised its importance. While their collective attempt to rehabilitate the faculty of imagination was most welcome, it also contained a danger. Since the poets and artists discovered and championed the cause of imagination, they predictably defined it in narrow artistic or aesthetic terms. As they understood it, imagination was an essentially aesthetic capacity and its exercise was deemed to be confined to aesthetic activities. Only the poets and the artists exercised imagination and, conversely, they only exercised imagination and no other human capacity. Unwittingly the champions of imagination retained the traditional dichotomy between reason and imagination. Further, since they conceived imagination in aesthetic terms they invested it with properties generally associated with art.

They identified imagination with creativity and said that only a creative imagination was 'truly' imagination. Like the rationalist philosophers they argued that imagination consisting in 'making images' and producing 'lively' and vivid 'impressions'. Since the images were designed to evoke feeling, they closely associated imagination and feeling and equated cultivation of imagination with cultivation of feeling.

For several centuries then, imagination was ignored or feared and not regarded as a fundamental and crucial human capacity. When it was finally rehabilitated in the eighteenth century it was conceived and defined in narrowly aesthetic terms. The Romantic impact was so powerful that even today we continue to think of imagination in aesthetic terms. The moment someone talks about imagination we immediately think of poetry and the arts. Several recent books and Schools Council reports have discussed imagination in exclusively aesthetic terms. This surely cannot be right, for we know from experience that imagination is at work in all human activities and not merely the arts, and that all areas of life and not merely the arts suffer in a society which neglects imagination. We know that a child can be imaginative or unimaginative, a historian's account of an event can be imaginative or banal; a politician can provide an imaginative solution to a problem or peddle banalities; and so on. We know also that no scientific, philosophical, mathematical or other discoveries are ever possible without imagination. In short, imagination cannot be equated with aesthetic imagination, which is but one form of it. Different forms of imagination operate differently and, unlike the aesthetic, do not at all involve feelings, emotions, vivid impressions, sensual images, and so on. The cultivation of imagination is not therefore necessarily the cultivation of feelings; it may instead be the cultivation of intelligence and even of reason. Unless we liberate it from its narrow aesthetic confines, we will continue to think that only the arts can develop imagination. The unfortunate educational consequences of such a view are surely too obvious to need elaboration.

It is not relevant to my purpose to undertake a general inquiry into the nature and forms of imagination. I only wish to draw particular attention to one form of imagination which plays an exceedingly important part in human life and has received little attention from educationists. For convenience I shall call it sympathetic imagination.

The sympathetic imagination is very different from the aesthetic. This becomes clear if we compare a poet with an imaginative historian. A poet offers us a new way of looking at an object or an aspect of experience – perhaps by illuminating those features of it that had never before occurred to us, and comparing and assimilating it to objects which we usually consider too dissimilar and disparate to share anything in common. He presents the object in a totally new light and transforms and recreates it. In giving us a new way of seeing it, 'it' is no longer what it was. With new eyes we see a new object. In other words the poetic imagination, like the artistic imagination in general, is necessarily transformative in nature.

Now take an imaginative historian trying to understand, say, classical Athens. He endeavours to transcend his own and his society's values, prejudices and ways of looking at man and the world, places himself in the position of the ancient Athenian, seeks to view and experience the world from the latter's perspective and tries to capture the ethos and spirit of the Athenian society. If he finds himself projecting the prejudices and values of his society into Athens, he struggles to rise above them in a determined effort to get as close to the heart of his subject matter as his abilities permit. If he is gifted and lucky, he might in the end offer a highly sensitive and faithful account of Athens 'as it really was' and help us make sense of its social and political institutions – including even such odious and apparently incomprehensible practices as killing weak or female children by exposure.

Our historian is as imaginative as the poet, but in a different way. His imagination does not 'transform' Athens into something it was not; rather it gets to the heart of Athens and presents it as it was. No doubt, like a poet he offers us a new way of looking at Athens; however the new way is also intended to be the true way of looking at Athens. Unlike the poet the historian uses his imagination to get closer to the object, to apprehend its truth. And consequently we judge his powers of imagination, but not those of the poet, in terms of his ability to help us grasp the truth of his subject matter. A poet's imagination is creative; a historian's imagination is re-creative and sympathetic.

We simply cannot understand other cultures, societies and historical epochs without sympathetic imagination, that is, without rising above our own values, preferences and views of the world and entering into their world with an open mind. We cannot understand others if we refuse to recognise their identity and respect their individuality, but insist on seeing them in our terms. It is only by means of sympathetic imagination that we can cross the space that separates us from other individuals and understand why they view and respond to the world in a certain manner. Without sympathetic imagination we remain prisoners of our own limited worlds and lack the ability to enrich and expand them.

Not reason nor intellect but fantasy is the opposite of sympathetic imagination. Sympathetic imagination releases and liberates a man from his subjectivity; by contrast fantasy is a form of self-indulgence. In fantasy one considers the world as one pleases, in sympathetic imagination one transcends the self and revises one's thoughts and feelings until they are fit enough to grasp one's subject matter. Fantasy represents a rejection of and escape from the world; imagination represents an attempt to get to the very heart of it.

In some respects, sympathetic imagination is much more exacting, although not more important, than creative imagination. In creative imagination one simply transcends the conventional ways of looking at an object; in sympathetic imagination one transcends oneself, suspends the values, preferences, ideas and prejudices that constitute the self and becomes a different self. Unlike the creative, sympathetic imagination is a slow and painful process, for it involves entering another world and appreciating modes of thought and behaviour that might be profoundly different from one's own and even repulsive. Unlike the creative imagination, sympathetic imagination is not free to wander as it pleases, but remains subject to the objective restraints of its subject matter whose innermost essence it struggles to comprehend.

It is my contention that in general the English educational system does little to foster imagination, and that while creative imagination is at last beginning to receive some attention, sympathetic imagination is almost entirely neglected. The cause of creative imagination has been championed for over two hundred years by eminent writers and philosophers and has had the organized support of artists, poets, novelists and others.

Even so, that the English educational system does not foster creative imaginative is relatively easy to substantiate. Creative imagination is developed by the arts and crafts, and by universal consensus these do not occupy an important place within our school curriculum. Both Newson and Plowden Reports provide ample evidence. As the Plowden Report puts it, the attitude that art is a 'frill' subject is 'still widespread' (para. 680). The Bullock Report remarks that 'in many schools it (poetry) suffers from lack of commitment, misunderstanding and the wrong kind of orientation'. And it quotes a survey according to which poetry is so badly taught that over eight hundred out of a thousand 'O' and 'A' level students said that they could not imagine themselves reading any more poetry after leaving school. The neglect of creative imagination is substantiated and persuasively criticised by Ruth Mock in her *Education and the imagination* Chatto, 1970.

The charge that the English educational system does not foster sympathetic imagination cannot be so easily substantiated. Since the importance of sympathetic imagination has rarely been appreciated, its absence has rarely been noticed by either the teachers or the government committees. Besides, unlike the creative imagination which has an intellectual home in literature and the arts, sympathetic imagination is less localised and more pervasive and therefore there are no disciplines to whose absence one can point in order to substantiate its neglect.

Nevertheless, there is indirect evidence for the relative neglect of sympathetic imagination in our educational practice. The importance of learning foreign languages, for example, has yet to be enthusiastically appreciated in all schools. An attitude to a language reflects an attitude

to the people who speak it. If one valued and took sympathetic interest
in other cultures, one would wish to know more about them and make an
effort to learn the languages involved. A certain degree of narcissism
that pervades Britain might at least partly explain its attitude to foreign
languages as well as its unwillingness to get foreign names right and
pronounce them correctly. In my experience more foreigners are in-
duced, pressured or even told to change their names in England than
in any other country. Foreign names and surnames must submit to the
baptism of Anglicisation before the Englishman can deal with them; that
is, the English do not raise themselves to the level of others; instead they
reduce others to the limited proportions of their own linguistic habits
and conventions.

The relative lack of sympathetic imagination is evident also in the
way English itself is sometimes taught. A literary text is taught in many
schools as if it were little more than a body of more or less useful information. Pupils are asked to summarise its 'content', briefly describe
the main characters, outline and discuss its various interpretations,
analyse the author's style, examine his basic 'message', and so on. Little
attempt is made to enter into the world created by the author, to explore
the experiences and emotions that inform his work, to imaginatively
participate in his vision. In other words the pupil is not encouraged to
transcend his subjectivity, lift himself to the level of the text and open
himself to the full impact of its vision. Instead the text is reduced to the
pathetic proportions of his limited experiences and ideas. The Bullock
Report observes:

We saw lessons in which a novel was treated as a hoard
of factual information with the pupils scoring marks for the
facts they remembered. How many sheep did Gabriel Oak lose?
What was the name of Bathsheba's maid? Where had Fanny
Robbins been working before she walked to Casterbridge?

And it sadly concludes, 'The explanations and summaries have
expanded to take-over point; the literature has receded.' Even when the
teaching of literature is not as crude as this, I suggest there is too great
an emphasis on criticism. A pupil is asked to criticise an author rather
than appreciate and enter into the spirit of his vision. No doubt, criticism and evaluation are very important. However, by themselves they
are blunt and dangerous instruments, blunt because one cannot criticise
what one has not fully grasped, and dangerous because an impression
is created that a literary text is valuable only as a punching bag, as a
device to exercise the pupils' intellectual muscles, and not as a window
to a whole new world of experience.

Our history curriculum is little better in most schools. It is often
heavily Euro-centred and includes little about the great non-European

cultures and civilizations. There are history textbooks still in use which proclaim the glory of Europe and present other societies as if they had neither history nor culture before the Europeans 'discovered' them. Professor Hugh Trevor-Roper writes:

Perhaps in the future there will be some African history to teach, but at present there is none, or very little: there is only the history of Europeans in Africa, the rest is largely darkness, like the history of pre-European, pre-Columbian America, and darkness is not a subject for history.

Trevor-Roper, who only reiterates here views articulated by Hegel, Marx, J. S. Mill and others, does not care to explain what he means by history, why he defines only certain types of events as historic or even historical, why *his* ignorance of the African history should be taken to imply that the latter does not exist, nor why we should accept his impertinent assumption that what does not exist for *him* does not exist *at all*. A child raised on such a narcissistic diet can hardly be expected to develop sympathetic imagination and acquire much respect for or even curiosity about non-European cultures. Mercifully we are becoming increasingly sensitive to the narrow nationalistic bias of our history books. We need to go on to combat Eurocentric and racist bias as well.

Does not our geography curriculum pay too little attention to people, their culture, their modes of dress, habits of food, arts, and forms of social organization? Should it not explain how their different ways of walking, talking, dressing, eating, treating animals, worshipping mountains and rivers, make eminent sense within the context of their climate and natural habitat? We should locate other societies against their natural background, bringing them alive to our pupils, lifting the latter out of their prejudices and conventional stereotypes, and stimulating them to imaginatively participate in the vastly diverse forms of life created by intelligent men in other parts of the world.

The religious education in our schools is even more disappointing. Christianity remains the pupil's staple diet, as perhaps it should be, but other religions are often treated simply as adjuncts about which an 'educated' child should know 'something'. The pupil is taught their 'basic' tenets, 'interesting' forms of worship, and how they compare with Christianity. It is rare to find attempts made to raise him above his own religious beliefs, to enter into the spirit of other religions, to appreciate and come to grips with their visions of human predicament, comprehend their complex systems of symbols and imagery and enjoy them as diverse and fascinating achievements of the human spirit. A child educated in our schools may, with luck, learn to tolerate, perhaps even respect, other religions, but is unlikely to appreciate, enjoy and enter into a sympathetic dialogue with them.

My view is that our educational system at its best cultivates the virtues of decency, tolerance and some degree of respect for those different from us. This is greatly to be welcomed. However, tolerance and respect are negative virtues. They stop us from harming others, but they also stop us from appreciating, enjoying, entering into and learning from a dialogue with other religions, cultures and societies. Unless we can enter into the spirit of other societies and cultures, we cannot appreciate their strength. And by failing to appreciate their strength, we fail to appreciate our own weaknesses and limitations. A nation that ruled over the largest empire in history, retained its political and territorial integrity against the worst of external threats and became rich without the benefit of vast natural resources, is understandably prone to cultural parochialism, the lack of intellectual curiosity about others, an unwillingness to learn from them and the absence of sympathetic imagination. These are all reflected in and perpetuated by our educational system.

A seventeenth century writer, Murault in his *Lettres Sur les Anglais* discovered a paradox in the English character. The English were gentle and hated cruelty, yet they committed a good deal of cruelty both in England and abroad. He resolved the paradox in terms of the Englishman's lack of imagination and remarked that the latter's cruelty was not a product of evil design, but a simple lack of sympathetic imagination. More recently, W. H. Auden has been among those who have commented on what he called the 'suffocating insular coziness', intellectual 'laziness', and lack of imagination in English life. These commentators are, no doubt, guilty of exaggeration. However there is a grain of truth in their remarks and we cannot but benefit from pondering over them – especially when we look closely and critically at our educational practices in general, and the curriculum in particular.

9 Ourselves and others in world perspective

We have given plenty of examples so far of teachers getting away from 'suffocating' and 'insular' anglocentrism by incorporating elements of many different cultures in the syllabuses of their individual subjects. They have usually taken these initiatives as a response to the presence of ethnic minority students in their school. But we now give some accounts of multi-cultural curriculum changes made in schools which have not had that particular incentive. As 'all white' schools they lack the cultural diversity which students in racially mixed schools bring to school and can share in the class.

The teachers at these schools aim at a multi-cultural approach across the entire curriculum, something that requires organised inter-departmental co-operation. Some of the ways this has been achieved at Stantonbury Campus, three integrated twelve to eighteen year olds comprehensives on a single site in Buckinghamshire, are illustrated in the film 'Anglo-Saxon Attitudes'. (A rewardingly full account of this school's 'Tanzania Link' project, featured in the film, describing how and why it was set up; what was discovered about Tanzania; how it was related to all the faculties; and how the trip was finally evaluated – direct from Stantonbury Campus, Milton Keynes, MK14 6BN.)

Stantonbury is among those schools which have moved from offering a 'Third World Studies' course towards a more general scheme of 'development education'. What is interesting is that this not only seeks to bring a world perspective into the British classroom – it also seeks ways to compensate, in its treatment of racial matters, for the students' lack of face-to-face familiarity with people of different cultures. We asked Deputy Head, Mervyn Flecknoe to convene a discussion with his colleagues on how they seek to achieve these aims. Here are extracts from the report on what was said:

Organising for curriculum change
Our 'development education' work at Stantonbury is partly the product

of a working party which spans all faculties. It is certainly monitored by this group and improvements result from working party discussions. Essentially, the working party seeks to secure the co-operation of teaching teams in the faculties and to suggest ways in which they might include material in their teaching time.

We set it up because three factors came together: the 'Third World Studies' curriculum, as we used to call it, was looking dated – it was orientated very much towards the population *problem*, the food *problem*, the colour *problem*, and we felt it needed reassessment to convey a more balanced picture of the rest of the world. It happened at about the same time that the National Front headquarters moved to Milton Keynes briefly. This meant that obscenely decorated Union Jacks appeared around the city (both members must have spent several weeks at it!), and, of course, students were talking about it. Thirdly, those of us who had worked in racially mixed comprehensives in London before, were coming to see more clearly that education for a multi-cultural society was every bit as important in our nearly all-white school.

Two working parties were set up, one to discuss the multi-cultural curriculum, and the second to consider development education. We soon realised that the extensive overlapping meant that they should be working together. We were influenced here by Mary Worrall's very important article *Multi-racial Britain and the Third World* (*The New Era*, March 1978 p. 47–52), which is still the most precise statement of the relationship between the two.

We had then to look at what the whole school was teaching. Simply introducing a new subject into an already crowded curriculum would have been quite wrong and ineffective. We wanted to convey a concern right across the curriculum – less a new subject, than a way of seeing the world. So we set out the whole school curriculum in a matrix: a grid with school years down the side and subject areas across the top. In the thirty-odd spaces this made, we wrote down what was already being taught in terms of multi-cultural or development education. This immediately revealed gaps in the most surprising places. Having talked to the people who taught the courses in the first place for the information to fill in the boxes, it was relatively easy to go back to talk about the gaps and how to fill them in. Thus, instead of producing just a report, which could be ignored, the working party had found a way of creating change. (The process is detailed in *Ideas into action*, see page 100.)

You can go to the home economics or biologist doing diet and nutrition and ask: 'Would it be possible to consider other cultures, for example, some less wealthy than our own?' English teachers will often introduce African literature, for example, once they are given the stimulus and advice on appropriate material. It's not threatening; there's no resistance. The scope for change may not be wide in maths, or in modern languages, but small changes can still be significant:

'The three most common European languages, French, German and Spanish, have all been used by colonial powers. I take French, and I've never actually seen a textbook that talks of any other country than France being Francophone. There's never a student who isn't surprised when I tell them I'm going to mark in the French speaking parts of the World on a map on the board, and then put in France last – after those vast areas of North America and West Africa where French is the native language. Simply putting France up last, I find, has a memorable effect, supporting a global perspective – and it is something any languages teacher can do in a few minutes of their next lesson'.

The Africa-England week
It is all too easy to 'do mud huts' in English, or Science, or European Studies and so forth, all at different times and in an unrelated way. We find co-operation between different subject areas vital. By getting different subject areas to co-operate with each other at the same time to do something significant, the children get the idea of continuity. It means drawing teachers of different disciplines together as a team to plan the week's activities, for a particular year group. We have used East Africa mainly of course because of our Tanzania Link, but it could just as well have been South America. Each faculty produced co-ordinated materials and work connected with Africa. We used the matrix system of visiting teachers individually, rather than a top down hierarchical approach. It is quite exciting to see teams of five teachers from very different subjects making a coherent plan of activities for the week for each class. The exercise really seems to broaden their own views within their specialist subjects as much as seeing how the subjects can relate across the curriculum.

So much for our organisation – what sort of ideas
lay behind the working party's motivation?

'I think it's a question of expectation. A school has a percentage in-fluence on children's attitudes, you can argue about what percentage, but it has some influence, so let's think about the things that kids get expectations about through school: they get expectations about careers, they get expectations about what examinations mean, they get expec-tations about literacy and numeracy, and now a measure of success is whether they get any expectations about the 'developing world' issue.'

'There is the empathy thing you know, putting yourself in the position of somebody who hasn't experienced prejudice. It can be a harrowing thing to talk about. I remember being in Tooting when a Neo-Nazi group met during the 1972 election, and seeing a kid of twelve, a black kid, wandering in because she'd been playing in the park around the periphery of the meeting. It was harrowing to see how she began to pick up what was being said and started to cry.'

'I have really moved away from the idea of a recessive chairman. The idea that a teacher can be neutral in the face of some of the myths and misconceptions put about on race and immigration is so erroneous as to be positively harmful.'

What teaching techniques do our staff find effective?

'Relative wealth and poverty isn't easy as a concept, but I've found it's worked extremely well simply with ten biscuits and ten children at the front of the class. I say I have ten biscuits which I am now going to distribute in exactly the same way that the wealth is distributed in the world, giving nine to a single child, and telling the other nine to share one biscuit. This creates a great deal of discussion immediately amongst twelve year olds. You get "this isn't fair!". From that start you can work very quickly from your nine biscuits to the broad facts they represent and from there move to map work, seeing the areas of the world amongst whom the very small proportion of the wealth is shared. That's one I use with a mixed ability group of twelve year olds.'

'With sixth formers, among the top thirty per cent of the ability range, I've used a set of photographs taken in Eastern Africa. The idea is to teach the students to interpret visual material by asking basic questions about the photograph, which is all they have in front of them. Where was it taken? Why was it taken? Who is this person? What is this object? What time of day? What is the weather like? Then I put the factual answers on the board alongside the guesses and hypotheses of the students – so indicating their accuracy. Then I move on to a wider range of photographs that cover themes I want to raise: for example, I might want to deal with simple technology and understand why a hand operated water pump can be much more successful and more appropriate as a piece of machinery than a diesel pump in many places. By examining a photograph and thinking about the facts and details in it, the immediate assumption that a diesel pump is always much better than a hand operated one, is questioned. It is a good way of getting behind what "better" means here, and that's the important point.'

'I also take a less able group – fifth year students who will take no exams at all. I show slides and without giving any answers at all, I simply ask the sort of questions I use with the sixth formers – where? why? – but point out the problems much more, toning the voice to suggest that here's a puzzle that needs unravelling: why is it, for example, that that

94

person is standing where she is? In one case I have two pictures, one of a traditional central Tanzanian house which is no higher than the average person's shoulder, another a big modern concrete and aluminium house with corrugated iron roof. We accompany these with a tape of an interview with a woman living in the traditional house of the region as to why she was so desperate to move into a new housing development which was coming into the village, when as far as we could see, her traditional house was cool inside and it was strong, whereas the modern house would seem amazingly hot, subject to all the problems of construction where people were not used to using new materials, and you couldn't hear yourself speak when it rained. The point here is for the group to see the problems and the reasons for the housing without my help. When I asked why is this woman's house was only shoulder high, there were two or three guesses, and somebody said because it was made of trees and there weren't any tall trees. This was a person who quite frankly normally I find very difficult to teach, but once he'd got this answer, he was watching everything I did. He'd suddenly realised that from nowhere at all he had found the right answer to a problem facing someone in Eastern Africa.'

The value of drama

It is easy enough to set up drama in development education. As long as it avoids stereotypes, educational drama has powerful potential for giving insight, understanding, and empathy. And writing which follows practical drama is, as many teachers know, an extension of the same. Here are just some of our examples:

'I was working with a group of fourth year mixed ability students. I chose a newspaper article about how systems of birth control in India weren't working. The general line of the group was: "Surely it is good for these people if they don't breed so much". In terms of looking at a country that seems overpopulated, they took it that the failure must be something to do with the way people there feel about birth. So I set up an imaginary situation where we were a group of people in a community facing a problem of no more births. What did this mean to us? It produced some strong drama among children to whom abstract questions and statistics about world population don't mean much. Although some would say it was chauvinist, there were remarks like "Well I'm no longer a man if I can't produce children", and "She's hardly a woman if she can't have children"; "What's the point of marriage?" But through the drama they began to empathise with feelings of men who saw themselves as "failing" and of women thinking "We're failing ourselves, and the men" and identifying these problems with the drug that the local doctor had been giving them.'

'As a teacher I'm not particularly good at ordinary discussion, but I remember setting up an imaginary factory with the pupils with a workforce which had a group of relative newcomers. The industrial process needed human experimentation and our drama was the discussion among the management as to how to get people for the experiments. It wasn't long before the decision emerged that they should be chosen from among the newcomers – and we pretended that they came in and were given forms of diseases. However crude as a starting point, it led to real reflection on how well we – and people in other countries – treat people as newcomers. Are they treated as servants, as people you just experiment with, or do you accept them on a fully equal basis to yourself? How long does it take communities to reach such acceptance?

In another drama example I took a big risk. David was the only coloured student in the group and we'd never tackled prejudice of any sort. I knew from one or two students in the group that there was a great deal of resentment about David, less I think because he was coloured, than because he was very intelligent and had tended, as a new student, to come in and rather take over drama. We imagined living in a derelict house; how were we going to run this house together? It was decided David was to get the food, I was to get the money, someone else was to get the clothes etc. Because I knew the group very well, I thought I'd break through this comfortable drama and I directly confronted David, saying 'I'm not sharing a house with you, you're black! I don't trust you!' There was an electric silence while people tried to think out whether this was the make believe world or suddenly a piece of the real world. The drama went on but afterwards we talked out that moment. I said that's the difference between the real world and when someone takes a role – you can say things in a role that you'd never say in the real world. I told them that I had had similar experiences, having a mixed background (my father is Cypriot) and I had been through exactly this thing in the 1950s and 1960s when the Cypriots got their wack, moving into North London. It was important to call on that experience, to match David's experience, so that it wasn't a question of me the white man playing against blacks as an issue, it was me as someone who had already felt this using it in the drama situation. It was probably the most useful drama moment I've ever used for raising an excellent and thoughtful discussion about racialism.'

'Sometimes we sit the class in a circle, and as teacher, I start off a role-play with the student opposite me. The roles could be countries, it could be people in a family, it could be teacher and student, or it could be on any issue that we want to bring up. It could be a racialist issue, for example – a father saying to his daughter "I don't like you going out with that boy, he's black". An exchange develops and when I decide to

96

stop, I move to the next chair. We all move around in a wheel and two others pick up the role-play. It may need only one exchange to get the thing going. If the teacher knows his group he can make the sort of outrageous comment that can spark emotion. It's when students become emotionally involved in an issue that imagination and personal feelings take their proper place as part of the understanding that these multi-cultural themes require.'

The value of games

Drama techniques require some specialist skill and training, but any teacher can use games! We use them a great deal because talking at a purely rational level does not ensure that memorable learning and understanding is taking place. And games allow students to experience situations and emotions which wouldn't normally come their way. We use the Aid Committee Game, the Co-operation Game, the Grain Drain Game, the Energy Game, the Trade Game, Star Power, Gronks and Friends, the Poultry and Poverty Games, and Ba Fa Ba Fa (all available through Oxfam). These games don't just give information, they give practice in feeling and seeing the world through others' eyes. There are other techniques to achieve this: an example from our history course is a study of the Opium Wars from the Chinese viewpoint. There is a saying 'The tales of hunting will always glorify the hunter – until the lions have their own historians'. Using documents from the period, we compare the Chinese and the English histories. Again, when the BBC showed East German news programmes, we used them to show that perspective on the 1980 Polish trade union crisis. We also use newspaper articles published in different countries on the same subject, and study the differences in what events each country chooses to report. These activities will help children to be slower to make simplistic or stereo-typed generalisations. We of course avoid an impression of all the 'Third World' as poor and downtrodden – that is just as stereotyped as thinking of all Arabs as oil-rich sheiks. In using the games we show the extremes of wealth *within* as well as *between* countries. But there is one final example of a particularly useful game for development education: it involves making simple templates out of card. The children divide into groups. The teacher has four templates: a bicycle, a car, a star and a television screen, together with pieces of white paper, coloured paper and scissors, pens and glue. Each group is given some money. You can load it in the way that the real world is loaded by giving different groups different amounts. They come to the teacher to buy their template. They also buy their raw materials, the white and coloured paper, scissors etc. and they go into production making goods to sell back. You can say to one group 'you don't have any access to white paper, but you have money to buy some'. Some have templates but no paper; others have plenty of raw materials but no technology. We find this produces excellent discussion and evaluation, and students are keen to devise their own variations of the game as follow-up.

How we played the machinery and materials game

That account from the staff at Stantonbury Campus shows the value they attach to games, giving children vicarious experiences on which to build multi-cultural understanding. That such teaching methods are appropriate and important when broadening the curriculum to include a global picture of the contemporary world, and an understanding of racial matters within it, comes through in our next account of teacher practice, from Groby School in Leicestershire. But first, for teachers who have not tried using such techniques, here is the 'write up' by second year pupil Anthony Alexis after playing that last game mentioned above. He had played it as part of the integrated studied course at Hackney Downs School in London, the course introduced by Frances Magee at the start of this section, and his response illustrates the sort of enthusiasm and awareness the game can produce on subjects often found too abstract or irrelevant by twelve year olds:

Our group had machinery (such as scissors, rulers, and pencils); we were better off than some of the others, and even better because we organised ourselves. Everybody in our group was equal, but each of us had a certain job – for example a purser and a maker; and we sold and bought things. If we played the game again and I had the choice whether to start as a country with more machinery or with more materials, I would choose to have machinery because it would be worth more than the materials (like paper).

When the second 'harvest' came, our group altered its tactics, because the price of paper went down – well, actually the price of finished goods went up and as we were making quite a lot, and had already made a lot of money, we could easily buy lots more raw materials. We also changed our production line.

We did not go in for unfair deals; and I never got angry. Reubin's group got angry when he sold me a pencil and paper for one counter and then I sold it back to them (because they desperately needed it) for five counters. We were very controlled and organised, and we had offers coming in all the time; we could protect our territory and our output. The real countries of the world do the same sorts of things with security and protection laws.

The smaller countries with the raw materials were too simple; they didn't realise that if they increased the selling price of their raw materials they could have made money enough to invest in some machinery for themselves. As it was, they always needed us, and we kept control of both their materials and the market for selling. We were more flexible than them.

There are some rules I would like to put into the game: I think that there should have been a wider market, with more things to be made. There should have been more than just a gentleman's agreement about security, there should have been something really strong like an international law against trespassing. Blackmarketing should be outlawed too. I also think that there should have been some kind of quality control; there were poor quality goods on the market and even some that were unfinished! Some of the bad practices should have been forbidden; there should be no bribery, no blackmail, no forging.

I got very involved in the game. I think I got overexcited because I was doing well, and I was beginning to think what it must be like in the real world with similar things going on. There are swindles, and there are high prices which have nothing to do with the real value of the goods. I went rushing around like businessmen must do, anxious to see if my product was high or low on the market.

I think that it must be very like the real thing because we all had our separate territories for making things, and there was something like a common or world market for what was made. Buying and selling got very competitive and for some people it became like a way of life just to make a profit, not minding how they did it. Money has got something to do with it. In my opinion the world would be better without money, but we still need to trade.

Some resources
The games mentioned, along with relevant booklets, fact sheets, etc are obtainable from:

1 Oxfam, 274 Banbury Road, Oxford OX2 7OZ (0865–56777 for free catalogues).

2 Christian Aid, PO Box 1, London SW9 8BH (01-733 5500 for free catalogue).

3 The Commonwealth Institute, Kensington High Street, London W8 6NQ (01-602 3252 for free lists).

4 Centre for World Development Education, 128 Buckingham Palace Road, SW1 9FH.
   This offers *The Development puzzle* by N. L. Fyson, a two hundred page book on world development questions with notes on simulations, speakers, school linking, and a list of local Development Education centres.
   CWDE issues a monthly bulletin *Action for development for teachers*.
   A particularly interesting article, 'Sensitivity or censorship?' by Michael Storm on apparent tension between Development education and Multi-ethnic

education appears in the issue of August 1980. It critically analyses the fear that to teach about poverty and famine in the 'Third World' risks damaging the self-image of British black children.

5 World Studies Project, 24 Palace Chambers, 9 Bridge Street, London SW1A 2JT (01-930 7661). This offers many important resources for teachers:

Learning for change in world society (1976), a book on the why and how of studying world society with many suggestions for classroom methods and lists of materials.
Debate and decision: schools in a world of change, a valuable handbook of discussion exercises relevant for multi-cultural education.
Ideas into action – curriculum for a changing world (1980). This handbook for teachers, written by teachers, gives case studies of many useful approaches, including, again, recommended resources.
The New Era journal about world studies in schools which gives case study descriptions of projects and news of recent publications.

6 School of Oriental and African Studies, Extra Mural Division, Malet Street, London WC1. This can supply *Development studies: a handbook for teachers* by P. Jones, (1977).

7 The Geographical Association, 343 Fulward Road, Sheffield, is a source of advice and can supply reprints of articles like *Multi racial education and geography*, by Michael Storm in ILEA *Geography Bulletin*, July 1978.

8 The Birmingham Development Education Centre can supply *Priorities for development* a teachers' handbook for development education (Spring 1981). This outlines school-tested work and ideas by teachers in the Birmingham area.

9 Council for Education in World Citizenship, CEWC, Cobham House, Blackfriars Lane, London EC4V 6EB, provides advice and resources for teachers and organises conferences for fifth and sixth formers.

Development Education Centres

For details of new member groups of the National Association of Development Education Centres, telephone the general secretary on 061-445 2495

Birmingham
Development Education Centre, Gillett Centre,
Selly Oak Colleges, Bristol Road, Birmingham B29 6LE
(021-472 3255)

Bracknell
Bracknell Committee for World Development Education,
c/o 'Constables', Windsor Road, Ascot, Berkshire SL5 7LF
(0990-21167)

Bristol
Development Education Centre, c/o The Breadline, Central Hall,
Old Market, Bristol 1
(telephone c/o Mary Hazelwood, 0272 34 644)

Cheltenham
Centre for World Development Education,
Adult Education Centre, Shaftsbury Hall, St Georges Place,
Cheltenham, Gloucestershire GL50 4AZ
(telephone c/o J. A. Hawkins, 0242 20969)

Derby
Derby Third World Resources Centre, c/o Elvaston Vicarage,
via Borrowash, Derbyshire, DE7 3EQ
(telephone c/o Peter Harding, 0332 71790)

Edinburgh
Scottish Education and Action for Development,
9 Union Street, Edinburgh, EH1 3LT
(031-556 0267)

Exmouth
South West Development Education Centre, Rolle College,
Exmouth, Devon EX8 4LR
(03957-5344 Ex. 69)

Hove
Third World Information Centre, c/o Oxfam Sussex Centre,
31 Western Road, Hove, East Sussex BN3 1AF
(0273-777338)

Leamington
Third World Information Centre, 32a Bath Street,
Leamington, Warwickshire CV31 3AF
(0926-26476)

Leeds
Development Education Centre, 29 Blenheim Terrace,
Leeds LS2 9HD
(0532-33300)

London (North)
Archway Development Education Centre,
173 Archway Road, London N6
(01-348 3030)

London (North)
One World Shop, 78 Evershott Street, London NW1 N6 5BL
(01-388 5809)

London
Africa Centre, 38 King Street, London WC2 8JT
(01-836 5809)

London (South)
Ujama Centre, 14 Brixton Road, London SW9 6BU
(01-582 2068)

Londonderry
World Development Education Project, 45 Clarendon Street,
Londonderry, Northern Ireland BT48 7ER
(0504-69183)

Manchester
Development Education Project, Didsbury School of Education,
9a Didsbury Park, Manchester M20 8RR
(061-445 2495)

Manchester
Shanti Third World Centre, 178 Waterloo Place,
Oxford Road, Manchester M13 9QQ
(061-273 8717)

Milton Keynes
Tim Bartlett, Stantonbury Campus,
Stantonbury, Milton Keynes, MK14 6BN
(0908-314055)

Norwich
Third World Centre, 17 St John Maddermarket,
Norwich, Norfolk NR2 1DN
(0603-610993)

Oxford
Development Education Centre,
72 Cowley Road, Oxford OX4 1JB
(0865-726216)

Southampton
World Studies Centre, St John's School, Castleway,
Southampton SO1 0AS
(0703-30634)

Workington
Cumbria Schools World Development Project, 28 Finkle Street,
Workington, Cumbria CA14 2BB
(0900-63621)

Experiental techniques in multi-cultural education

For our second example of a curriculum development aimed directly at
giving a 'global perspective' and at the same time sensitising students to
the realities of living in a multi-racial society, we turned to the Humanities Faculty at Groby Community College, a fourteen to eighteen
Leicestershire upper school. It operates an O/CSE World Studies
course as its contribution to the compulsory fourth and fifth year core
curriculum. The head of faculty, Dr David Selby who is seen teaching
in 'Education versus prejudice', offered this account:

CSE students take the College's own Mode III examination in World
Studies; students of 'O' level potential follow the Joint Matriculation

Board's Integrated Humanities syllabus, which is extremely flexible both in terms of content and mode of assessment[1] – a flexibility which enables the Groby staff to follow a mixed ability policy.

Our World Studies course is based upon the assumption that there are certain definable problems of human organisation on this planet which can only be understood from a global point of view and which can only be treated on a global basis. Central to the syllabus is the concept of the 'global village' and the conviction that the most salient feature of the contemporary world is the interdependence of its inhabitants. After examining the idea of 'global village' and other background information, including the terms 'First', 'Second', 'Third', and 'Fourth World', we invite students to explore a number of themes using a problems/solutions/alternatives approach: 'Population', 'Poverty and Affluence', 'Conflict and Violence', 'Structural Violence' which includes 'North-South' relations, 'Reactive Violence', and 'Destruction of the Environment'. In addition, in the second year of the course, students are given the opportunity to involve themselves at a local, personal level in one or more issues to which they have been introduced. An account and analysis of their involvement can be written up as their 'major project'; alternatively, those not wishing to get involved can attempt a library-based research project.

Race relations, the nature and effects of prejudice, discrimination and oppression are practically leitmotivs of the World Studies course. They are dealt with directly under the 'Conflict' and 'Structural Violence' components of the course and more tangentially under almost every other section of the syllabus. Indeed, Groby teachers have often claimed that the nature of the syllabus carries real advantages for multi-cultural education in a virtually all-white school. Consideration of topics such as 'Hunger and Malnutrition', 'Illiteracy', 'Disasters', 'Apartheid' and 'North-South', inevitably means that racial issues frequently present themselves in the classroom and give the teacher the opportunity to develop discussion of them. Given that race thus arises apparently inadvertently, the skilled teacher can withdraw from any counter-productive classroom confrontation, knowing that many other chances to explore the issue will occur before the course ends.

We feel that for a World Studies programme to maintain its credibility, medium and message must be in harmony. The mixed-ability classroom would seem to be the essential medium for teaching about relations globally and within our own multi-cultural society; it is a demonstration of interdependence and togetherness in action. Can teachers concerned about de-streaming, globally and nationally, appear credible to setted or streamed groups? This thinking led to the team's decision to work within a mixed-ability context. That decision inevitably triggered off a whole range of problems connected with class management and the resourcing of World Studies. In the event, we prepared a 'mainstream' booklet for each topic, together with a simpler version written in conjunction with the Head of Compensatory Education, and a *Readings and Things* pamphlet containing a range of more advanced material for the ablest students. The booklets provide the backbone of the course, but to avoid 'suffocation by workbook' and also to try to bring a democratic and participatory approach to World Studies, many other techniques are also used. These include discussing films[2], filmstrips and slides, debates, large and small discussion groups, individual work programmes both inside and outside school, simulation games, and – most importantly – experiential activities.

Amongst the experiential units used at Groby are a number devised by a group of educationalists, psychologists, and sociologists brought together by UNESCO in 1972. The units are often referred to as '3.01' units and are based upon the proposition that a deepening understanding of human behaviour – one's own and one's peer group in particular – is an essential prerequisite if international understanding is to be achieved, and racist attitudes eschewed. Each unit involves a class or group in an exercise or experience which is followed by discussion and, if appropriate, work on paper[3].

An example is the 'Cat and Mouse Fantasy', shown in the film 'Education versus prejudice'. This involves reading a story to the students, who we find can exercise their imagination most readily if asked to make themselves comfortable by lying on the floor and closing their eyes. The story invites them to think of themselves walking into a dark empty room, in an old deserted house. The student imagines feeling a strange bodily sensation, and begins to shrink and change shape, eventually becoming no more than a mouse. After examining the room, the mouse sees a cat coming through the door. The cat begins to stalk the mouse and stops right in front of it ready to pounce. At the critical moment, the mouse is asked to think of the options open to it and decide what to do. But then as the cat is about to spring, both cat and mouse tremble and begin to change shape. The cat becomes a mouse and the mouse becomes a cat. The new cat is asked the following questions:

How do you feel being bigger and no longer trapped? How does the mouse look to you? Do you know what the mouse is feeling? What are you feeling? Decide what you're going to do and then do it. What do you feel now?[4]

After experiencing this 'Fantasy', the teacher draws out the students' reactions. They usually have a lot to say! After a while, discussion tends to focus on the changing relationship between the cat and the mouse, the questions above being of crucial significance. Some students will have decided to eat the mouse in case the changing happened again; some will have slunk away 'to avoid further danger'; some will have remembered what it was like to be a mouse threatened by a cat and will have decided to leave the mouse alone or even to try and enter into friendly and constructive dialogue.

From such simple, imagined experiences, the discussion broadens to questions of dominance and submissiveness within international, inter-group and inter-personal relationships. Far-fetched as it might seem, the film I think demonstrates how the fantasy is an excellent starter unit for work on Race Relations, Minorities, Apartheid and North-South Conflict. These issues are suddenly matters of intense interest, even in the all-white school. For what happened when the 'mouse' became the 'cat' in Zimbabwe? Was the Oil Crisis of 1973 the moment when the 'mouse', globally-speaking, changed into the 'cat'?

There are also a number of very useful 3.01 units which explore stereotyping. In a unit called 'Faces', students are encouraged to inspect nine pictures of male and female faces and to decide which face fits one of seven occupations listed on the board: diplomat, criminal, student, comedian, policeman, teacher and musician. For the two extra faces, they are asked to suggest occupations. Once students have completed the task, a table of results can be written up on the board.

In the ensuing discussion, the processes by which we begin to form stereotypes can be explored, along with our reactions and behaviour upon the basis of stereotypes. An interesting alternative exercise involves asking students to respond to descriptive titles such as 'German', 'Irishman', 'Squatter', 'Dog Lover' and 'Women's Libber' by writing off-the-cuff pen portraits or by drawing quick sketches. Again, a teacher with a good personal knowledge of a class might attempt a role-playing exercise involving a plastic surgeon and his team 'remaking' the face of a 'patient' so the face accords with a particular occupational role. This exercise can actually be quite anxiety-producing and the teacher needs to be sure of her/his relationship with a class and its individual students.

UNESCO 3.01 units are not the only source of experimental exercises. Periodicals such as *New Era*[5] and the *World Studies Journal*[6] carry accounts of simulation games from time to time and the catalogues of organizations such as Oxfam, Community Service Volunteers, Third World Publications, Christian Aid and CWDE[7] all offer games and exercises as a basis for a multi-cultural perspective. CWDE includes in its list *Ba Fa Ba Fa*, a game devised in the USA about the problems which arise when different cultures meet each other. It is often worthwhile, too, to approach the local Community Relations Council to see what simulations they know of and/or have in stock. The Leicester Community Relations Council, for instance, has copies of *Passport*, a simulation game on race relations and immigration, devised by Keith Bradford, once of Coventry CRC[8]. Education Officers from the

Leicester Council visit Groby from time to time and involve World Studies classes in playing Passport.

Teachers can also work out their own experiential unit or simulation game. Social Studies teachers at Hartcliffe Comprehensive School, Bristol, produced 'Cake and Coke', an exercise giving students first-hand experience of apparently being discriminated against, of denial of their 'rights' – as also shown in the film. The teacher gratuitously distributes fizzy drink, cakes and biscuits to a random few, finds an excuse to leave the class, allows a few minutes for them to react, then returns to discuss the behaviour and feelings of the 'haves' and 'have-nots'[9].

At Groby, I developed the 'Purple Armband Experiment' based upon an American idea. It involves creating a clearly visible minority in a school and in the community by asking a small number of students to wear an armband. Student participants must be prepared to keep the secret of why they are wearing the armband from everybody, including teachers, friends and family. If questioned about the armband, they are asked to respond by saying 'I'm afraid I'm not at liberty to tell you' – or to use some similar but possibly more colloquial formula. The aim of the experiment is, firstly, to observe how people react to the presence of a minority group, identified by a superficial sign and, secondly, to explore the internal dynamics of the minority group itself.

My class not unexpectedly leapt at the chance of attempting the experiment. Fifteen students volunteered to wear the purple armbands – purple because the colour had no immediate or readily-understood political or religious significance (save, perhaps, to a High Church minority in the community). The remaining fourteen students were likewise sworn to secrecy and agreed to act as observers of the experiment which was to last for three school days. Their role was to note down significant incidents and also to move in upon any situation threatening to get out of hand. Techniques for dealing with such situations – whether involving fellow-students or teachers – were con-sidered at length. Indeed much of the briefing session was given over to emphasising the potential hazards of wearing an armband; the wearers were told to expect verbal confrontation at the very least and conceivably, actual physical violence. For this reason, I had, prior to the lesson, obtained the consent of the College's Executive Team (the Principal and three Vice-Principals) to the experiment taking place. No other colleague was privy to the experiment.

The students came to the debriefing session at the end of the experiment keen to relate stories of how those wearing armbands had been singled out and subjected to name-calling, emotional blackmail, boycott, threats and, in a few cases, physical intimidation. Equally, there was a lot of discussion about how the armband-wearers – the visible minority – had quickly developed their own solidarity, empathy and interdependence as a group. This phenomenon was not merely a response to threats, real or imagined, from the majority; it also arose out of a sense of shared knowledge.

What came out most clearly from the students' comments and subsequent writing, however, was that their own experience of being part of a visible minority had given them a clearer understanding of how readily we all lapse into discriminatory behaviour; also they gained a more vivid appreciation of what life can be like for the many minority groups in the world who face persecution because they fail to fit in with the norms and values of the society in which they find themselves. As Judith put it:

'I enjoyed taking part in the experiment, but I do not think I would enjoy permanently being a member of a minority group. If you wear a purple armband, you can take it off if you do not like the way you are being treated, but if you really are different, either by the colour of your skin or by your beliefs, you cannot unpin and discard them. You must live with the intolerant attitudes of other people. While most people in my class would now say that they think to prejudge and then to discriminate is wrong, most will continue to do these things, perhaps not against those of a different colour or who have a different religion but more likely against those who have certain inadequacies which make it impossible for them to fit in. I think people of my own age are most guilty of this because it is so important to them to be accepted by the majority that they find it necessary to reject and riducule a few'[10].

Such writing is surely indication enough of the potential of experiential techniques for multi-cultural education in 'all-white' schools.

References and sources
(1) For details of the Groby World Studies CSE syllabus and the JMB Integrated Humanities syllabus, cf. *The New Era*, vol. 59, no. 4, July/August 1978, pp. 134–9; *The New Era*, vol. 60, no. 6, November/December 1979, pp. 212–29 and *World Studies Journal*, vol. 1, no. 1, Winter 1979/80, pp. 27–33.

(2) For a first-rate handbook on using films in world studies, cf. Taylor, N. and Richardson, R. *Seeing and Perceiving* Concord Films Council, 1979 (see p. 211).

(3) '3.01' units are described in detail in Wolsk, D. *On experience – centred curriculum* UNESCO, 1975 available from HMSO.

(4) *Ibid.*, p. 45.

(5) *The New Era* is obtainable from the Distribution Secretary, 54 Fontarbia Road, London SW11 5PF.

(6) *World Studies Journal* is available from the Distribution Manager, Groby
     Community College, Ratby Road, Groby, Leicestershire.

(7) Education Department, Oxfam, 274 Banbury Road, Oxford OX2 7DZ;
     Community Service Volunteers, 237 Pentonville Road, London N19NJ; Third
     World Publications, 151 Stratford Road, Birmingham B1 1RD; Publications,
     Christian Aid, PO Box 1, London SW9 8BH; CWDE, 128 Buckingham Palace Road,
     London SW1W 9SH.

(8) For further details of *Passport*, write to Community Relations Council,
     Tudor House, 14 Spon Street, Coventry.

(9) Cf. *Rights and responsibilities* in Fisher, S., Magee, F. & Wetz, J., *Ideas into
     action* (Ikon/World Studies Project, 1980), p. 23

(10) For a fuller description of the experiment, cf. Selby, D. E. *The Purple Armband
     Experiment: An Experiential Unit in discrimination* in *The New Era* vol. 61,
     November/December 1980.

A note on examinations

Many teachers fear that examinations will constrain attempts to develop
a multi-cultural curriculum, though the schools represented in these
pages have not allowed them to do so. There seems to be some impasse
between that teachers' viewpoint and the examination boards'
declaration that there is little demand for them to modify and change
subjects and content of examinations. For discussion of these issues,
detailed evidence on questions of how far examination syllabuses have
been reviewed from a multi-cultural viewpoint is given in *The way
forward*, by Alan Little and Richard Willey, see page 175.

A summary and analysis of the available evidence about the
performance of pupils of West Indian origin in CSE and GCE
examinations is given in section 9 of *Caught Between* by Monica Taylor,
see page 160.

10 A school policy on racism

In 1978, a number of teachers at Holloway School in North London felt the need for their school to adopt a formal and public stance in favour of a multi-cultural curriculum and against racism. It was a time when there had been a disturbing increase in electoral support for the National Front, which had launched a specific campaign of recruitment in schools. After a copy of a National Front leaflet was found in school, this policy statement was drafted by the Head Teacher, George Spinoza, and put to a full staff meeting:

The discovery of this leaflet makes it necessary to have a school policy on the subject to enable us to deal with possible problems in the future. At the same time we must be careful not to over-react. It is true to say that the racial harmony in the school is far better than in most London schools and that the staff are united in the opposition to all forms of racialism and racist ideas. However, we must not be complacent. Racialism outside schools is becoming gradually more respectable and this development will inevitably have repercussions inside schools.

In view of this, we should consider the adoption of a number of specific proposals:

1 We should undertake a campaign of education in assemblies, in lessons and during form periods. Such a campaign should seek to achieve the following:

a Impress upon the pupils that discrimination against people because of the colour of their skin or place of origin is wrong;

b Explain why black people, Cypriots and Asians have a right to live in this country. This is particularly important because of the numerous myths that are perpetrated about immigration;

c Prevent any racialist abuse occurring inside the school wherever we possibly can. For example if epithets like 'coon', 'nigger', 'wog', 'yid', or 'paki' are heard, they should not go unchallenged. We should explain why they are offensive and prevent them from becoming common currency inside the school.

2 The use of materials like films, television programmes, factsheets and stories that assist in the furtherance of the above aims should be encouraged.

3 If any racialist literature appears or is circulated in the school it should be confiscated. Obviously confiscation on its own is not enough; it has to be accompanied by a clear explanation of why we cannot allow the circulation of material that is designed to incite racial animosity and it is clearly dependent on the education programme outlined above. Some may argue that such positive action will create more problems than it will solve. To allow the circulation of such literature in school is an affront to all the black and Cypriot pupils in the school and it would undermine their confidence in the educational system. It would also lead directly to tension and possibly open conflict among the pupils. If any attempts at the circulation of such literature are nipped in the bud it will establish that racist ideas are not 'respectable' and give some credibility to our aims of running a harmonious, multi-racial school.

Confiscation of racialist literature would be consistent with our current practice. We do not hesitate, for example, to confiscate pornographic material, hopefully explaining why. By the same token, racialist literature is directly offensive and degrading to many of our pupils. Similarly we often confiscate sweets and drink inside the schools. If chewing a toffee is regarded as being disruptive of normal school activities, how much more so is the circulation of racialist literature?

By adopting these suggestions as school policy we may seem to be inviting an unwarranted intrusion of politics and political ideas into school. Leaving aside the obvious point that many subjects we teach already deal with a wide range of political ideas and arguments, we need to say specifically why the brand of politics represented by the National Front merits our active opposition.

The National Front are not just one extreme of the political spectrum, they are qualitatively different from all other organised groups.

They are openly and proudly racist: they believe in the compulsory repatriation of all black and coloured people even though many of them have been born here; they would ban multi-racial education, a school like ours would cease to exist; they even want to see reggae and soul music banned. They are in fact unique in British politics, their racism sets them apart.

Finally, the point is bound to be made that by making a stand against racism we are attracting publicity and even hostility from some quarters.

This is true. We have to make a choice; do we ignore the problem of racism and racialist organisations and hope they will disappear, or do we as a multi-racial school take a principled stand against them? The same dilemma presented itself to the German people in the early 1930's and they took the former course with disasterous consequences. We cannot afford the same mistake.

The ILEA has a clear policy on multi-racial education as outlined in a recent document from the Chairman of the Schools Sub-Committee. We should attempt to operate in the spirit of this policy by building a campaign against racism not only at Holloway and the rest of Division 3, but throughout the whole of the ILEA.

What happened at Holloway School when that statement was put forward? We asked Shaun Doherty of the English Department:

Many different points of view were put forward at the staff meeting, and some teachers expressed apprehension that if we took a public stand we may attract unwarranted attention to the school, perhaps making it a focal point for the National Front. But after lengthy discussion the document was unanimously adopted as school policy and subsequently discussed with pupils. We found, incidentally, that it received favourable publicity in the local press, despite some somewhat lurid headlines ('Head canes Racist Poison'), and it was sympathetically reported in two national newspapers.

There is no doubt that the policy contributed to the morale of the pupils, by externalising the already harmonious multi-racial atmosphere in the school. It was not, however, implemented on any very systematic basis – much depended on the initiatives of individuals and departments. It would be unrealistic to imagine that such a statement will somehow transform the entire existing curriculum overnight. In fact, perhaps the most immediate implementation of the policy was carried out informally, for example in confronting racist remarks in the corridor or classroom and explaining to the pupils why it was necessary to do so. This type of intervention demands both vigilance and flexibility as well as a sensitivity to changing social and political circumstances outside the school.

Let's look at an extreme example: 'You fucking paki curry eater, I'll kill you'. When I heard this remark in a second year class I was doubly disturbed because it combined racist abuse (often, we've noticed, directed at the eating habits of particular ethnic groups) with an apparent threat of physical violence. I stopped the lesson and called the speaker out to the front, making my own sense of outrage clear to the rest of the class. This was necessary in order to reassure the pupil at the receiving end of such language that teachers are not neutral to it, and are ready to protect any pupil from apparent physical threats. I then publicly explained why his remarks were offensive to me; fortunately he was receptive to argument and in fact was ready subsequently to apologise. Of course, it's not always easy to respond effectively to remarks in the middle of a lesson – one has often to follow the case up afterwards; but it is important that there is some kind of *public* reaction to that kind of remark. I personally disagree with Robert Jeffcoate when he argues that some expressions of white racism in the classroom should be accepted by the teacher. (R. Jeffcoate 'Positive Image'.)

A less obvious, and more typical, example occurred with a class of fourth year boys: 'Sir, I think black people should be sent back home because this country is overcrowded'. If I had failed to respond to such a view with the facts to indicate the ignorance, as well as insensitivity, it is based on, I would be guilty of fostering racist attitudes through omission. Silence may not imply agreement, but it does imply no serious disagreement, and so serves to create an atmosphere in which racist attitudes are apparently an acceptable part of classroom discourse. The intervention need not be heavy handed and should seek to win over the offender, but it is so important that the teacher makes his or her attitudes clear.

Our approach is clearly interventionist and is presented to pupils and parents as such; it has met with no opposition from parents and very little from pupils. However, even if such opposition were to be expressed we would feel obliged to stand up to it.

As can be seen, the policy is not simply about reacting to expressions of racism. It seeks to establish within the school a firm commitment to a multi-cultural curriculum – something just as important as the immediate response to surface expressions of racism. Some of the ways this was done were:

1 A first step was to communicate the policy to the pupils and involve them in it. Informal discussion in form periods and year assemblies took place. Yearmasters explained the reasons the staff were adopting the policy, and while such large gatherings are not conducive to real learning, the effect on pupils was noticeable. Coupled with press publicity, and given the possibility of the National Front focusing its propaganda upon the school, we found these discussions generated enthusiasm among pupils for the ideas of anti-racism. There were no hostile reactions.

2 Films. Largely under the auspices of the Sociology Department, films were used with third, fourth and fifth years, including 'Last Grave at Dimbaza' – a documentary filmed illegally in South Africa with a chilling insight into a racist society and 'Divide and Rule – Never!',

which captures the mood among young people at the Anti-Nazi carnivals of the late 1970's. (For films, see page 211.)

3 Outside speakers from anti-racist and minority group organisations and political parties were invited to put their points of view and discuss them with the pupils.

4 Syllabus content. The History Department revised the unit of the third year syllabus on African and Caribbean History to include:

a Dispelling misconceptions concerning the 'primitive' state of Africa prior to the coming of the Europeans, and developing awareness of the complexity of traditional African societies;

b Examining the economic basis of racism;

c Introducing the methodology used by African historians;

d Studying Jamaica as an example of a multi-racial society;

e Reviewing the causes and the problems associated with migration.

In the fourth and fifth years the general title of the syllabus is 'World Affairs 1919 to the present day'. In contains fifteen units which include 'Aspects of Apartheid in South Africa', 'Population and Race in South Africa', 'Genocide', 'The Road to the Second World War', and 'Civil Rights in the USA'.

The Sociology Department has also introduced a course unit on minority groups which reviews the experience of West Indians, Cypriots, Turks, Pakistanis, Indians and Chinese in Britain.

The English Department emphasises that it is not enough to use material portraying black people, that children must be given opportunities to express their own identities through writing about their own experience.

5 Language. The boys bring a spectrum of language backgrounds to the school that are sometimes at odds with Standard English. The natural language of the child is received positively and not regarded as something to be corrected; acquiring skills in Standard English does not involve rejection of this natural language. The Language Policy Group is formulating a policy to take account of all the uses of language in school. The use of transcripts of spoken language to assist with writing has been explored.

6 The hidden curriculum is equally important. The basis for organising groupings in the school is on the principle of mixed ability, to obviate ethnic minorities occupying a disproportionately high number of places in lower streams, as research has shown happens where streaming exists. Discipline is equally important. We have opposed the creation of

Disruptive Units and set up our own support unit. Although it has few facilities and is understaffed, it represents an alternative to the 'sin bin' notion of separate units outside school. There is no caning in school.

It would be misleading to represent these initiatives as unproblematic; we see them very much as a tentative first step towards establishing a curriculum that does not just have multi-cultural components but which can itself be properly described as multi-cultural.

Nevertheless, they do represent a clear acknowledgement that the problem of racism exists in society and, by extension, in schools. As NFER research for the Schools Council has revealed (New Society, 16th February 1978), many school children, even in infant and primary schools, have openly racist attitudes and many more accept racist assumptions and myths. Teachers can only make this problem worse by pretending that it does not exist. Although simply accepting that there is a problem doesn't solve it, it makes the conditions for tackling it possible. Even if teachers can't persuade their school to make a public stand on the issue they can raise the arguments in the staffroom and at least begin to challenge existing assumptions.

Other sources
Teaching and racism: All London teachers against racism and fascism (ALTARF), 1978: (see p. 56).
Race in the curriculum reprinted articles available from the CRE free (see p. 211).

11 From school to work

This section raises questions about careers guidance in schools with ethnic minority pupils. But it is not for careers teachers alone. It brings out basic issues to do for example with contact with parents, and with advising pupils on subject options, that concern all staff in schools at secondary level. It has been prepared by John Twitchin, incorporating draft material by Denise Abbott of the Commission for Racial Equality, and ideas and suggestions from Ted Murray, the Job Liaison Officer, and Maureen O'Connell, the Head of Humanities, at Tulse Hill School in South London; and from Evelyn Davies, Principal of the Pathway Centre in Southall:

In 1978, the fifth year tutor and careers teacher at an Ipswich High School did something all secondary school teachers could do: they made a simple check among their school-leavers. They found that one month before leaving school none of the black students (twelve per cent of the school's population) had jobs to go to, compared with nearly a quarter of the white students. The next year, the Ipswich Association of the NUT did a larger scale survey for all secondary schools. Again young people from ethnic minorities were shown to have much less success in finding employment – little over ten per cent, compared with over fifty per cent of white school-leavers. And they were careful to check that neither lack of effort in their job-search, nor lower qualifications, could be identified as significant factors to explain this (See *Job opportunities in Ipswich for* black school-leavers, NUT Ipswich Association, December 1979.)

The findings of the Ipswich teachers are confirmed by other surveys in Bristol, Leicester, Bradford and London. In 1978 in Lewisham, for example, a careful and detailed study found that black school-leavers were three times more likely to be unemployed than their white peers. And those who did get jobs had made more applications, attended more interviews, and had taken longer to find work than their white contemporaries, even when they had comparable qualifications. Despite this extra effort, fewer black school leavers had found the kind of work they wanted, so they were less satisfied with their jobs. (This important report: *Looking for Work* is available from the CRE, 10 Allington Street, London, SW1 – which can also supply *Half a Chance?* the disturbing report of a study of one hundred firms in Nottingham in 1979, which proves the extent and nature of the discrimination young blacks still face in finding work.)

So it is not just disproportionate unemployment figures. Young people from ethnic minorities who do get work achieve lower status and lower paid employment than their white peers with equivalent qualifications. Their difficulty in achieving even modest and realistic ambitions leads to some young people becoming disillusioned, and from their discontent the generalisation is made that young blacks are trouble-makers and potentially unreliable employees. Thus in many places a vicious circle has developed.

It is a vicious circle, as many teachers will know, that gets reflected in school. If pupils at the age twelve or thirteen see older brothers or sisters, and other relatives or neighbours, stuck in low status work, this will affect their own view of their chances. Many will form expectations lower than their own potential; some may react by adopting unrealistically high ambitions. If expectations are left unmodified by careful advice from that age onwards, based on a teacher/pupil relationship which means the advice is respected, then pupils may drift into lower streams, or demand to be placed too high. A resistance may develop to just that sort of self-assessment process that is the basis of the careers staffs' work.

Careers guidance has many problems. It is difficult enough to help school-leavers to make informed choices of occupation on an assumption of fairly full employment in the economy. Even that task is complicated by the question of how to promote the idea of recurrent, lifelong, education and training for job flexibility. On top of all that, in the 1980s we have the serious dilemma: how far should pupils be prepared for possible long-term unemployment, or forms of under-employment, resulting from structural and technical change in the economy? What possible alternative to the traditional work ethic is there to offer for the pupil who may never find work?

These are major questions for all pupils in all schools, and in tackling them, teachers can show their ethnic minority pupils how they share with their white peers a range of difficulties and frustrations. But the main issue for this chapter remains the teacher's role in helping equalize opportunity in securing jobs. Ethnic minority pupils can be particularly dependent on what the school offers in career counselling, especially if the community groups they belong to have not lived in Britain long enough to establish the 'unofficial' or informal job-finding channels and contacts (eg with supervisors or union representatives, through their relatives and friends) that many of their white peers can rely on. This is one reason why the quality of the counselling and other supportive preparation for work offered by the schools is so crucial, if the equality of opportunity that they have the right to expect by law, is to mean anything at all in practice.

This is no narrow, technical problem for careers teachers alone. It is part of the very meaning of multi-cultural education to recognise the key responsibility of all teachers to enable their pupils to compete on equal terms in the labour market. If as a result of an inappropriate curriculum, damage to self-esteem, inadequate counselling or stereotypical low expectations, other teachers have sold ethnic minority pupils short in terms of qualifications they finally achieve, then the careers staff start with a major disadvantage. And this is compounded by the undoubted widespread discrimination on grounds of race and colour which – whether intentional or not – still afflicts the job market.

The researches mentioned earlier established at least three facts of disadvantage for ethnic minority school-leavers, additional to the problem of acute jobs shortage that they share with their white peers – three facts that run against some teachers' impressions or assumptions:

1 *They try at least as hard to find work, but are less successful;*

2 *Even when they are not unrealistically ambitious, they tend not to achieve their aspirations;*

3 *They suffer discrimination on the grounds of race or colour;*

Put very simply, careers education can help off-set these additional problems by:

Ensuring that when they do apply for jobs, black school-leavers present themselves as effectively as possible.

Making sure that they and their parents are aware of as many employment options as possible.

Encouraging employers to have a positive attitude to recruiting ethnic minority school-leavers for types of work for which they have not previously been considered; encouraging school-leavers to have realistic attitudes to working life; making known the procedures available to counter instances of discrimination.

Such general observations may seem all too obvious, or all too easy to make: we need to look in more practical detail at what they mean.

The first step of course is for teachers to know the facts about the jobs search for ethnic minority pupils in their local area, and then to see if there are any more particular reasons than those we've indicated so far for any additional disadvantage that those facts reveal.

Further reasons to identify might include:

1 It may be that pupils' career ideas are too narrow or inflexible. For example, parents and boys from a West Indian background often lay heavy stress on the need for a trade. (In the West Indies, as used to be so in Britain, it is a common saying that if you have a trade you never go hungry.) This may work against the school-leavers' suitability for the type of work chosen. Boys with a clerical, artistic or literary persuasion may be pressured by parents towards trades in building, construction, or electronics.

2 Both pupils and their parents may suffer from a poor knowledge about the types of jobs available locally and nationally; and about when and where and how to apply for jobs. As another example, many West Indians who acquired their skills in the West Indies did not undergo a formal apprenticeship, and although now skilled craftsmen, many entered their trade without having any formal academic qualifications. Hence, *some* parents find it difficult to accept the need for CSE (and in some cases technical apprenticeships or 'O' Levels). *Some* parents may assume that the academic requirements for apprenticeships are actually a tool to block the entry of black school-leavers into some trades.

3 Reflecting their teachers' or parents' low expectations, some ethnic minority school-leavers may lack the confidence to find work worthy of their abilities. Others, perhaps as a reaction to anxiety about acceptance in British society, may develop a conscious desire to aim high in what is still 'a white man's world', and thus be led to hold on to over-ambitious aspirations about jobs.

4 Based on the experiences of neighbours and relatives, many may have a debilitating expectation of discrimination against them; and they may lack the clear ability to identify themselves as black Britons, and to bring up and discuss the difficulties this poses for them in searching for work.

5 Many who have come to Britain fairly recently may still have obvious linguistic difficulties, which can hinder even the simple routine of writing applications.

6 Less obviously, but no less importantly, many may be ill-equipped for the ritual of presenting themselves for interview – something which requires familiarity with British cultural traditions and the conventional expectations in the minds of employers about procedures of selection and training.

7 There is a problem for some – more often Asian Britons – who gain more qualifications, by staying on at school, than they need for the jobs they want, and which they should have started up to two years earlier (though very often there's little guarantee they would have got the job

then!). But much more commonly, young people from ethnic minorities who want to remain at school for as long as possible still don't achieve enough, in staying on till eighteen, in terms of academic or vocational qualifications to obtain a job with good prospects and/or status. This poses a very serious problem – since to be eighteen plus, black/brown, and both unqualified *and* inexperienced, statistically now gives a high probability of long-term unemployment.

So what kinds of assistance does all this suggest?

To take the last point first, some consideration is needed in schools about putting pressure on the Further Education sector to provide recurrent educational opportunities through courses that are realistically related to local job possibilities. This would help ensure that pupils are not retained in school to leave at eighteen with inadequate and/or irrelevant qualifications.

Equally, careers staff need to have a voice in the quality and design of any 'compensatory sixth form' at their school. Really helpful individual advice to pupils on the best mix of qualifications and experience to aim for – by staying on after sixteen; by taking an FE course; by going to work at sixteen; by taking a work experience placement, etc. – obviously depends on what range of available options there are. Helping to extend these, in collaboration with the rest of the staff, the youth employment service, the careers service, the community relations council, and local community workers and organisations, may itself be a vital condition of successful careers teaching in multi-ethnic schools.

One important and suggestive model, is Operation Springboard, a job training scheme set up by Camden Committee for Community Relations in the winter of 1979 to help young people from various ethnic minority groups to compete in the job market on equal terms. The Operation Springboard project was particularly interesting for the way it brought together language support training with new kinds of work experience in local firms. The report on their first year experiment, *A chance to work*, is available from the CCCR, 1 Robert Street, London NW1 3JU.

Another interesting model is South Liverpool Personnel, an independent employment agency which has been catering mainly for young Liverpool-born black people since 1972. Its report *Black Prospects*, (available free from 2 Rialto Buildings, Liverpool L8 1TB) gives clues on how to help black school-leavers get into work, and into better jobs.

But while helping encourage 'second chance' schemes may be very important as a short-term measure, it shouldn't distract teachers from the real task: improving the first chance learning at school, so that ethnic minority pupils don't leave with lower, or differential, success rates.

The question is how the ideas and methods of second chance projects like 'Operation Springboard' can be adopted and applied within the secondary school system. Apart from obvious implications like tackling linguistic difficulties, and designing a curriculum that encompasses rather than ignores the needs of ethnic minority pupils, it seems that any adequate preparation for leaving school to work will depend on how teachers relate to parents, give direct help to their school-leavers, and liaise with local employers.

Parents

Section 3 underlined the need for as much communication as possible with ethnic minority parents about their children's educational progress – a communication in which the school must take the initiative. Such contact is a crucial element in school-to-work preparation, and needs to have been established on entry to school and re-inforced at the time of choosing exam courses in the third year – well before school leaving year.

Aspirations Recognising the importance of this contact, some schools give parents handouts in simple English, setting out the choice of subjects to be made at the end of the pupil's third year, and the relation of these choices to careers. They also encourage parents not only to attend parents evenings, but also to come along to special events and talks arranged by the careers teachers. But as many teachers will know, more informal contact – perhaps through class tutors, or the pastoral system, or even through letters home – is needed on two problem points which can strongly affect parental aspirations for their children, especially parents from ethnic minorities:

1 *Interpreting school reports.* Bitterness and misunderstanding will all too often arise if a child in a weak set has been graded A1, as a reflection of effort and ability in the context of the set group – rather than compared to the whole year group. Such a child might get A1 and A2 in all subjects in the first three years, but then his/her parents are told (when making end of third year choices) that he/she has little chance of exam success at CSE above a grade 4.

The teacher may have been trying to encourage the pupil, but without discussion of the relative value of the grades related to the whole year group, the result may be misleading and unfair on both pupil and parent. Teachers need to check on parents' understanding of grade marks – rightly or wrongly, some parents take them extremely seriously.

2 *CSE and GCE* Equally, many parents may not understand that statistically a percentage of children won't even gain CSE grade 5, and that only twenty per cent have GCE potential. Parents will be very suspicious

if the first they hear about this twenty per cent is when they ask why their child is not 'down for GCE'.

Again, good and frequent communication, which gives the parents real confidence in the school is the only answer to this. It goes without saying that such confidence depends on there being the right proportion of ethnic minority children among the twenty per cent – or whatever the school's success rate – who get GCE. Without this, anything said to ethnic minority parents about the top twenty per cent is going to sound pretty hollow – and rightly so!

The cultural background Another reason for relating closely to parents is the need to be familiar with the cultural assumptions and pressures which will be influencing the pupil outside school. As one example of this, a study *The employment and training needs of the Bengali community in Tower Hamlets* found that the Islamic concept of performing one's duty, especially to one's family, was a significant limiting factor on the job choice of local school-leavers. It meant they chiefly tended to enter small family-run clothing businesses industry.

'That so many young Bengalis wanted to enter the rag trade was not to say that they or their parents regarded this as the ideal choice. It was more their recognition that this was virtually their only choice: their only salvation from unemployment or employment on shift-work in a factory. Careers advice in school seemed to have had no impact on the aspirations of these young people.'

To take another example: a firm which became concerned at the very low percentage of successful ethnic minority applicants for their apprenticeship scheme, found that cultural misunderstanding in the recruitment interview sessions was a key factor. In one section, candidates could be highly marked for 'positive self-projection in discussion'; but this by some cultures is considered inappropriate behaviour in such a situation.

The point of finding out about such different cultural values is not, of course, that they should be regarded as 'exotic' ideas, which need to be broken down, or from which pupils need protection. After all, some minority groups' cultural views may well prove more in tune with current socio-economic trends than the set of now out-of-date class and work ethics that most teachers have assumed up till now.

A useful piece of background reading (available from CRE) is the report on a study made in the mid-1970s of Asian and white school-leavers in the Midlands, called *Aspiration versus opportunities*. It put this general point in these terms:

'In multi-racial schools, careers teachers need to be aware of, and sensitive to, the cultural and ethnic background of ethnic minority pupils and the effect that this can have on pupils' self-perception, career choices, and ambitions. Local education authorities should ensure by in-service training and briefing that careers teachers have a real understanding of the value systems and background of their pupils.'

But teachers don't need to wait around for in-service training to be supplied – they can go for themselves to visit the local mosque, or community bookshop, or Pentecostal church, or CRC office, or temple, or Harambee Youth Centre, etc, to consult with community leaders about their cultural traditions. Equally, they could talk to parents. This is all the more vital, since it is only when parents, in turn, better understand the school system and the role of careers officers and teachers that they can play a full and realistic part in helping the school give their children a fair preparation for working life. Thus, as with all parent/teacher contact, the aim is for more dialogue, whereby both sides can learn something from each other, for the pupils' benefit.

Again it is worth bearing in mind that many Asian and West Indian parents not only have no personal experience of British educational practice – their assumptions and expectations about choosing jobs will have been formed by their own upbringing in very different societies. Some Asian parents, for example, especially middle class East Africans, have brought to Britain their strong commercial traditions, and have built something of a social and business network of their own, rather like the Jewish community, so that professional jobs in fields like hotel management, accountancy, or commercial law, are often arranged informally for their school leavers. Strong family expectations in that direction may determine such childrens' subject options at school, and may well mean that the pupils make little use of the careers staff. Other Asian parents, however, may have had their expectations formed in parts of India, where among the middle class the premium is on being a doctor or a barrister. As a result, their children may seem over-ambitious in British terms. Asian parents from rural areas of India or Bangladesh on the other hand, who have always expected to be workers, may not always influence their children to be ambitious enough in British terms. Careers staff may need to be ready to draw attention to that intermediate realm of jobs – jobs like television engineering, or nursing, or physiotherapy – which either didn't exist or were not familiar to many Asian parents when they were being brought up.

Asian girls, and their parents, sometimes make stereotypical assumptions that certain jobs may conflict with their community cultural or religious values. If career choices for girls are not to be restricted, the teacher may need to be able to give reassurances about this. When ethnic minority pupils are heard to say 'I want to do ... but my Dad says . . .' this in effect places the careers teacher in the position of an alternative father figure, whose advice becomes much more than merely informational – he or she becomes the society's 'long arm', shaping the place of West Indian and Asian-descended children in it. This is why a review of the nature of expectations in teachers' minds, and the quality of their understanding and handling of parental assumptions, are especially vital on the careers guidance side.

Pupils
Ethnic minority school-leavers need and deserve to know what they're up against. This means at the very least that teachers should share with their pupils:

facts about local and national job prospects in a changing labour market;

their understanding of the socio-economic background to ethnic minorities' place in the workforce;

the facts of racial discrimination – or, indeed, the lack of it – in local industry, and the implications of this for their job search.

It may be neither fair nor realistic to leave them operating only on impressions about these matters gained from their parents' or relatives' personal experience. If there does appear to be discrimination in local companies against job-seekers from minority groups, it is important for school-leavers to be aware of this, and to have thought out strategies for dealing with it. If, on the other hand, such discrimination does not exist, it is equally important for school-leavers to realise this. What is essential is for them to have as clear a view as possible of the real situations they will encounter. They may well need a strategy, for example, for finding out whether an employer has a formal equal opportunity policy, agreed with the relevant unions.

More particular help is needed for many school-leavers in presenting themselves as effectively as possible as job applicants. This could mean building 'social and life skills', including self-determination and decision making, into the curriculum, together with communication skills, particularly interview techniques.

In some schools which recognise the importance of this, there is an allocation of extended registration time, or one period a week, sometimes in both the fourth and fifth year, sometimes in the fifth only. It gives a period which lends itself most readily to informal counselling. Some teachers have found it useful to begin by talking over questions like:

1 What do you see as your good and bad points?

2 What do you think you have to offer – a friend? – an employer?

3 What sort of skills will you leave school with?

4 Are there any situations you find intimidating – and how do you cope with this?

5 Have your families had experiences that confirm that there *is* racial prejudice among employers?

These are difficult questions, more searching than those in the self-assessment profiles used as a preliminary to careers interviews in many authorities. Success depends on pupils feeling they can talk freely to someone who is well informed and has their real confidence. Such 'personal development' questions need to be tackled. More than anything else, this chapter is about building pupils' *confidence* in the face of the difficulties and opportunities they will soon be experiencing. If confidence is not built up, ethnic minority pupils stand in particular risk of not doing themselves justice.

There are various ways to help pupils with the process of finding work:

1 Mock interviews between teacher (as employer) and pupils in turn, which the rest of the group observe and comment on at the end;

2 Practising form completion (pads of duplicated Government forms can be bought, or make up your own);

3 Looking at and interpreting newspaper advertisements, and asking pupils to write out applications based on the information in the cuttings;

4 Using the telephone, encouraging pupils to make real calls to find out information about jobs;

5 Asking pupils to write out a personal biography for use in job applications later on;

6 Discussing issues like punctuality, conforming to standards of appearance, coping with an authoritarian boss, the dangers of frequent job changes, etc;

7 Watching and discussing relevant television or radio programmes, like the BBC television schools series *Going to Work*;

8 Working with pupils to check out local conditions (the Careers Officer should be able to provide information about what happened to last

year's leavers; what jobs are available locally; what amount of travel is needed for a job, etc);

9 Looking positively at unemployment: eg Do you know how to sign on? Re-training as a feature of working life now and in the future. A project to review what is available at AEI's or other community schemes and leisure activities, in mornings, afternoons and evenings, – ie plan a programme to keep busy, as well as allocating time for job hunting and perhaps further study.

A series of school exercises in interviewing could be capped by asking an outsider – a personnel officer, or someone from the Job Centre – to conduct interviews, as if for real, for jobs of each pupil's own choosing. It is interesting that as part of Operation Springboard, it was arranged for a supervisor from Marks and Spencer to come in and give the school-leavers practice in recruitment interviews. In this way, not only could misunderstandings about the implications in employers' questions be sorted out, and the candidates practise their language and communication skills, but also the effects of some different cultural behaviour patterns came to light. A few candidates, as a automatic reflex to being in the position of asking for something, simply never met the interviewer's eye, but looked down throughout. This gave a chance to point out that this is not expected behaviour in a job-seeking interview.

Here again, as with the cultural assumptions of parents, the idea is not to 'train' pupils out of such behaviour patterns, or to ask them to denude themselves of cultural attitudes and values that are part of their identity just because these may be different from those of most employers. Rather, the aim would be to help those pupils who can, to become 'bi-cultural' in their approach to job-searching and dealing with employers, and to help any who find this flexibility difficult to achieve, at least to be aware of likely expectations in the minds of employers, and to be able to explain why they may not be meeting these in the conventional way. This is needed to ensure they are not being misunderstood, or that their way of conducting themselves is not seen as a deficit in assessing their abilities. For example, in the case mentioned earlier where a firm was calling for 'positive self-projection' an agreement was made with the union to work out another, more culturally neutral, entrance procedure. This gave more attention to manual dexterity and qualities such as ingenuity, and modified the initial training to give opportunities to catch up with qualifications. For employers to give school-leavers fairer chances to demonstrate their potential is actually simply to act in their own enlightened self-interest.

A selection of materials on job finding and interview techniques is listed at the end of this chapter. Here we should perhaps say, that one positive idea is simply to invite ex-pupils who have had success, to come and talk about what they found was needed, and how they coped. We should particularly mention Community Service Volunteers job-hunting game *Hassle* as a good aid to bring out the multiple problems likely to affect the job-search, especially for ethnic minorities. (CSV, 237 Pentonville Road, London N1 9NJ)

Hassle is also useful for giving school-leavers a knowledge of their rights, and of the appropriate procedures, *if* they meet discrimination. It incorporates four specific instances involving discrimination during the job-search. While it is obviously a traumatic step for any teenager to initiate legal proceedings – especially if his or her faith in the working of the law is already less than unbounded – a knowledge of one's legal rights and how to go about achieving them, is a vital first step. But in addition to this, they will need help to recognise the different guises discrimination can assume. It can be *direct* – as where two black school-girls applying in person for part-time vacancies at a chain-store were told by the Staff Manager that the posts were filled. They confirmed with the store's switchboard that vacancies were still open, and asked a white friend to apply. She was duly considered for the job. Or it can be *indirect* – stipulating employment requirements which have a disproportionately adverse effect on certain racial groups, like the company just mentioned which revised its recruitment procedures, or like the furniture store in Liverpool which was found guilty of discrimination by an Industrial Tribunal for refusing an application from a black school-leaver because of his address. (They would not, they said, employ residents of districts 1 or 8 in the city, which are both areas of concentrated ethnic minority population.) Again here, ex-pupils might usefully be invited to talk of their experiences, perhaps alongside a speaker from the local Community Relations Council. The CRE is the obvious source for free information leaflets on the Race Relations Act and other equal opportunity legislation which can be worked through, and explained with school-leavers.

Local trade union officials, or the TUC Regional Education Officer, can be called upon in helping ethnic minority school-leavers to understand not only the purpose and traditions of trade unions, and the vital role of contracts of employment as part of the protection against unfair dismissal, but also the strengths and weaknesses in practice of the local trade union organisation as a defence against exploitation or discrimination at work.

Employers
Pressure of work may act as a real disincentive to careers teachers in finding the time to get to know their pupils' parents. In fact, it may be necessary to remind the LEA that there is Section 11 funding available for

specialised careers teaching posts. But one of the most dangerous results of work pressure is that teachers slip into limited and stereotypical thinking about the job options and employment potentialities of ethnic minority school-leavers. This will all too easily be reflected not only in the pupils' own perceptions, but in those of local employers. This places a high premium on working to build up links with local employers in both public and private industry, so that they contribute much more in terms of work experience and job tasting *outside* school, than just through employers' visits inside school.

1   This would give pupils a more realistic experience of what jobs entail than they get from one-off idealized visits or talks.

2   They would also see a wider choice of occupations than the 'old favourites' to which they've previously been limited, but which may be obsolescent, over-crowded, or below their abilities.

3   It would also help employers to get to know school-leavers as individuals, rather than in terms of group stereotypes. This is the only real way of modifying any prejudicial assumptions in their recruiting.

The Operation Springboard Scheme offers interesting evidence on this last point. In response to direct requests and persuasion, local employers in Camden agreed to provide some work experience for unqualified ethnic minority young people, with poor command of English – the sort of candidates they would never normally consider as job applicants. The project gave tuition not only in basic language, but in the more sophisticated vocabulary related to the individual placements. But this language support cannot entirely account for the surprisingly high proportion of trainees who have been offered permanent jobs, and have been kept on by these employers. Given an opportunity to demonstrate their ability, the trainees were able to rebut many employers' preconceptions about what type of person was capable of doing particular jobs in their employment. For example, one young Chinese boy being given some work experience in the store room of a large hardware concern was soon offered a job when it dawned on the manager that it was a positive business asset to have a fluent Chinese speaker on the staff, in a locality where a significant proportion of the customers were Chinese.

This confirms that a vital part of preparation for school to work lies in building more and better liaison between the school and local employers. In doing this on their pupils' behalf, teachers can encourage employers to check that they are not losing capable job candidates, either because their entry procedures work to narrow cultural assumptions, or to criteria which are not strictly job-related. They may also not have noticed that they are indirectly discriminating, perhaps by recruiting mainly through existing employees, or only through schools with a low percentage of ethnic minority pupils, or not notifying vacancies to the Careers Service.

At the same time, of course, employers say they want school-leavers with realistic attitudes towards work. Here again, careers teachers can point out to them that the best way of achieving this is through arranging for much more direct job-tasting. After all, the occasional industrial visit, where everything is presented to best advantage, may serve only to reinforce somewhat idealistic illusions about how work compares to school; realistic attitudes can only result from realistic experience. It is a point underlined in one of the conclusions of *Black Prospects*, the survey on local-born black youth in south Liverpool:

'Our respondents had not resigned themselves to low status jobs – they were now very keen to get qualified or trained. They did not seem to be getting much help from their employers. Most felt that subjects taken at school had not prepared them for their jobs. But this had not deterred them, except in the short-term, from wanting and taking more qualifications. The stimulus for getting trained or qualified comes for many people only after finding out what work is all about and what jobs are available.'

An afterword to Head Teachers and Heads of departments

Effective careers guidance to school-leavers from ethnic minority groups can only be achieved if at least one person can be allotted time in the timetable for:

1 Setting up work experience, and conducting the necessary *follow up* with pupils and 'employer';

2 Ploughing through the existing materials, disseminating the ideas, and *producing* new materials for use by teachers in the classroom (a chapter of ideas alone can only be a start);

3 Liaising with local community based schemes for young people seeking work, skills, or qualifications;

4 Carrying out surveys of the school's own leavers, and publicising the results to staff;

5 Working with the careers teacher and careers officer to obtain the up-dated local information, and to pass it on.

Two last thoughts

Firstly, if it is not already your standard practice, would it be a good idea to invite the local Careers Officer to attend parents evenings, and to interview all 5th year boys and parents about jobs, training etc.?

Secondly with his/her help, would it be a real help to your pupils – and their parents – to produce a booklet of useful local information and addresses for each leaver – including addresses relating to civil rights? Should these be translated in various languages?

Some resources

Community Service Volunteers, 237 Pentonville Road, London N1, can not only supply *Hassle*, but other materials – eg their *Life skills training manual*.

Garnett College, Roehampton Lane, London SW15, has a good deal of material on interview techniques, job applications, etc.

Wolverhampton CCR have developed two week courses for YOP 'graduates' who find their inexperience of the techniques of the job searching a handicap which work experience had not remedied.

Careers Consultants Ltd, sponsored by Midland Bank, have produced *Exercises in career education* (by D. Cleaton, 1976). It includes a wealth of material and work sheets, and a set of teacher's notes.

The National Institute for Careers Education and Councelling (NICEC) have an exhibition of materials and schemes on permanent display. They will also offer advice. NICEC Resources Centre, Bayfordbury House, Lower Hatfield Road, Hertford SG13 8LD (Hertford 59001).

The ILEA Learning Materials Service, Publishing Centre, Highbury Station Road, London N1 1SB, offers a wide range of games, booklets, videos and packs – eg *Work it out, Making a living, You in the seventies, Living in a city, Working in a city, I'm here* and *Race for Times.*

The National Youth Bureau, 17–23 Albion Street, Leicester LE1 6GD, offers YOP – *Information and resource pack.*

The NUS, 302 Pentonville Road, London N1, offers *16–19 education pack.*

The National Extension College, 131 Hills Road, Cambridge, offer a *Job hunter kit* – a series of booklets for group discussions with a counsellor's hand book.

The Careers Research Advisory Centre (CRAC) Bateman Street, Cambridge, offer the widely used source book *Exercises in personal and career development.*

Tottenham College of Technology's Community Service Unit, have hand-outs for students on ways of finding out about available jobs.

12 Mother-tongue or 'community languages'

At the very start of this book, Barbara Roberts spoke about languages in her primary school classroom:

I encourage talk about accent and dialect. We talk about how dialect relates to where we all come from and how we should never be ashamed of the way we speak, as it is part of ourselves and our personality. We go on from accent and dialect to different languages. I am very proud of the bi-lingual children in my class – some of them read out stories in their mother-tongues and translate them for us. We are making a book on languages together. I feel this helps create a respect for each other and it can foster a feeling of pride in those children who are learning English as a second language, rather than leaving them only with a feeling of inadequacy in their reading and writing of English.

Barbara Roberts was giving recognition to the linguistic diversity in her classroom – valuing and building on the range of linguistic resources brought to school by pupils who are habitually bi-lingual and bi-dialectical. We have already had some suggestions (pages 45 to 48 and 71 to 75) about how bi-dialectical children, particularly those of Caribbean origin, can be helped to explore and expand their range of language skills within school. This section, edited from draft material supplied by Clare Demuth and by Maggie Ing, picks up issues surrounding mother-tongue teaching (or as some prefer to put it, teaching community languages). These issues are presented in the films *Your Community School* and *Languages for Life*. Broadly, we review the arguments for mother-tongue support within the curriculum; then look at some research evidence on the effects of mother-tongue provision; we then move to ways mother-tongue teaching relates to the teaching of English as a second language.

Much has already been said along the lines that multi-cultural education is to do with treating others' cultural values with the respect that we would normally expect to be shown towards our own. But so far we have not properly confronted the fact that it is not possible to respect the culture of any community without recognising the significance of that community's own language, or, indeed, the characteristic ways in which people in that community speak English. More even than religious traditions, or social or domestic customs, it is language – the way people communicate and share their thoughts – which symbolises and embodies a culture and its values.

Linguistic facts of life

It is a fact that a traditional assumption of many educators, and indeed of most parents, has been that apart from offering European languages such as French or German, the business of schools is to teach pupils the spoken and written variety of English known as 'standard' English. This reflects the importance of standard English for public purposes, as a tool of learning and as a means of communicating between and across different communities. It is a fact, too, that most employers expect their employees to have a command of the country's standard form of communication. But it is also a fact that life outside the classroom, the law court, the factory or the office, is not only conducted in a wide range of varieties of English, but also in a number of other languages. Research by Rosen and Burgess (*Languages and dialects of London schoolchildren*, Ward Lock Educational 1980) has shown that only 15% of pupils in a sample of London schools were perceived by their teachers to be standard English speakers; in some schools the proportion was even less. The dimensions of linguistic diversity reported were impressive: twenty different varieties of UK based English; forty-two overseas dialects of English; and fifty-eight named world languages. Schools in inner-city areas had pupils with a wider range of linguistic backgrounds, but few schools anywhere in Britain have a strictly monolingual population who are speakers of standard English. This pattern of diversity is not a temporary phenomenon; many communities long settled in Britain continue to speak their own language at home and, as a result, many of the children born in Britain are bi-lingual to some extent. The impression of such diversity from that research project raises a fundamental question: should teachers be finding ways to help their potentially bi-lingual pupils to build on *all* their language skills, while at the same time acquiring a sufficient mastery of standard English to enable them to operate successfully in this society?

Bi-lingual education and teaching community languages

There is no justification for debating the place of community languages in school without first recognising the viewpoint of the minority language communities. The importance they attach to it is evidenced by the fact that in almost any town where there is a linguistic minority they have organised forms of supplementary schooling, associated perhaps with the local religious centre, or organised by parent groups, to support it. Some of the schools, for example, the Polish School in Ealing, have been long established. The minority communities' viewpoint is clearly expressed by Rashida Noormohamed, a Birmingham Community Worker, and by Dr Ranjana Ash, an E2L specialist teacher in London, in the film *Languages for Life*. In speaking to the Afro-Caribbean Teacher's Association in 1980, Dr Bhikhu Parekh also stressed the importance of a mother-tongue in a child's development:

First, to teach a child his mother-tongue is to open to him a door to a culture. A language is not just a vocabulary and a body of grammatical rules but a vehicle of culture, and embodies a particular way of looking at the world, understanding human existence and conceiving inter-personal relationships.

Second, mother-tongue is the necessary basis of the child's self-esteem and self-respect. An Asian child who only speaks English and whose habits, attitudes and patterns of thought are all English, is English in every respect except colour. He has nothing that he can call his own as a British Asian child, in terms of which he can define and distinguish himself from his white peers. If we are not to presuppose total assimilation, such a child needs that independent basis for self-respect and pride, without which he may lack the confidence and willingness to learn from other cultures.

Third, the family plays an extremely important role in the education of the child. Given the history and pattern of the Asian migration, it is the case that many Asian parents do not speak English well enough to discuss matters of common concern with their children in English. Unless therefore the children acquire adequate mastery over their mother-tongues, their communication with their parents is bound to remain restricted to a limited vocabulary adequate only to express a few basic needs, and a source of frustration and agony to both parties.

Dr Parekh went on to give reasons for integrating the teaching of mother-tongues into mainstream education:

It implies a recognition by the school that a child's mother-tongue is an integral and essential part of his or her education and therefore the responsibility of the school. Not to include it conveys the impression that learning a mother-tongue is somehow peripheral, or optional, and of such marginal relevance that it can be left to the voluntary supplementary schools, sometimes run by ill-qualified teachers. Its inclusion assures the child that the school respects his or her language and culture and indirectly encourages its white pupils to do so as well. Further, to teach mother-tongue within the school curriculum removes the extra burden on the child who would otherwise have to devote his or her free time to attending supplementary schools. Finally, it would help establish adequate teaching standards, the stocking of necessary books in school libraries, and would direct attention to the best method of teaching mother-tongues.

It is universally agreed that teaching languages is one of the educational functions of schools. In our schools we teach modern European languages – why should only these languages be taught? We should teach any language which is rich, for which there is a demand, and in which children and their parents are interested. We could therefore introduce Gujarati, Urdu, Hindi, Bengali etc., all of which satisfy these criteria. Their teaching need not be confined to those whose mother-tongues they happen to be. An English child or for that matter a Gujarati child can benefit from learning Bengali or Urdu just as much as a native speaker.

Even when the number of students involved is extremely small and the teaching of mother-tongue has to be undertaken outside school hours, it should still remain the responsibility of the school itself. It is the school, not the parents or some other agency, which must be expected to organise, conduct and supervise its teaching. Since mother-tongue teaching is an integral part of a child's education, its teaching is an integral part of mainstream teaching and cannot be called supplementary teaching. And since mother-tongue teaching is not supplementary teaching, it cannot be assigned to so-called supplementary schools. When carefully analysed the expression supplementary school turns out to be self-contradictory. If a subject is educationally important, it should be taught in and by the school. And if it is not important, it should not be taught in schools at all, be they mainstream or supplementary.

In case it is argued that the ethnic minorities are seeking a privileged treatment in asking for mother-tongue teaching, it must be said that they are only asking for the same treatment that is accorded as a matter of right to the white British child. English is taught in our schools to the children whose mother-tongue it is. In other words, mother-tongue teaching is already an established and cherished practice of the British educational system. The ethnic minorities ask for no more than that this practice be extended to them as well.

As a footnote to that, it is worth noting that mother-tongue teaching has now (Summer 1981) been given official recognition in an EEC Directive. In preparation for this Directive, the EEC funded the Schools Council in producing materials for primary teachers in Greek and Bengali.

No teacher would deny that good education depends on respect for the child and for the knowledge and abilities the child already possesses. Equally no-one would deny that a bi-lingual person has more resources and can communicate with a wider range of people than someone with only one language; someone conversant with two languages and cultures can be enriched by both. This means that a child's competence in a mother-tongue is an accomplishment, rather than a 'problem'. Unfortunately, mono-lingualism has long been the norm in most parts of Britain, with the exception of Wales and parts of Scotland and N. Ireland. For those who speak only English, with perhaps a smattering of French or German, it is hard to understand how schooling in two or more languages is taken for granted by people in many parts of Europe, Asia and Africa.

It is sometimes assumed that pupils' mother-tongues are at best irrelevant to their education, and at worst can actually 'interfere' with the learning of English. To regard it as irrelevant is educationally wasteful, in denying children the opportunity to further develop skills in which they have a grounding; and far from interfering, research shows that confidence in mother-tongue – the first language of emotions and imagination – may well be a prerequisite to adequate second language development.

The Bradford project: Mother-tongue and English teaching

This was a project, funded by the DES in 1979, which among other aims, set out to test the claim that developing first language skills interferes with acquiring English as a second language. It is featured in 'Languages for Life'.

Two infant schools, using no extra staffing resources, reorganised their teaching so that groups of Punjabi-speaking children could be taught through the medium of Punjabi for half the school day. In each school there was also a control group of children from Punjabi-speaking homes who were taught only in English, but with the same range of activities and the same timetabling. The work was monitored over a year. After testing both the experimental and the control groups, the research team found that the children who had been taught in Punjabi had developed their skills in their mother-tongue to a far greater degree than those who had been taught only in English. The research team also found that the children who were taught in Punjabi did not suffer in their acquisition of English. In fact, their skills in English had developed slightly faster than those of the control group. One interpretation of these results is that linguistic and conceptual growth in the mother-tongue naturally fosters second language development.

There were other, less easily quantifiable gains – both researchers and teachers noted the general liveliness of the experimental group and their confidence in the use of Punjabi in school and playground. For these children it seems that learning in two languages was nothing difficult or extraordinary.

While the Bradford Project points to both the educational and social advantages of forms of bi-lingual education in the early years of schooling, there has been no equivalent research into the language development of junior and secondary age children. The only evidence available is from an educational project mounted by the EEC in Bedford from 1978–1980.

The Bedford project: Teaching the mother-tongue

Groups of children of Italian and Punjabi origin, aged 5–9, were taught the home language of their parent's country of origin, every day for one hour during the normal school timetable. They learned the standard/ national language although at home they spoke a local/regional variety. Despite this disparity it seemed that the children's ability to use the standard language enabled them to communicate more easily with their parents.

The children were also taught to read and write in either Italian or Punjabi. After the 4 years experiment the teachers were satisfied that the children had made good progress in both oral and literacy skills. As would be expected from only one hour's instruction a day, the experience in no way detrimentally affected their learning of English. This suggests that even a few hours of mother-tongue teaching within the junior school curriculum will give the opportunity to maintain fluency and learn to read and write in a community language.

The Bradford study demonstrates some of the potential gains from bi-lingual education; the Bedford experience shows the value of schemes for maintaining community languages through a regular, school-based programme of teaching. Both depended, to a greater or lesser extent, on the presence of qualified teachers who are themselves bi-lingual. Does the absence of such teachers mean that schools can 'opt out' and remain determinedly mono-lingual? This would be to ignore the conclusion of most observers that giving recognition of home languages in school can enhance self-esteem and a general motivation to learn as well as contributing to a closer relationship between school and the community. But more to the educational point, mono-lingualism slams the classroom door on all that everyday experience which, in the case of the native speaker of English, is accepted as a natural resource for school activity.

Even at the level of 'news', 'diaries' and 'my hobby' compositions, the teacher is asking pupils to communicate in one language what they may have experienced in another.

However, we have already noted that it is not so difficult to take the first steps in narrowing the gap between the language of school and the home. If community languages are not spoken by teachers or ancillary staff, they certainly are by parents, secondary age students and many adults in the community. These were the kinds of community resources drawn on by Rosemary Clarke for her Bengali-speaking children (see pages 13–15, and the film 'A Primary Response'). In Birmingham, Tindal School (pages 30–34, and 'Your Community School') responded to the enthusiasm of parents, community and pupils for community language education by making provision for teaching in school, though only outside time-tabled hours. This meets one of the arguments pressed by Dr Parekh: the work is provided by a community project which works closely with the school, takes place on school premises, and has the clear support and involvement of the head and other teachers.

Mother-tongue versus community languages

At least for junior age pupils it may be worth noting that *mother-tongue* is not necessarily the most appropriate term to refer to the language taught. Standard Italian, standard Punjabi, or Urdu are not languages, or varieties of languages, commonly spoken in the intimacy of the home in bi-lingual communities in Britain. They are more truly *community languages* in the sense of accomplishments necessary to participating membership of large and widespread groups in the United Kingdom and other parts of the world. The examples at Tindal and in Bedford point to another important distinction between mother-tongue and a community language. In the former, literacy is not necessarily important, whereas for the latter, it is. For some communities, literacy in the community language is more highly valued than literacy in the mother-tongue. This distinction comes out in comparing the work in Tindal School shown in 'Your Community School' with that in Bedford shown in 'Languages for Life'.

The latter film also shows the importance of literacy teaching to community language education in the secondary school. From examples in Manchester and Peterborough, it illustrates the growing awareness that schools and local authorities can collaborate to provide classes in modern Asian, South European or Near Eastern languages in addition to those of Western Europe. Teachers and materials can be provided on a shared or consortium basis and lessons offered at the very least in free-study or immediately outside school hours. The real need is for more schools to accept that a qualification in a modern Asian language can be at least as useful for their pupils as one in French or a second 'foreign' language. CSE Mode 3 syllabuses can be submitted in almost any language. The London and Oxford Boards offer papers at 'O' level in all the main Asian languages (which can also be 'borrowed' by other Boards). Most FE colleges and universities now accept any subject taken at 'O' or 'A' level among qualifications for admission (except for a few specific courses). So this is another sense in which there is educational waste, if not actually an imposed disadvantage on pupils, if their grounding in speaking languages other than French and German is not built on in school. Apart from that, the UK now has at least 100,000 Punjabi speakers and as many Urdu speakers; Britain also has many commercial and other links with Asian countries. Ability to communicate in a language spoken locally would have obvious advantages for people who meet the public in their work – in the national health service, industry, education, law and, indeed, almost every sector of British life. There are schools where these advantages are pointed out to the pupils, and community languages are offered as well as, or as an alternative to, languages such as French. Even so, some of these schools have found that such opportunities will not be taken up if the timetable forces difficult choices. In Coventry, one scheme provided part-time language teachers (including one for Cantonese) but the 'O' level class was timetabled to clash with physics and maths: only five pupils opted to study their mother-tongues. But in the following year, when the language classes were moved to the lunch time, no less than ninety took up the opportunity. This proved that there was a demand, though it is still less than ideal – any class offered during the lunch-hour is bound to be seen as somehow 'non-essential'.

At the time of writing (1980), the appropriateness of the 'O' levels in Asian languages for individual students needs to be considered carefully. Ralph Russell, who appears in 'Languages for Life', has argued that the examination papers still assume that candidates will not only have the language in question as a mother-tongue, but can read, speak and write it well. In fact, while children may have spoken *mother-tongues* at home, many will have had no opportunity to develop skills in *community languages*, unless they have been sent to community schools. According to the Rosen and Burgess survey, only half of the first year secondary pupils in their sample who were loosely described as 'bilingual' had some facility in reading or writing other than in English. The proportions may vary in other parts of Britain, but in London, forty per cent of the sample which speaks Urdu could actually read and write Urdu, while twenty per cent could read but not write it. Of the Punjabi speakers, seventeen per cent could read and write it, while five per cent could read but not write it.

So for pupils who come to classes with little or no literacy skills, CSE examinations might still be more appropriate – at least until 'O' level syllabuses reduce the demands they make to an equivalent level to those made in French or German – ie, the level it is possible to study to from scratch. Courses at more basic levels also open the doors for children whose mother-tongue is English to learn modern Asian languages, a development which Ralph Russell argues should be encouraged:

Firstly, for exactly the same reasons that we encourage them to take exams in any other foreign language, and secondly, because of the particular relevance that knowledge of an ethnic minority language has to the building of a truly multi-cultural society.

That last objective can be fostered in other ways. Eric Hawkins argues in *Modern languages in the curriculum* (Cambridge University Press, 1980) for a tripartite language curriculum in which all children study their mother-tongue, a second language, and – together – follow a course on language awareness. He argues that once there is curiosity about language and serious study of it in the school, the bi-lingualism of some class members will be established as an asset and a skill rather than a problem or handicap. In an appendix to the book, Eric Hawkins outlines a model course with questions to ask, and ways for their pupils to approach the answers.

Language as culture
These ideas for studying linguistic variation clearly overlap with the spirit of the earlier accounts from teachers who incorporate material on non-standard English dialects. As this section began by saying, study of languages and dialects offers a direct way to engender interest in the cultural norms of their speakers, and as such is not for language teachers alone. It is a means of gaining access to a wealth of culture all too often ignored in British classrooms. here is part of an account in ISSUES newspaper by E2L teacher, Maurice Oliphant, of how he responded to finding one of his pupils was carrying around a copy of *Three hundred poems of the T'ang dynasty*:

She knew a lot about Chinese poetry and its historical development, and she described her own favourites – telling us what the poems actually said, and what kind of ideas the poets were trying to get across.

The other students were very interested, and keen to stress that they knew poems in their own first languages which they could bring in to the centre. I asked them to bring in just one favourite poem to begin with. One boy said he didn't have a favourite, but that he would bring in his father's favourite!

From then on we had fairly regular poetry readings (in a variety of languages) and discussions about the poems in English. First, some of the students wanted to read their poem to the class and this often gave the group the opportunity to talk about rhythm. Then the reader would paraphrase the poem into English, and we would talk about the kind of things the poet might have wanted us to think about. The students wrote their poems out for display – and then I had to take my turn with the students at reading some of my favourite mother-tongue poems. I chose some short poems which had been influenced by the 'imagist' movement because they are often easy to understand on the surface yet allow a lot of scope for interpretation. Here are two of the poems I read them; both resemble Chinese poems in that they present concise images, leaving the reader to infer any implications; and they are poems of understatement.

'In a station of the metro'

The apparition of these faces in the crowd;
Petals on wet, black bough.

Ezra Pound

'The red wheelbarrow'

so much depends
upon

a red wheel
barrow

glazed with rain
water

beside the white
chickens

William Carlos Williams

That took place in a language centre but, as Maurice Oliphant points out, all the work could have been done in the mainstream English lesson and many of the poems he read came from standard CSE anthologies. And sensitivity to the range of languages spoken by pupils need not be the prerogative of the English Department alone. John, one of the boys of Greek Cypriot origin born in Britain, and seen in 'Does School Hurt?', remarks in the film on how his Science teacher draws on his knowledge of Greek:

'I'm in the sciences now at school and a lot of the words come from the Greek. They say to me, 'Is this word from the Greek?' and I say, "Yes". And they say, 'What does it mean?' I explain what it means, and how it was derived. And that helps the whole class, because those words, a lot of them are self-explanatory if you know the meaning, and it's another way of helping you remember.'

Resources for bi-lingual teaching

Many LEA language centres provide books, worksheets or project packs which are written in the main local community languages, some of them bi- and maybe multi-lingual. Some consist of stories for a bi-lingual adult to tell in the classroom; others are for groups which include fully bi-literate children; while some are written primarily for recent immigrants who are literate in another language but not yet in English. *The World in a City*, produced by the ILEA Bi-Lingual Education Project is an example of this last category. The workcards, printed in eight languages with the parallel text in English, are designed to allow secondary age children to follow ordinary classroom work rather than be permanently withdrawn into special groups. Those materials are available from the ILEA, Learning Materials Service (for London schools) or from the CRE (for all others).

Two pamphlets, also from ILEA, draw together ideas touched on in this section. In *Bi-lingualism in education* (CUES Occasional Paper 1), John Wright, director of the project which produced *The World in a city*, offers some guidelines for incorporating minority languages into the activities of primary and secondary classrooms. His central argument is that the motive for their introduction should be utilitarian not tokenist, that the minority child must be expected to use his language and not have it merely displayed. *Languages* from the ILEA English Centre, Sutherland Street, London SW1V 4LH, contains topics such as different languages, dialects and accents, the history of language, playing with and inventing words, the ways in which languages affect the way we think about others. The booklet is accompanied by a cassette tape and teachers' notes.

Several school broadcast series have programmes on variety within languages spoken in Britain. They include the Thames Television series *The English Programme*, and, from the BBC, radio series such as *That'd be Telling* and *Web of Language* and television's *Communicate*. The BBC Schools television series *You and Me* has included stories for four and five year olds in mother-tongues from India, Italy, Greek and Turkish Cypriot, Vietnamese, Chinese and West Indian dialect. The *You and Me* book has printed the stories in both mother-tongue and in English. For details of these stories, in seven languages on audio cassette, contact BBC Cleveland, 99 Linthorpe Road, Middlesbrough, Cleveland. Further details can be found in the ITV and BBC annual programmes for schools and in a BBC leaflet *Broadcasts for multi-cultural education*, obtainable free from The School Broadcasting Council, BBC, Portland Place, London W1.

Schools wishing to buy minority language reading materials for their libraries should seek advice on how best to cater for the wide range of reading abilities that will exist among their bi-lingual pupils. The best source of advice may well be a local teacher, or a member of the authority's language or multi-cultural support service. Many local library services will be able to help and many more may well be open to suggestions. One source is Soma Books (see page 71).

The Library Association has produced *A public library service for ethnic Minorities in Great Britain* (E. Clough and J. Quarmby for the LA, 7 Ridgmount Street, London WC1E 7AE, n.e. 1979). This large book includes useful information on specialised library services and lists of publishers and booksellers. The school of librarianship at the Polytechnic of North London has produced *The Cypriots of Haringey* by J. Leewenberg (Polytechnic of North London, School of Librarianship, 1979) which includes information on booksellers and publishers of Greek and Turkish materials.

The National Council for Mother-Tongue Teaching is the only national organisation specifically concerned with the promotion of mother-tongue teaching within the educational system. It keeps information on ILEA policy initiatives, teaching projects and teacher education, together with lists of advisory staff on mother-tongue teaching, and lecturers available for courses and seminars. It should be able to tell you whether there is any organisation in your area producing mother-tongue materials. NCMTT, 5 Musgrave Crescent, London SW6.

13 English as a second language

Over the past decade the teaching of English as a second language has been serviced in many LEAs by teams of specialist teachers and well-resourced language centres. In the early days, most of their work was with children in withdrawn groups or 'immigrant reception centres'. Now, E2L services increasingly direct their attention to the support of class teachers in developing the language of whole classes in the main-stream. There are two sound reasons why primary teachers should welcome co-operation with the specialist E2L staff, and draw upon their accumulated expertise. First, very nearly all the second language learners in school are now British born and enter the school system at the bottom through nursery and reception classes. This means that language development in a multi-lingual context is central to the work of teachers of these classes and throughout the infant and junior school – although this aspect of teaching may have played a very small part in their initial training. Second, there is evidence that children who learn English only, or mostly, in specialist groups do less well than those retained in ordinary classes for the majority of their time. For a report on U.S. research in this field see Ann K. Fathon, *Variables affecting the successful learning of English as a second language*, TESOL Quarterly, vol. 10, no. 4 (December 1976).

To get a clearer and more practical idea of these points, we asked Neil Parr of the Haringey English Language Resource Centre to outline some of the approaches the Centre has supported at primary schools:

Over the past fifteen years the views of teachers working in multi-lingual classrooms have changed – from seeing children who speak English as their second language as a problem requiring some kind of specialist 'therapy', to recognising that children are learning from all around them and particularly from other English speaking children. This is not to say that specialists are unimportant – far from it – but to signal a welcome gradual change from the state of affairs where children are withdrawn from the class or even the whole school for some 'mysterious' work which the class teacher is then expected to follow up. Such specialist follow up work means the class teacher devising individual one-off lessons which make it difficult for the child to feel part of the class, and to join in with the work others are doing around him/her.

Happily, there is a growing movement towards the specialist being in support of the class teacher by devising the specialist programmes to match what the teacher hopes to do. This leaves the class teacher freer to focus on the learning of *all* the children. Most effectively, they would be talking and exchanging information among themselves.

The teacher's aim should be to find activities for the group which will allow second language learners to play a full part and encourage the intellectual development of the children.

In the following examples of ways teachers have done this, there is a common emphasis on meaning, understanding, using judgement, reasoning and predicting. If the children know what they want to say or talk about, it is much easier to provide the words, phrases, and structures to allow them to do so. A useful motto to remember is 'meaning comes first'.

In the diagram opposite, a North London Infants School teacher shows how she used the *Story of Motilal* with her class of six and seven years olds. (The story had been adapted by the Wolverhampton Language Service from a picture book published in India but available in this country). The story, as adapted, is retold simply and is full of the language of comparison. The theme is 'Pride goes before a Fall'. A typical sentence reads: 'He had the biggest cows and the fattest chickens and he had more cows and more chickens than anyone else in the village'. The teacher first chose the story with the needs of her bi-lingual children specifically in mind, but found that so much could be developed from it that the whole class soon became involved. The diagram shows how it developed.

Some general principles of storywork can be drawn from this example:

1 Choice of story – a 'good' story with clear, interesting episodes;

2 Presentation of the story – with clear visual support using a flip book, flannelgraph figures, slides or pictures;

3 Having a taped version of the story;

4 Follow up work to involve children in the meaning content. In the case of 'Motilal' this included art/craft, drama, puppet work;

5 Follow up work with children retelling the story and devising alternative endings;

6 Using the tape for the children to listen to the story repeatedly with or without the text, and have a taped version in children's first languages.

144

Telling the Story

Tell the story to the whole class, using large scale illustrations to help children derive the meaning, and encouraging them to predict the events.

Groups of children could listen again to the story using a cassette recorder and an accompanying flip-book of the illustrations.

Artwork

Individuals painted the episodes from the story. Decisions, about who painted what, were made in group discussions.

The class made a large scale collage of Motilal, for display in the class and to use as a base for further visual aids – reminders of events in the story, interesting words from the text and children's opinions of Motilal's character (he is not a very pleasant person!)

Individual collage work where group talk revolved around planning and organising what materials and implements the children would need.

Talking

Retelling the story on tape.

Groups discussed the story to get the right sequence for their paintings to make a wall story, and other charts showing the sequence of events.

Children worked in pairs to plan and put on puppet shows of the story using card figures.

A group of children wished to act out the story.

Alternative endings were discussed and devised by the children.

All material was collected together and presented to the whole school as an assembly.

The children discussed some of the more complex moral issues which arose.

Reading

Children followed the text while listening to the taped story, or read the text themselves.

Pictures had captions and labels.

Reading games were made based on the words used in the passage.

Children read their own and other children's written versions of the story and the alternatives devised by groups.

Writing

Describing the characters using a word bank made for use with 'Breakthrough'.

Linking words – then, next, suddenly – were discussed and their use encouraged in the children's story-writing.

The children made their own story booklets, helping each other in groups to find words and read over each other's work. Here the 'Breakthrough' approach was very important.

Five children made a group book of the possible alternative endings to the story.

The whole developed into other curriculum areas, particularly maths with children discussing the relationships between size, weight etc.

Access to a tape recorder can be very important. It can be a means for all children to make a permanent record of a story without interrupting the flow by writing. It also allows children to judge objectively what they have said as to its 'correctness' or whether it makes sense to an audience. A child compiling a story for others to hear or read becomes more fully involved with getting the sense right and sees a real purpose in putting in the effort.

Ideally, all schools would equip each classroom with a cassette player permanently set up in the reading areas. A central store of taped stories can be built up using both commercially produced tapes and tapes which the staff themselves have made from reading schemes or school library books. The children are able to select tapes to listen to and follow with the relevant book. The Language Service can support the school and perhaps provide tapes in some first languages of the children.

This approach allows for two children to listen to a story while following the text or spotting events in the illustrations. Where the two children have different abilities in English the collaboration can be of benefit to both, with one pointing out events to the other. In a school where a child, only able to speak Urdu, was new to a class, the teacher borrowed a story tape in Urdu for the child to use. The teacher was interested to find that each child in the class demanded to hear the tape even though no other child spoke Urdu.

This helped build respect for second language speakers in the class and additional tapes in other languages spoken led to group projects (in English) on the different alphabets and sounds of languages.

Using language for learning

Apart from working with stories, most other primary school activities benefit from collaboration. Groups of children may ask members of the class or school their opinions of television programmes, colours, clothes, hobbies, etc., taking it in turns to ask the questions, record the results, or operate a tape-recorder. There is nothing in this to exclude a second language learner who benefits from planning the wording of questions. But it is the *follow up* work: recording, interpreting and using the results, which has the greatest value.

For example, one class was looking at properties of different materials. A group, including a child just beginning to learn English, were investigating how different materials bounce. They took a rubber ball, a ball of wool, a golf ball, a large football and a ball of plasticine. Then one child let each ball fall from a fixed height by a wall marked at regular intervals with different coloured horizontal lines. Another child watched how high the ball bounced and called out the result to a third child who recorded it on paper.

Here all the participants are benefitting from experimenting with these materials, yet in order for the task to be successful the children need to communicate to each other information about conducting the investigation – disagreeing about whether the ball was dropped from the correct height, and deciding how high the ball bounced: 'the rubber ball bounced up to the purple line' or 'the ball of wool bounced below the green line'. The language for the task comes from the children themselves and in this instance each participant learned from the other especially when they swopped roles so that each had an opportunity to drop the balls, observe the bounce, and record the results.

Each was required to talk and justify what was observed. Most important is that all were involved in a task that meant something to them and gave a reason for communicating. In this instance, the bilingual child learned more relevant English than if he had been taken aside and made to repeat structures without this meaningful context.

In another class, a group including two second language learners were comparing weights of different materials as an introduction to density. On one pan of a class balance was a sizeable piece of plasticine. A number of common objects – glass jars, a large ball bearing, a block of wood etc. were available and the child speculated from previous knowledge, whether the objects would be heavier or lighter than the plasticine. One child recorded their reasoned guesses. They then gauged the weight of the plasticine and an object in their hands and another child recorded their revised estimates. The objects were then balanced and results recorded by the third child. Similar group work was very successfully done by another teacher where children were estimating how many centicubes would full common household containers and packaging as part of work on capacity. They were then asked to justify and verify their estimates, again being encouraged to agree or disagree with each other and record each others results.

All such activities end up with results which can be recorded in a table, graph or diagrammatic form.

Sometimes such recorded results are left as the end product and form a pleasant display. But many teachers see that they can be a starting point for helping children to interpret the results through questioning. This can be a means merely of testing that children understand their results. Several teachers have taken this activity further and, after providing a model, encourage the children to make their own questions from the graph for each other to answer. It is generally from this activity that questions arise which are more demanding and which require reasoning skills. We are all guilty of underestimating our children's abilities, and if left to develop a task they will very often come up with very complex activities themselves.

This type of activity is one in which the second language learners can play a full part. This will, naturally, not only be of great benefit to the second language learners in the class but all children who are actively involved in developing their abilities to express ideas in English.

Of course, these sorts of ideas are the stock in trade of primary teachers. The important thing is that having little English is no indication of a child's intellectual development and that tasks for second language learners should be as intellectually demanding as for others.

There are many obstacles to successful teaching, ranging from classroom organisation and availability of resources to the willingness of the specialist and class teacher to work closely together. Despite these, many initiatives are being tried in classrooms throughout the country.

This principle is central to the work of projects such as the SLIPP project (Second Language in Primary School Project) developed in the ILEA Centre for Urban Educational Studies (CUES). Amongst its many aims, it attempts to 'support the child's learning of English through his or her involvement in learning tasks' with emphasis on collaborative activities within the curriculum. Further information about teaching and in-service materials is available from CUES. The watchword must be collaboration: between children in groups; between specialist and class teacher; between school and local authority; between teachers and publishers, and all other agencies involved in the teaching of children or the training of teachers be it in-service or initial training. Being bilingual is not a handicap, and in the rich diversity of multi-cultural, multi-lingual classrooms it is vital that our motto should become 'Meaning, understanding and collaboration come first'.

I personally find the best help towards this is given in Muriel Saville-Troike's *Teaching English as a second language: theory and practice for multi-cultural education*, (Prentice-Hall, 1978).

Language development resources

The first source to tap for any teacher is the Local Language Teaching Centre. Almost without exception they produce pamphlets of advice and materials for language related classroom activities.

Further information on the SLIPP Project can be obtained from the Centre for Urban and Educational Studies, 34 Aberdeen Park, London N5 2BL.

The ILEA Learning Material Service, Publishing Centre, Highbury Station Road, London N1 1SB has produced classroom materials designed for language development, including story telling pack, sequences of cards and 'action' pictures. It can also supply copies of the ILEA's guidelines 'Language and the primary school' (1979).

Teachers will find guidance on the methodology of teaching English as a second language to small groups in the teachers' book for the second edition of *Schools Council project in English for immigrant children. Scope Stage 1* (Longman 1978).

Joan Tough's *Talking and learning* (Ward Lock Educational, 1977) has a section on second language learning which focuses particularly in teacher/child dialogue.

English as a second language in multi-racial schools by Hilary Hester, Carol Wainwright and Mary Fraser (National Book League, 1977) contains a valuable and comprehensive annotated bibliography, describing the books and other materials that are available to support second language learning; it also directs teachers' attention to courses and useful agencies.

Chapter 20 of DES *A language for life* (the Bullock report, HMSO 1975) discusses children from families of overseas origin, and paragraphs 20.9 to 20.11 deal particularly with second language learners.

Daphne Brown's *Mother tongue to English: the young child in the multi-cultural school* (Cambridge University Press, 1979) is a closely observed account of bi-lingual children in a primary school. It includes information on activities in English and mother-tongue.

E2L at secondary level

Outside any special class the school may provide for him or her, the E2L learner at secondary school is faced with new demands on his language skills. He or she usually has to cope with the ways of speaking of a range of different teachers; with specialist subject languages or jargons; and with text-books and worksheets which make no allowance for his or her level of English.

Apart from giving words of encouragement and support, the class-room teacher in secondary school can help the E2L learner in much the same way as the primary teacher – by being aware of what stage of English the pupils are at, adjusting his or her language accordingly in making sure instructions have been understood, and by providing opportunities for the student to talk and listen to the spoken language. As at primary school, stories with a strong repetitive element seem to be especially useful.

But even more perhaps than at primary school, the premium is on co-operation between staff, and the involvement of all teachers in some across-the-school policy on E2L. Making a language audit, to be cir-culated to all staff, would be a useful first step, indicating the range of English language competence of children entering the school. Questions for school policy might include the relationship between language and streaming or setting; by what criteria do we distinguish between 'slow learning' and inadequate English? Do we need a curriculum policy that ensures that first year children are taught by relatively few teachers? Most of all, what is the right interplay between E2L teaching and all other subject teaching – for example, are subject teachers indicating to the E2L staff any particular English forms what are crucial to the subject? And conversely, are subject teachers aware of what the E2L staff are teaching, so they can give further reinforcement and use of the language in the class? Are science teachers perhaps, failing to realise that some pupils, however adept they may be in specialist jargon of the subject, may yet be failing exams through misunderstanding the English formulation of some of the questions? And in turn, do E2L teachers in special classes sufficiently relate their work to the language the pupils will be meeting in their classrooms? Should they rather be teaching subjects, with attention to English language difficulties, to help compensate for learning missed? Should E2L staff 'follow' the progress of children with English language difficulties when they go into the main stream? Working alongside the mainstream teacher in the normal classroom, could not the E2L specialist spark off new ideas and strategies?

To establish this kind of collaboration may need a great deal of discussion, but if it works, it can be exciting and creative, as well as effective. We asked Stuart Scott, who has done E2L work at Tollington Park and Barnsbury Schools in Islington, North London, to give an idea of how he works:

I started six years ago, as the 'language specialist' in two secondary schools. The title sounds impressive, but all it meant was that children with language problems were withdrawn from mainstream classes and met me in twos and threes in a stock cupboard once or twice a week. For one third of the children at the schools English was not their mother-tonge. Most of the remainder speak a very different dialect from that of their teachers. Forty distinct languages were spoken in the schools. So if language was a problem, I only encountered a tiny part of that problem. In those early days, I didn't feel at all happy about the way I taught the few children that I did see. I was isolated from the mainstream classes, though mainstream teachers were probably comforted in feeling that the language problems were being dealt with by an expert. How my work changed from that isolation would take a long time to relate.

At home, children speak their mother-tongue with their family and friends. Even if they are not particularly adept at reading and writing it, they have certainly become skilled in using it for a variety of spoken purposes. At school they can also use their mother-tongue with some of their friends. Some of them may speak a different version of it (eg Cypriot Turkish or mainland Turkish), but they soon learn to cope with the differences. If they are lucky, the school will make arrangements for them to continue learning their mother-tongue. They also begin to speak English and become familiar with the London English used by other children. In class they listen to teachers whose English is often different from what they hear in the playground. When they don't understand, it's the teacher's job to explain. If they get specialist English teaching, it will emphasise a different variety from that used with other children. Every child in the class speaks differently. E2L children are learning to see whether those differences affect meaning. Through dialogue they can get a chance to check out their understanding. Slowly, through contact with all those varieties, their control of English will develop. Class activities can actually encourage this process. Differences between their mother-tongue and English will grow more distinct. Becoming bi-lingual can actually give them a greater awareness of language use than mono-lingual speakers have.

When we want to learn a foreign language we may take a course that enables us to practise the language in artificial situations without the interference of our mother-tongue. Exactly the opposite holds for children in school. There, language will only develop if their own mother-tongue and the values and skills that accompany it becomes a resource and not a problem to be dealt with.

Home economics and E2L

I worked to establish mother-tongue classes during the school day. This was a tremendous confidence builder for the children, and incidentally had a good effect on the subject teachers. I worked with teachers in all the subject areas to create situations where all the children could through talk learn from each other. Home Economics proved one of the most exciting areas, because every child felt that he/she had a lot to offer the subject. The HE staff and I together decided on aspects which high-lighted the different experiences and values the children brought to the preparation of food and to home management. Some examples were: different meal patterns; attitudes to raw and cooked foods; views of relative importance of meat as against vegetables; the different forms and names around the world of food made from the common ingredients of bread. Apart from the differences between cultures, and between generations, on questions of nutrition, we also looked at different reasons for wearing different kinds of clothes – particularly at the intended effects of styles within different cultures. In all this, the important point for teacher collaboration is to rehearse the themes in advance, to anticipate any points on which the children's own ex-perience will be in conflict. For this reason it is valuable to talk over proposed lessons with ethnic minority teachers on the staff, or with the staff running local supplementary schools.

We encouraged the children to discuss such different cultural values between themselves, usually in small groups. We often recorded their discussion, and written work developed from this talk after there had been some time for reflection.

We found that we quickly moved away from notions that there were a basic set of skills to teach, or some fixed body of knowledge to impart; but the results emphasised the fully equal values of Home Economics (considered by too many teachers to be a low status subject) in devel-oping concepts, as well as language in use. Our collaboration provided the needed strategies for encouraging pupil talk; and the encouraging results in HE, were a useful basis for informing and discussing similar approaches by other subject teachers.

Further resources

Teaching language as communication, H. G. Widdowson, Oxford University Press, 1978). This relates teaching ideas to the structure of the language and the needs of pupils in the classroom, and offers detailed analysis of scientific prose, and how to teach young children to understand it, which is as useful for the science teacher as for E2L specialist.

On the question of creating an awareness of language throughout the school, there is the Open University Language Development Course (PE232 Block 6) which contains a useful section on language policies and practice.

Among supplementary readings for that OU course is an article by Katharine Perera, *The language demands of school learning*, which describes a number of the difficulties pupils find in understanding textbooks. One example she points to are difficulties with sentence markers – expressions such as 'furthermore', 'that is', 'similarly', in the structure of factual prose. Without clear understanding of such markers, the sense of even the simplest argument is lost.

More examples for language policies are given in:
Language policies in action: Language across the curriculum in some secondary schools, by Michael Torbe, Ward Lock Educational, 1980.

Language across the curriculum: the implications of the Bullock Report in the secondary school, Michael Marland, Heinemann Educational, 1977.

14 The power of teacher expectations

In November 1980, the HMIs brought out a report on the ILEA, the largest authority in the country. It was based on five years of inspections and discussion about the facts that nearly a quarter of all pupils leave London schools with no graded exam result at all (compared with 13.8% nationally) and that only 4.9% of pupils leave with five or more higher grade 'O' levels or CSE (compared with 9.1% nationally). 'These schools frequently blame their pupils' background for the poor results', said the report. 'This is largely unjustifiable. The fault lies in low teacher expectation'. Such under-expectation has been found by the HMIs in other national surveys of both primary and secondary education.

We thought it might be useful to have a brief reminder of what is known in general about how far a teacher's view of his or her pupils, and particularly, expectations of their success, has a powerful influence on their progress and performance in school. According to many experts, these researches have important relevance for teachers of ethnically mixed classes. However, we leave the reader to decide exactly what this relevance is. We have met some teachers who apparently have particularly high expectations of ethnic minority pupils. We have met others who say they find it difficult to avoid discriminating between minority groups, based on an assumption that some bring a stronger 'culture of learning' to the school than others. There are certainly very many teachers who are concerned that minority pupils are often perceived (usually by their colleagues!) as too intellectually or culturally disadvantaged, or as deprived and burdened with too many personal and social problems, to succeed well in school. These questions are seen to be a serious concern to teachers in the film 'School Report', and brought out again in 'Teacher, Examine Thyself!'

There is no doubt that many parents of British Caribbean children feel that pupils are encouraged to achieve in the West Indies, whereas they are still expected to underachieve by many teachers in Britain. We asked Maggie Ing of London University's Institute of Education, to give us a brief summary of the classic research on the effects of expectations. The question her summary raises, in the context of multi-cultural education, is this: Are minority children failing to make the most of their abilities in our schools, not just because of the language difficulties and cultural differences our schools have yet properly to come to terms with, but because many teachers underrate their potential on the basis of stereo-typical thinking – whether consciously or not?

'Smart and dumb'

Most teachers have heard of R. Rosenthal and L. Jacobson's classic research *Pygmalion in the classroom* (Holt, Rinehart and Winston, 1968) but it is not so generally known that the authors first tested out their hunch four years earlier in a small scale study of psychology students training rats to learn their way through a maze. Eight students were told that their animals had been specially bred to learn quickly; six were told that their rats were from a slow-learning strain. In fact, the animals were randomly drawn from the same strain and no great variation in their speed of learning would be expected. The 'smart' rats, however, learned better and the students reported that they enjoyed working with them. The 'dumb' rats were slower and disliked by their trainers. It is possible that the students did not record their animals' progress with perfect accuracy (which in itself would be significant if we transpose the findings to teachers with children) but it is highly likely that the differences in handling the animals, frequently and gently for the bright' ones, rarely and brusquely for the 'dim' ones, had an influence on the rats' performance.

If expectation can affect the performance of creatures who can be hardly influenced by the subtler social and cultural messages inherent in the way they are handled, we might expect it to be even more true of people. Too much has perhaps been made of the original *Pygmalion in the classroom* experiment, where teachers were falsely informed at the beginning of the school year that some children would bloom academically. There were increased IQ score for the bloomers, but this was only in the first two grades and there are several interpretations of the results. However, Rosenthal subsequently (*Psychology Today*, September 1973 pages 56 to 63) collected data from two hundred and forty-two studies in all sorts of situations where the Pygmalion effect might operate. Eighty-four studies showed the predicted results, where by the rules of statistical significance only twelve (about five per cent) would have turned out by chance alone.

Teachers' impressions

These data indicate that, at least some of the time, the expectations of those in control of situations affect the outcomes. They do not tell us how expectations are expressed in action and just what goes on between the persons involved. A few studies to date have explored the details of contacts in the classroom and Ray C. Rist's paper *Student social class and teacher expectations: the self-fulfilling prophecy in ghetto education* (*Harvard Educational Review* Vol. 40, No. 3. August 1970) is one of the most sensitive and saddening.

A single group of children, half of them black, just starting their kindergarten year in a North American urban school, were observed closely twice a week for the first year and a half, and their progress followed up for a further year. By reputation their teachers were both experienced and competent; in interviews they were seen to be committed and without prejudice.

As early as the eighth day in the kindergarten of schooling, the children had been assigned to one of three tables, according to the teacher's assessment of them as 'bright', 'average' or 'below average'. Two and a half years later, these labels were still firmly stuck.

The kindergarten teacher's first impressions had decided the children's fate. Intelligence tests of young children are notoriously poor predictors, but the teacher had not referred to even this attempt at objective classification. The teacher, Rist found, like so many others had in fact formed impressionistic opinions from social information – on who was on welfare; on who was from a single parent family; on an initial interview with the mother; on any experience she had of children from the same families; and on whatever she gathered of the child's abilities after eight days in school. Tables 1, 2 and 3 in fact turned out to represent a clear stratification of social class, with Table 1 children neatly dressed, clean and better off and Table 3 children scruffy and shabby (and, as it happens, darker-skinned).

Life on Table 3

Once allotted to Table 3, the children had very different experiences from their class-mates. The teacher talked less to them and they talked less to her. On the Friday after Halloween, for example, she announced that she would allow time for *all* the children to come to the front of the class and tell their experiences. In fact, she then called on only six children, five from Table 1 and one from Table 2. On another day in May, Rist noted that for a whole hour, she made no communication at all with Tables 2 and 3 save two commands to 'sit down'.

Although the blackboard extended along a wall parallel to all three tables, the teacher tended to use the part of the board nearest to Table 1, even occasionally reprimanding Table 3 children who stood up to see it better. Her assessment towards the end of the first year was, 'Those at Table 1 gave consistently the most responses throughout the year and seemed most interested and aware of what was going on in the classroom', and 'It seems to me that some of the children at Table 2 and most all the children at Table 3 at times seem to have no idea of what is going on in the classroom and were off in another world all by themselves. It just appears that some can do it and some cannot. I don't think that it is the teaching that affects those that cannot do it, but some are just basically low achievers'.

Rist's findings however, were that the children on Table 3 were trying to learn; cut off from much direct contact with the teacher, they sometimes tried to learn from each other, or from listening to what the teacher was saying in her dialogues with the more favoured pupils. But when the frustrations were too great, many of them switched off.

When the children moved up to the First Grade, they were allotted to the new table groupings according to their performance on 'readiness materials' at the end of the kindergarten year. No child from Tables 2 or 3 was promoted to the 'fast learners'. The same process, with additional information from reading tests, was repeated when they progressed to the Second Grade. All three groups were now using different reading schemes and each child had to complete one book before tackling the next in the series. As they were not allowed individual reading time to finish a book on their own and move ahead, a child designated as 'slow' would of course always remain 'slow'.

The Second Grade teacher was found to be using more controlling and fewer supportive contacts with the slow learners. This Rist saw as a reflection of the more disruptive behaviour of children with two years' experience of neglect and low expectations by their teachers.

The IQ scores for these children, taken at the end of the kindergarten year, had showed no statistically significant difference among the children at each table. The Table 1 scores were slightly higher, but the highest individual score was from a Table 2 child and several Table 2 and 3 children scored higher than some from Table 1.

Whatever the basis for the initial stratification of the children, it was not their academic potential. Nor could it be ascribed to any racial antagonism by the teachers towards the Table 3 pupils – for the teachers in this study were themselves all black. However, in interviews with the teachers, Rist found that they had a picture of the 'Ideal pupil' which reflected their own cultural values and experiences.

Ideal pupils

What this perception of the ideal pupil can mean is that a child from a comfortable middle class background, speaking standard English and relating easily to adults, is all to easily perceived as a potentially 'success-ful' pupil. Those who fit the ideal least closely may be perceived as unable to learn or, in extreme cases, as unteachable. When we add factors of race to the social indicators operating against some children, the effect of teacher expectations is likely to be magnified.

It is not a matter of being overtly racist; it seems to be more a matter of checking whether we have an 'ideal pupil' cast in our own image, and as a result perhaps unconsciously categorise children who are 'different' as less educable and treat them in subtly different ways.

Not much research has actually been done on the sensitive question of how far teachers' stereotypes of the abilities of different ethnic groups affects children's progress, but the few studies available do confirm that the stereotypes exist.

Rubovits and Maehr (*Pygmalion black and white, Journal of Person-ality and Social Psychology* Vol. 25 No. 2 on pages 210–218, 1973) set up experimental lessons with sixty-six student teachers, each of whom had four pupils, two black and two white. One white and one black child in each group were randomly labelled 'gifted', setting ex-pectations to which the student teachers' responses were studied. The particular responses observed were: teacher's attention to pupil statements, encouragement of pupil statements, elaboration, ignoring, praise and criticism. The pupils in fact initiated contact with the teacher about equally, but the teachers clearly favoured the 'gifted' white pupils, followed by the 'non-gifted' whites, then the 'non-gifted' blacks and, last, the 'gifted' blacks. If this finding is at all representative of what goes on in schools, it is profoundly alarming. It demonstrated a racial stereotyping so strong that ability is a positive quality in some teachers' eyes *only* if it is shown by a white pupil; an able black pupil is likely to have even more negative teacher contact than a slow one.

The 'teachers' in the experiment were students, but in previous interview they had all expressed entirely 'liberal' beliefs.

Expectations into action

There are at least four ways in which a teacher can communicate a good or bad opinion of a child's potential. First, by a range of non-verbal as well as verbal cues, she can create a warm or cold *climate*. Smiling, nodding, looking into the eyes, leaning towards or away from the child, tone of voice, can all convey as much as words of approval or disap-proval. Second, the 'ideal' students tend to get more *feedback* about what they are doing. In one study quoted by Rosenthal, researchers observed how teachers behaved towards the pupils they (the teachers) had named as high or low achievers; only three per cent of the high achievers' responses were ignored, but fifteen per cent of the low achievers'. Whether they are right or wrong, the 'good' pupils get more information, which obviously makes it easier for them to learn. Third, it appears that teachers tend to give *more, and more demanding, material* to their 'good' students. Victor Beez, working with teachers of preschool children in the Headstart programme, told half of them that they could expect exceptionally good progress from their children and the other half that they could expect very little. Observers, who were not told the teachers' expectation, noted the subsequent interactions. The teachers who thought they had 'bright' children attempted to teach them far more, and the children actually learned far more, than the group of whom poor performance was expected. Closely linked to this is the fourth factor of *output*. Teachers tend to give favoured pupils more chance to respond; they are asked more questions, given more time to reply, and more guidance.

Classroom interaction

What happens in classrooms is not just a matter of communication between teacher and pupils, but also between pupils. Very early, children pick up how the teacher views them and their classmates and the effects of expectation spread. Rist details the ways in which the kindergarten children responded to one another. The Table 1 children soon felt safe in ridiculing those at Tables 2 and 3. When Tony (Table 3) was asked a question and didn't know the answer, Gregory and Ann (Table 1) called out 'He don't know. He's scared,' and 'It's sixteen, stupid'. Jim (Table 1) was heard saying over and over to Tom (Table 3): 'I smarter than you. I smarter than you.' When the observer asked Lilly (Table 3) what she was drawing, she replied 'A parachute', but Gregory (Table 1) interrupted, 'She can't draw nothin'.

Table 1 children tended to be given responsible jobs and quickly imitated the teacher's more disciplinary approach to the Table 3 group. 'Girl, leave that piano alone', Pamela ordered, when the teacher was out of the room. Then, in time, it was noticed that the children at Tables 2 and 3 turned on one another the same kind of cruelty that they had themselves experienced.

The research evidence is that the hidden assumptions within the classroom, and the subtle or gross differences in the way that the teacher treats different pupils will readily be perceived by the whole class and are likely to be incorporated into the pupils' attitudes towards themselves and others.

Strategies for change

How can we avoid creating or reinforcing poor expectations of some of our pupils? Every teacher must start with his own perceptions and attitudes. As the science teacher confirms in the film 'School Report', well-meaning teachers tend to deny that they or their colleagues or, sometimes, their pupils, do have stereotyped expectations of different groups, yet half-an-hour of staffroom conversation will often reveal quite blatant categorization. Among remarks heard from kindly, concerned Primary school teachers: 'The black kids are boisterous and can't settle'; 'The Asians work hard but show no initiative'; 'You can't expect much creative work – they're mainly Irish'.

Honest reflection on our own half-buried assumptions may be revealing. Better still, feedback about our own *behaviour* in the classroom makes it more difficult to imagine that we do one thing, yet behave in a quite different way. A video tape recording of a classroom session, or a sound recording, or a colleague acting as observer and making notes may be needed to help us become conscious of which children are attended to and which are ignored.

Some points to consider in such observation:

Who is asked questions?

Who is not?

How long do you wait for an answer?

When a child initiates communication, do you: Ignore it? Acknowledge it? Expand it? Ask for more information?

Do you ever try to give more difficult tasks to your 'slow' learners?

What do you do if one child speaks contemptuously of another? Ignore it (and so tacitly agree)? Or reprimand him?

How do you check that your pupils have understood instructions?

Which children do you consider fast, average and slow learners?

On what grounds do you make those distinctions?

How would you list the characteristics of your 'ideal pupil'?

How closely does that list relate to your rating of pupils' ability?

Which children tend to be nearest you most of the time? Why?

Which children do you like best? (Honestly!) Are you fair to the others?

Positive expectations

No-one can avoid forming expectations of others, and a lot of social interaction is eased by our knowing roughly what to expect. Teachers have a duty to provide their pupils with *appropriate* work, which involves some judgement of what they can do. But the research shows that damage to some pupils seems to come from *poorly-based* judgements (the state of a child's clothes is not an adequate indicator of his mental capacity; nor is his accent), *made too soon* and *inflexibly* held. If we can be slow to label a child, insist on gathering more evidence, be prepared for him or her to surprise us and give him or her plenty of chance to show what he or she can do, the negative effects of expectation might be much reduced.

For every reported instance of failure following upon a teacher's low expectations of pupils there are positive results from those whom the teacher expected to do well. Table 1 children with a measured ability lower than some of their Table 2 and 3 classmates prospered in school. This effect would obviously not be unlimited, but we have got nowhere near expecting *all* our pupils to learn and giving them all the attention, input, feedback and opportunity to make it possible. The positive power of teacher expectations has still to be harnessed.

Further reading

Able to learn? The pursuit of culture-fair assessment S. Hegarty and D. Lucas NFER, 1979. Research on alternative tests of ability among children of West Indian and Pakistani background.

The education of the black child in Britain M. Stone, Fontana, 1981. Interesting related evidence and discussion on expectations.

West Indian children in our schools. Interim report of the Committee of Inquiry into the education of children from ethnic minority groups Chairman: Anthony Rampton OBE. Cmnd 8273. HMSO, 1981. This report draws particular attention to the importance of teacher expectations. Several sections of *Caught between* – the review of research made for that Rampton Committee report, prepared by Monica Taylor – summarise further evidence related to teachers' expectations and pupils' achievement levels. *Caught between* NFER/Nelson, 1 Oxford Road East, Windsor, Berks SL4 1DF.

15 Racism awareness in the school system

This chapter, written by John Twitchen, has been expanded for the 1985 reprint, to describe and comment in more detail on some of the exercises shown in the 50-minute film '*Anglo-Saxon Attitudes*' (see page 4). These were carried out by a group of West Yorkshire teachers in 1980 at the first Racism Awareness workshop run as part of its in-service training by an LEA. Some of the exercises are developed from ideas given in a book by Judy Katz[9], and have also been used in workshops run for members since 1982 by the NUT. The overall aim of those workshops is given in the NUT's letter of invitation:

'The workshop is designed for teachers who wish to develop an awareness of the operation of racism in society in general and in the education system in particular at an institutional and personal level. It will be specifically focused around 'white' attitudes and the professional responsibilities of white teachers in a multi-racial, multi-cultural society. It is hoped that through an exploration of the processes involved in 'unlearning' racism, and exercises aimed at strengthening participants' anti-racist understanding and techniques, teachers will be provided with information and skills which will help them to make an effective contribution to anti-racist strategies in their own schools, colleges and local associations.'

This chapter has a similar aim: it offers a set of suggestions for using the BBC film as a training aid, and outlines some introductory and follow-up exercises which could be used with it, whether in staff rooms, at Teachers' Centres, union/association, or on teacher training courses. It should be emphasised that the suggestions reflect only one of many current approaches to racism awareness (or as some now call it, 'developing anti-racist strategies,) for teachers, and that they are necessarily experimental at this stage, given that the 'state of the art' of racism awareness training is still in evolution and there has been little in the way of systematic evaluative survey of either the short or long term effectiveness of different methods and materials. The film, however, reveals something of what a group of teachers who are already sensitised to multi-cultural approaches can yet discover by careful reflection about how much school practice is at best unwittingly patronising or tokenist, and at worst, unintentionally racist – at least by omission. The critical point is that they looked behind the customary assumption that racism is simply a matter of individual prejudice or misguided behaviour, whose main expression is in extreme violence, to examine the more significant concept of hidden forces of institutional racism – something we can't avoid participating in, and actually reinforce by inaction or indifference towards it. In one workshop exercise, the teachers set out to invent a school system deliberately designed to be subtly racist: defined in the sense of preserving in practice a white majority's advantages over a black minority in a society which in theory outlawed discrimination and held publicly to principles of equal opportunity for all. Through the film, we share their moment of realisation that our actual school system – even including many of the efforts to adopt multi-cultural approaches – is scarcely distinguishable from their invented system.

The PEP reports on racial disadvantage[1] have demonstrated the low relative position of most of the ethnic minority communities in terms of the main social indicators – especially employment and housing. The findings of the 1980 report *Half a Chance?*[2] gives chilling proof of the nature and extent of outright discrimination faced by black school leavers seeking jobs, despite the equal opportunity legislation. This difficulty of discrimination is added to the educational disadvantage most ethnic minority pupils share with working class children.

Of course, schools cannot themselves rectify major inequalities in society at large. But the Bradford teachers came to see it as a form of racist attitude to use that fact as an excuse for not examining whether the school is unwittingly reflecting within itself the racial disadvantages of the wider society, or is failing to do what it can, both as a social organism and through its curriculum, to avoid reinforcing the attitudinal and institutional factors which cause those facts of racial disadvantage. Among the recurring questions at the workshop were these:

Why are matters of racism so rarely discussed openly and frankly in school staffrooms and departmental meetings?

What is it we're afraid of?

Why does it seem so often to need an outside event, like National Front leafletting of the school, to provoke that discussion and review of school practice and policy without which we cannot be sure that we are not leaving children prey to influences and attitudes based on misconception and ignorance?

Are we inhibited by fear of perhaps upsetting colleagues' sensibilities?

Should we not fear more the possibility that, however efficient and committed our teaching, our schooling is not giving many children, especially those who are members of an ethnic minority, the kind of self-image and the respect they need and have a right to expect?

It is clear from the account of the school policy of Holloway School (page 109 to page 114), from the film on Birley High School ('School Report'), and from many of the schools represented in this book, that these questions have been tackled squarely in many cases. However, several facts are equally clear from those same accounts. First, that strong support from the headteacher is required, together with a good deal of discussion to break down deep defensiveness on such questions among many of the staff. Second, that some strong group support is needed for any exercise that involves self-examination of unconscious attitudes. We all feel ourselves to be 'worthy', and our self-esteem is dented if we find we have elements of racist thinking or attitudes, however unwitting they may be. It is a real problem that the term 'racism' carries so heavy a pejorative load: this deters many from tracing the ways its institutional forms affect the results of what we do, however well intentioned. And thirdly, the films show how a thought-out conceptual framework or analysis is needed if the issues are to be raised constructively. It was such an analysis, based on looking at themselves before looking at others, that the Yorkshire teachers were seeking.

New approaches to setting up discussion of racism

Many schools now (1985) are grappling with the concept of racism (a) as a development of concerns with multi-cultural approaches, (b) because the LEA has asked them to produce a whole-school policy on the subject, or (c) because the LEA has a policy which includes the word, but its full meanings and implications are not clearly spelt out – and commitment to implementation depends on making any policy 'one's own'. Many other school staffrooms have yet to see the need to consider racism. Because it is a matter of attitudes, as much as of information, 'racism awareness' cannot be effectively achieved by attending a few talks or lectures. It seems to require at least an intensive two/three day workshop, and a process of research and discussions with staff colleagues over a period of a year/18 months, if it is to result in significant change in school practice towards an anti-racist overt curriculum, and a non-racist hidden curriculum. The following exercises can help teacher groups, especially in all-white or mostly white staffrooms, to start to make their own examination of racism, either as a first step to articulating a whole-school policy, or to securing the commitment to make an existing anti-racism policy effective in practice. They are some suggestions for 'do-it-yourself' in-service staff development, as part of a process involving all teaching and non-teaching staff along with representatives of parents, governors, community spokespeople, and not least, the pupils.[15]

The role of group leader

In a school where these are new issues, it can sometimes be helpful to invite an outside adviser to conduct the initial stage of racism awareness, leaving the staff to get on for themselves with the second stage – determining their next steps of action. A suitably sensitive outside catalyst can absorb and 'take away' the defensive feelings commonly aroused in attempts to examine racism. You might seek advice on who has experience in doing this in your LEA, or who is used in other LEAs[16]. If, however, resources do not allow for outside help, it is important to note that in her book *White Awareness*[9], Judy Katz suggests that anyone acting as group leader needs

'a good understanding of racism. This includes both an awareness on a personal level of your own prejudices and assumptions and an ability to analyze and describe racism on an insitutional and cultural level.

You should be open to your own learning needs and should be a role model whose ideas, attitudes and values can be tested by individuals and the group. Your willingness to disclose your grapplings with racism and the areas that are still unresolved for you will be most helpful in the learning process of others.

A climate of trust must be established so that participants feel safe in exploring their attitudes and behaviours and comfortable in disclosing them to the group. It is essential to recognise how difficult it is for most white people to come to grips with racism – especially their part in it. Therefore, support and concern for the participants are critical. While dealing with the content issues – for example, those defining racism or exploring institutional racism – you must also be aware of the process issues: how people are feeling, how they respond to one another, and so on.'

The suggestions in the rest of this chapter presuppose a thoroughly prepared group leader, who can create an informal 'non-threatening' atmosphere in which staff can together share thoughts, feelings and experiences. The aim is to help you not to 'confront people', but rather to inspire staff to *confront the issue*, and through self-discovery within the group to become committed to effective action in combating racism.

In terms of preparation, you would be well advised to be aware of the differing ideological assumptions that may well underlie any group's discussions of racism and education and the 'map' on page 175 illustrates how 'facts' which may seem self-evident at first can actually be regarded from at least three different viewpoints. The main difference of emphasis is between those who subscribe to the 'cultural pluralist' and the 'anti-racist' schools of thought. And while it is important to focus attention on the need for white people to learn to accept responsibility for dismantling structural barriers to equality for blacks, this has to be done in a way that ensures that their actions are supporting any active resistance of the black oppressed and are not simply 'containing' that resistance. An overview could be gained from the M. Banton article (see page 12) and references 13, 14, 17, 18. It would also be useful to study the set of policy papers *Education for Racial Equality*, available from the Berkshire Education Department, Shire Hall, Reading, RG2 9XE; the NUT policy statement *Combating Racism in Schools* (see page 211); and the AMMA booklet *Our Multi-Cultural Society: the educational response* (29 Gordon Sq., London WC1H 0PX).

This chapter describes exercises that teachers' groups have found practically useful for developing their ideas, both individually and collectively, whatever their personal ideological perspective. Such development of 'racism awareness' is of course not sufficient on its own: it is only a step towards helping white people in particular to enter direct dialogue with black people on a non-racist basis of genuine equal respect. That in turn should be part of a springboard for action to address the needs of all children in a multi-cultural and multi-racial society, in a non-racist way. Such action could range from political lobbying, through school policy making, to classroom teaching practice.

1 Why do we need to talk about colour prejudice and racism in our schools?

This question is, of course, best raised by listening to black British experience. If this cannot be arranged on a face to face basis, some elements of the black perspective of Britain as a racist society are given in the tape/film strip, *The Enemy Within*, available from the British Council of Churches, 2 Eaton Gate, London, SW1 W9BL, or in the BBC documentary film *Black*. (Those materials, like this chapter, use the word black to mean British people of Afro-Caribbean and of Asian background.) However, it may be that an all-white group needs first to reflect on racial injustice in society as it has affected them – to explore the experience of being white in a multi-racial society – before being able properly to listen to what blacks have to say. One way to start is to invite each member to share with the group:

Where their own name comes from – and how they feel about it;

Any racist incidents they have witnessed or experienced for themselves;

Any evidence of racism or prejudice they have become aware of through talking with pupils in or out of school;

How they remember first becoming aware of how black British people feel about the way they are treated in their country;

Any steps towards anti-racist action they have already made or been associated with;

Any fears or expectations they have in being asked to join an exploration of racism as a professional concern.

That can be done as a 'listening' exercise, in pairs, with each person 'reporting' to the group what his or her neighbour has said. Apart from getting things started on a personal basis, that introductory exercise often brings in direct evidence of racism, which helps establish why we need to talk about it.

For a group which is particularly worried or defensive at the start, confidence can be built up by using the 'inoffensively amusing' film *Fred Barker goes to China* (see p12). Alternatively the 'Drawbridge' exercise detailed by Katz[9] has been found very helpful as an 'opener', as have exercises detailed in *Debate and Decision: schools in a world of change*, available from the World Studies Project (see p100), or at Teachers' Centres.

'Anglo-Saxon attitudes' (Part 1)

A common platform of understanding, on educational grounds, of the need to consider racism, is given by showing the first 15 minutes of the 50 minute compilation film 'Anglo-Saxon Attitudes' (see p4), which is designed specifically for this purpose.

As with all films, without proper introduction and frequent stops it is likely to be watched for the *passive entertainment* value of the *presentation*, rather than for *active learning*, which depends on the audience registering and responding to the *content*. For this reason, for any effective use, the group should briefly note their own individual answers, before viewing the film, to such questions as the following (of which nos. 10–15 are the most essential):

1 What is democracy – at least in theory?

2 How many people live in England?

3 How many of those people are black (ie of Afro-Caribbean and Asian background)? And how many are immigrants?

4 Where do most immigrant workers in Britain come from?

5 Since 1945, how much have immigrants added to the size of the population of Britain?

6 What, in your view, was the fundamental cause of the street disturbances in Toxteth and Brixton in 1981?

7 How were those disturbances described in the media?

8 How are those disturbances described by many spokespeople of the young black communities?

9 How many living languages are used in Britain by at least 100,000 people each?

10 What is your definition of prejudice?

11 What is your definition of racism?

12 What are the typical out-of-school attitudes of white school leavers in this area towards black ethnic minorities?

13 Was your answer to No. 12 something you feel, or something you know?

14 Do four-year-old children, both black and white, notice skin colour difference?

15 If you said 'Yes' to No. 14, then are four- and five-year-olds also aware of the 'social weight' attached by the adult society to being black or white?

16 Do black school students in our locality experience direct discrimination in trying to find holiday jobs or permanent jobs, as compared to equivalently qualified white students?

17 If your answer to No. 16 is yes, then what for you are the chief ways a school should respond to that fact?

18 How much do you know about Morocco?

19 This film begins with a primary school assembly; are we watching good or bad multi-cultural school practice?

STOP on Lord Scarman's words '. . . lack of job opportunities' to ask: Are not his observations, so far, both familiar and very obvious? If he is right about the conditions black people are living under, then is not the important question, *why* are most black people living in such disadvantaged conditions? What is Lord Scarman's personal view (and he is certainly no left-wing, black extremist!) of the fundamental reason for that? (Then run on with his words 'They are suffering from . . .'

STOP on the words '. . . ill-equipped for the job market' (station porter shot). Discussion of racism will be no more than emotional moralising if it is not founded on the facts of black disadvantage in Britain. So invite the group to research for themselves the place of black ethnic minorities in our society. You and they could obtain *Black and White Britain*, the third Policy Studies Institute survey (Heinemann, £8.00, paperback, 1984); or the summary in the Runnymede Trust Bulletin Number 169 (see page 211). Further sources of official figures are: *Ethnic Minorities in Britain* – Home Office Research Study Number 68 (HMSO); the White Paper reply to the Home Affairs Committee, made by the Conservative Government under Mrs Thatcher in 1982, *Racial Disadvantage* (HMSO); or the free fact sheets on Racial Disadvantage from the CRE (see page 211). The figures demonstrate forms of systematic and unchanging disadvantaging of black people additional to disadvantaging they suffer as working class and/or as women. Since democracy, at least in theory, is the settling of social priorities by the will of the majority, *subject to the full protection of the rights and interests of minorities*, then democrats must be concerned about this basic injustice in our community, and need to reflect whether many black people *as black* are somehow (perhaps, wholly unintentionally) being excluded from the power and decision-making which determine life chances in our society.

STOP at the end of the 'boys in bus' sequence. This section demonstrates that multi-cultural education is only partly to do with making school 'comfortable' for ethnic minorities; more essentially, it is to do with equipping white children with the 'conceptual tools' to understand, and not be victimised by, the adult, peer group and media influences that reinforce their negative images of the place of black British in our society. According to Gus Horsepool, the comments the boys make are the very least he hears in out-of-school sessions from every school he visits, with both boys and girls, and whether or not they have black personal friends. Some teachers seek to evade the implications of the sequence by raising questions of classism and/or sexism and/or criticism of the film-making, perhaps not seeing that these are red herrings in a discussion about responses to people *as black*. The boys are a mixed ability group, from a caring community school, so the evidence poses these challenges:

1 Are such views and attitudes typical of white school leavers in our area? Do we actually know (as opposed to guess) their views and attitudes outside school? How could we check if the film is representative?

2 How far are we agreed that those pupils – and many in our own area – express attitudes based on misconception and ignorance – and that they are inadequately educated for living in a multi-racial and multi-cultural society? To that extent, should it be one of our school's major aims and objectives to work out – on a whole-staff basis, and in collaboration between primary and secondary schools, and with parents' bodies – what kind of preventative schooling is needed against such myths and misconceptions?

3 Even in a school where social awareness is a high priority in the curriculum, the teachers' efforts inside school do not appear, in many cases, to have impinged on what their pupils think and do outside school. So by what methods can we directly relate what we teach directly to the pupils' social experience?

STOP at Graffiti on wall. How sure are we that any ethnic minority pupil leaving school in our area would not report similar hurts and apparent teacher indifference, as Suade does, if they were asked to comment on their schooling by a BBC film team – or indeed an LEA inspector?

Do we contextualise the sort of books and films children are bound to come across outside school (Robinson Crusoe, Dr Doolittle, Beau Geste, Tarzan, etc.) so that white pupils do not associate the out-of-date negative imagery of black inferiority in such materials with black British people (or other ethnic minorities) in contemporary society?
(See page 44.)

Do we need a whole-school policy on racist remarks, etc. (as we have on other harmful and anti-social behaviour, like smoking in classrooms or corridors) so that it is not left to individual staff to decide on their own, whether and how to deal with such incidents?

What is the harm (a) to black pupils (b) to white pupils, who pass such graffiti, especially if teachers ignore its existence and/or its effects?

STOP at the end of the Cumbria Nursery sequence. Jean Adams is acting in the light of researches documented in David Milner's *Children and Race – Ten Years On* (Ward Lock Educational, £4.95, paperback, 1982) which prove that attitudes are already formed before school age. Teachers in a multi-ethnic area could check with black parents or friends, whether it is common to find black children trying to scrub themselves white. If so, do we need to ask, what is it in the white children's words and behaviour in the nursery school or play group, that is giving the black child the idea that it would be better, growing up in Britain, to be less black? If teachers ignore the impressions and social experience children are bringing into school, then are they not leaving them prey to all the influences outside school, which currently tend to reinforce the myths and negative stereotypical thinking that Gus finds in school leavers? By secondary school age, is it not too late to do much to remedy this at an affective level? (David Selby describes some useful approaches on pages 102–107; and this chapter can be used in class.)

In discussion arising from the film, you may need to refer back to the pre-viewing questions. Some factual answers:

2 Approx. 57 million.

3 Approx. 2.9 million are black.

4 Ireland and South Europe (see page 22).

5 Less than none, since more have emigrated.

6 According to Lord Scarman, social disadvantaging deriving from white people's hidden racial prejudice.

7 'The riots'.

8 'The uprisings' or 'the first urban rebellions'.

9 12 languages.

16 See suggestions on pages 115–119, 123–126.

Leicester, incidentally, has 23% black population.

2   What is racism?

Words like racism are used as loose umbrella terms, meaning very different things to different people, so little of use will emerge from discussion, if some initial effort is not made by the participants to establish some common understanding (or 'working definition') of the terms 'prejudice', 'racism', 'black', 'white', 'discrimination', etc. Because 'racist' is commonly used as a term of abuse, and is often muddled with personal attitudes which should be more properly described as 'prejudiced', it has been found helpful in the following exercise always to start with the meaning of prejudice, before moving on to the key word 'racism'.

In introducing the exercise you might draw attention to the fact that 'racist' as a noun is sometimes used to mean 'racially prejudiced person', sometimes (especially by some blacks) to refer to 'whites in a racist system'. (Some people underline the distinction by saying 'racialist' for the first meaning.) It is for the working of a system that 'racist', either as a noun, or as an adjective for racism, is used in this chapter, If the distinction is not clear, many in the group are likely to assume that they are personally under attack, and may simply resist the exercises, rather than using them as an interesting and professionally important opportunity to explore previously unconsidered ideas in trying to improve the education of all children at school. (See also page 163).

What do we mean by the word 'prejudice'?

---

1 Any preconceived opinions or feeling, either favourable or unfavourable (*praejudicium* = before judgment);

2 Holding to an attitude despite contrary available evidence, information or experience;

3 An unfavourable opinion or feeling formed beforehand or without knowledge, thought or reason;

4 Unreasonable feelings, opinions or attitudes, especially of a hostile nature, directed against a racial, religious, or national group, identifiably different from our own;

5 Negative personal perceptions that discriminate against individuals seen only in terms of being representative of such a group.

6 Personal attitudes towards other people, usually based on negative group stereotypes, which are not inborn but learned as children from adults and reinforced by the media and peer-group talk;

7 A partial rejection of a person on the basis of his or her real or supposed specifiable characteristics.

8 A tendency towards biased judgements, normally perceived in others rather than ourselves.

9 An inability to move beyond an initial response of seeing someone in terms of a projected generalised label in one's mind rather than as a person.

What do we mean by the word 'racism'?

1a A belief that human races have distinctive characteristics that determine their respective cultures, usually involving the idea that one race is superior and has the right to dominate others;

b A policy of enforcing such asserted right;

c A system of government and society based upon such a policy – a system defined more by effects than motives;

2 Perpetuation of belief in the superiority of a particular race;

3 Assertion of rights and interests of a particular racial group, who assume superiority, however unwittingly, and have power to enforce this, to the detriment of other racial groups;

4 The treatment of a minority, identified by racial background, as scapegoats for social stresses, injustices, or conflicts of interests affecting the whole society;

5 Justifying the relative disadvantaging of a group, through an attempt to 'biologise' social structures;

6 A way of rationalising a fear that the privileged position of one's own ethnic group in society might be eroded;

7 An inadequately acknowledged residue of the colonial encounter between white and black, in which personal attitudes and behaviour come second, and institutional power and pressures come first;

8 The conduct generated by the belief that some races, however identified, are inferior, not in this or that respect, but *as people*, and that, therefore, their interests and feelings do not deserve to be regarded as equally important or worthy of respect as those of any so-called superior race;

9 Action that, regardless of the intentions involved, defends the advantages that whites have because of the subordinated position of black racial minorities, and based on, or fuelled by, culturally sanctioned beliefs, involving dehumanising stereotypes, and/or paternalism, and/or ethno-centrism;

10 A combination of prejudiced attitudes against black people and the power to implement action based on these, which leads, however unintentionally, to disproportionate under-privilege and disadvantage for black people in a white dominant society.

11 Racism, whether individual, cultural or institutional, is no less racism for being unintentional or unwitting.

Procedure for meanings exercise

Ideally, break up into groups of not more than ten with up to 45 minutes for 'PREJUDICE' and 45 minutes for 'RACISM'. If there is not time, then do

(C) below for 'prejudice', quickly in 15 minutes, before doing at least
(C) for 'racism' over 45 minutes.

A *Brainstorm*
   i) Ask the group to reflect on, and scribble down in keywords, what
      sorts of things they mean, and understand others to mean, when
      using the word 'prejudice'; and then 'racism', 'black', 'white' . . .
   ii) Ask each member in turn to declare their ideas, building up a list of
       all the overlapping concepts that emerge.

B *Discussion*
   Ask the group to review the list:
   i) is anyone unclear about any of the ideas?
   ii) does anyone disagree with any of them?
   iii) is there any agreement on which are essential and which inessential?

C *Stimulus*
   As an aid to discussion, circulate copies of the 'What do we mean by'
   list. Ask each member, over 5 minutes,
   i) to underline which to them are the most important words or ideas
   ii) to add anything significant they think has been left out.
   Then ask each in turn to declare what they have marked and added, and
   why. Some common ideas are deliberately not included on the definition
   sheets (prejudice as 'fear of the unfamiliar', racism as 'prejudice plus
   power') to see if they are added, or 'arrived at' by the group themselves.

D *Definition*
   If there is time, it can help to focus the discussion to ask the group to try
   to agree their own definition, however long or short, that could be
   reported back and compared with what other groups have come up with,
   although it is not essential to reach a consensus.

Comments on the meanings exercise
This exercise should help the group build its own understanding of the
interactive relationship between racial prejudice as a personal attitude,
and racist disadvantaging of blacks as a result of the white dominant
power structure of society. The question for education is to break the
circle of interaction.

Most of us recognise prejudice as attitudes built on negative
stereotypes which are hardened, and wide open to reinforcement, by the
media. A definitive analysis of research and ideas on prejudice is *The
Nature of Prejudice*, by Gordon W. Allport[4]. Stuart Hall, in the booklet
Five views of multi-racial Britain[3] documents the process by which
social stresses in Britain have been channelled into a concern with race
during the 60's and 70's. The apparent need for scapegoats in a society
with growing social tensions, is of course all too depressingly familiar. It
may be worth checking whether all the group agree that by any
philosophy, a basic purpose of education is to equip the next generation

to be able to operate independently of such a tendency to seek scapegoats; to distinguish between people *with* problems and people *as* problems; to modify assumptions revealed to be based on misconceptions or ignorance; and not to blame the victim of social injustice.

None of the 'meanings' on the lists above are necessarily 'right' or 'correct' – the point is that the group review together the possible variety of ideas as a beginning to a process of reflection on racism which will be further developed as a result of later exercises.

It may help some groups to narrow the focus to 'colour prejudice'. Discussion can profitably turn on the significance of the word 'learned' in no. 6 on 'Prejudice'. Only if it is accepted that we are not born with our prejudices – that they are socially conditioned – can teachers seek to 'unlearn' their own and their pupils' prejudices based on misconceptions and ignorance.

Hopefully, in discussion of racism, it will have become clear that the common use of 'racial', as in 'racial disadvantage' is, strictly speaking, a misnomer for 'black'. Also clearer should be distinctions between 'scientific' and 'popular' concepts of race; between 'colour' and 'race'; between 'blacks' and 'ethnic minorities'. Discussion could focus on the terms 'assumed superiority' and 'unwitting', and particularly on the recurrence of the word 'power'. The question might be put: While both black and white people can be deeply *prejudiced* as individuals, can black communities be *racist* in Britain? The group might consider the view that while blacks can of course be racially prejudiced, to the extent that 'racism' has a power element (ie, that racial prejudice becomes 'racism' when it is the basis for operating institutions with the effect, in practice if not in theory, of perpetuating forms of black disadvantage or 'blocking of life-chances') then on the whole, blacks can only be victims of racism in Britain, as they lack the power to affect white people's 'life chances', however prejudiced or otherwise they may be. After discussion, clarification of terms can be helped by viewing the first 40 slides of *Recognising Racism*[12].

This chapter uses 'racism' chiefly in the sense of number 10 on the list; and it assumes 'anti-racist' teaching or policies to be concerned not simply with personal prejudice or overt behaviour against black children in school, but also with the education of all children to live in a society characterised by 'racial' (i.e. black) disadvantage and widespread (illegal) discrimination. In other words, this chapter means 'anti-racist' adjectivally, to refer to education directed towards combating structural injustice in society – a society characterised by two facts needing resolute action: many whites have stereotypes of blacks which involve assumptions of white superiority, and are based on misconception and ignorance; and such attitudes underlie, or are (perhaps unwittingly) used to rationalise the ways the structures of power work to perpetuate forms of black (called 'racial' in the official documents) disadvantage. This chapter also assumes that there is one race – the human race – and that the main thing in common, apart from humanity, between black British people of Asian and of Afro-Caribbean background as such is that in practice (if not in theory) they suffer forms of discrimination on grounds of skin colour in this country (see pp7/8).

Mapping different views and perspectives

It is helpful for a group to build some framework for the recurring viewpoints and beliefs which are likely to be expressed in any staff-room discussion of multi-cultural education. The 'map' opposite arises from in-service work in Berkshire, and is reprinted with acknowledgement.

The map summarises three main perspectives. Column A emphasises assimilation, and reflects what is still the dominant outlook in the British media and in many schools. Column B presents the view that cultural diversity should be respected, and emphasises the importance of tolerance, understanding and information. Column C summarises the views about racism and prejudice which are presented in, for example, racism awareness workshops. (See also pages 6 to 9.)

A map such as this is useful to leaders of racism awareness sessions since it helps them to identify the perspectives which participants hold, and to focus attention on possible inconsistencies and contradictions. The map can also of course be shared with workshop participants in order to emphasise and clarify the difference between 'multi-cultural education' (column B) and 'anti-racist education' (column C). It can be used in an effective workshop exercise if it is cut up into its various parts, and if participants then try to piece it together again, working in twos and threes.

3 What is cultural racism – can it be unlearnt?

Individual racial prejudice is obvious enough, ranging from bigotry that consciously refuses to accept some individuals or groups as entitled to the full respect due to a fellow human being (that might come out in the staff room through remarks like 'I don't like teaching *them*') through to well intentioned paternalism (expressed in remarks like 'Don't speak *that* language here, you must practice your English'). Less obvious is *cultural racism*, the tendency of a group to feel that their way of doing things is the 'right' way. This may be simply because they are conditioned by upbringing to think so, and think that what is familiar to them is the best. (It is often said 'those who live in our country should learn our ways' but even on a narrow and ethnocentric interpretation, what *are* British ways? Scottish, Irish, Welsh, English, Protestant/Catholic, Southern/Northern . . .?)

History

Picking up the idea of assumed superiority as an element in racially prejudiced attitudes, an exercise which many find surprising and

A map of Tensions and Controversies

A	B	C
Immigrants came to Britain in the 1950s and 1960s because the laws on immigration were not strict enough.	Ethnic minorities came Britain because they had a right to and because they wanted a better life.	Black people came to Britain, as to other countries, because their labour was required by the economy.
Immigrants should integrate as quickly as possible with the British way of life.	Ethnic minorities should be able to maintain their language and cultural heritage.	Black people have to defend themselves against racist laws and practices, and to struggle for racial justice.
There is some racial prejudice in Britain, but it's only human nature, and Britain is a much more tolerant place than most other countries.	There are some misguided individuals and extremist groups in Britain, but basically our society is just and democratic, and provides equality.	Britain is a racist society and has been for several centuries. Racism is to do with power structures more than with the attitudes of individuals.
It is counter-productive to try to remove prejudice. You can't force people to like each other by bringing in laws and regulations.	Prejudice is based on ignorance and misunderstanding. It can be removed by personal contacts and the provision of information.	'Prejudice' is caused by, it is not the cause of, unjust structures and procedures. It can be removed only by dismantling these.
There should be provision of English as a second language in schools, but otherwise 'children are all children, we should treat all children exactly the same' – it is wrong to notice or emphasise cultural or racial differences.	Schools should recognise and affirm ethnic minority children's background, culture and language . . . celebrate festivals, organise international evenings, use and teach mother tongues and community languages, teach about ethnic minority history, art, music, religion, literature.	Priorities in education are for there to be more black people in positions of power and influence – as heads, senior teachers, governors, education officers, elected members; and to remove discrimination in the curriculum, classroom methods and school organisation; and to teach directly about equality and justice and against racism.

This table arises from in-service work in Berkshire, and is reprinted with acknowledgement.

revealing is simply to review alternative interpretations of Britain's imperial past, and of world history in general. These throw into relief the impressions we have gained from traditionalist history books. We have already seen (pages 60–66) two school history syllabuses being used to help pupils appreciate the past as an interplay of culturally autonomous interpretations, ie of interestingly different, and equally valid, points of view. Dr Bhikhu Parekh reminded us in Chapter 8 that study of history calls for open-minded powers of empathy. One aid to this are his own observations on some of the cultural effects of the British colonialist period in the talk *Asians in Britain*[3]. Many people have found that they were acting on unexamined and out of date assumptions, through reading accounts of African history like J. D. Fage's *A History of Africa*; Walter Rodney's *How Europe underdeveloped Africa*; Basil Davidson's account of the slave trade *Black Mother*; books and articles on universal history by Geoffrey Barraclough[5]; and most particularly, *Black Settlers in Britain* by File and Power (see bottom of page 61).

Many teachers are using the two booklets *Roots of Racism* and *Patterns of Racism*, available from the Institute of Race Relations, 247 Pentonville Road, London N1 9NG, along with the set of history posters *Whose world is the World?*[6] now available in most Teachers' Centres. A group could examine each of these posters individually or in pairs for five minutes; then report the content back to the group in sequence, 1–12. Next, seek reactions to the view of history presented. If some are critical of 'simplistic views', or 'bad graphic design', then invite them to work with the Teachers' Centre to make a better set of posters! The point to discuss is whether or not children and adults carry into their image of Britain today an inadequate and 'ethnocentric' view of history with overtones of black inferiority.

Do we need in our schools popular and vivid presentations of African history (social organisation, cultural achievements, linguistic and religious development, etc.) *before* the period of European exploitation (as has been done with S. American Indian culture)? How else can teachers displace images of 'blackness' based on negative stereotypes reflecting only caricaturing constructs of W. European culture? Is it enough to teach a view of 'Black' as equal to 'White', if that is still only in 'White' terms; without a sense of positive distinct identity can true 'equal' respect be established? (If not, then we need school resources drawn from the work of present-day African scholars and historians, who present their history in terms of its relationship with the present (post-colonial) African nations.) Vital documents for discussion here are Dave Hicks' *Images of the World – occasional paper No 2*, and *Bias in Geography Textbooks – working paper No 1*, both available from Centre for Multi-cultural Education, University of London, Institute of Education, 20 Bedford Way, London WC1H 0AL. Another stimulus to discussion is *Books that censor reality*, paper by Beverley Naidoo in *Racism in educational media* Jan 1984 Conference Report from 5 Eastfield Ave, Watford, Herts.

Language

One commonly used way of illustrating how assumptions are embedded in our language, as well as in our image of history, is the 'Black' and 'White' exercise. List on the board all phrases and uses first of the word 'black' and then of 'white', that the group can think of; then work through them deciding by general consensus if each carries negative, positive or neutral associations. Adding up the totals is a way of discovering just how heavily the word black is laden with the negative associations. What is the effect if such words are applied to people? In particular, what is the effect on white children's self-image if they feel white represents positive/good and black represents negative/bad? And what is the effect on black children's self-image? (See pages 37 to 42.)

The American black actor Ossie Davis made a study of the synonymns for 'whiteness' and 'blackness' in Roget's Thesaurus. He found that 'whiteness' had many synonyms that are favourable and pleasing to contemplate' and only 10 with negative connotations, 'and then only in the mildest sense'. 'Blackness' turned out to have no less than 60 synonyms which are distinctly unfavourable; and in addition to those, it has 20 directly related to race.

'The English language is my enemy ... Any creature, good or bad, white or black, Jew or Gentile, who uses the English language for purposes of communication is willing to force the Negro child into 60 ways to despise himself, and the white child 60 ways to aid and abet him in the crime'. Ossie Davis, 1967[7].

It was as a positive rejection of this that the US Civil Rights Movement adopted the slogan 'Black is beautiful'. 'Black' has now acquired a 'political' meaning in some contexts, symbolising pride in cultural background and self-assertion against unjust treatment.

Other simple examples of the way we can be victimised by our very language in trying to be non-racist, are the unconscious use of the word 'people' (see 21 of the assumptions exercise); the way we accept the media's exclusive use of the word 'riots' in relations to the street disturbances of 1981 (see pre-viewing questions 7/8, page 166); the use of the word 'racial' when we mean simply British people of Afro-Caribbean or Asian background (see also pages 40–44).

'Anglo-Saxon attitudes' (Part 2)

The next two sequences of *Anglo-Saxon attitudes* illustrate primary teaching which aims to combat cultural racism. After showing the Barbara Roberts sequence at Ecclesbourne Primary School, you could stop the film and note (a) her readiness to review her own attitudes; (b) how she is very far from ignoring skin colour differences, and how she risks no split between her teaching and the children's social experience in her project 'ourselves'; (c) that she 'legitimates' the idea of moving to find work, and of speaking in other ways than in standard English alone, by putting herself up front as a person, before asking any children about their family background (thus avoiding patronising or exploitative approaches, or insensitivity to children's self consciousness); (d) how she makes the point that to reject non-standard English accents or dialects is partly to reject the person; (e) how she teaches against stereotyping, by the simple device of putting hands on black and white paper; (f) how she supports mother tongue skills in the class-room as much for the respect it wins in the eyes of other children, as for the cultural support it gives to mother tongue speakers.

On this last point, you could introduce, if relevant, the issues and information on mother tongues or community languages offered in Chapter 12, and presented graphically in the film *Languages for Life* (see page 4). Especially important, however, is a point Barbara Roberts makes on pages 16–18 about *first setting up a context of similarity*, before referring to any differences. It is not clear from the film that she first asks the children to outline their fingers in pencil and to identify all the ways our hands are the same. Only then does she ask them to colour them in, so that colour differences are seen as a marginal extra difference, not the main thing about hands. In the same way, the children have read and discussed *Aesop's Fables* before Barbara asks the Turkish boys to share (bi-lingually) one of them in their mother tongue. This prevents any assumption that an initially strange sounding language must reflect 'strange' ideas or people; Barbara wants no children to regard differences of language or skin colour in a negative way as strange, exotic, or simply because different, threatening. Similar principles are seen operating in the next sequence of the film, the Leicestershire Primary Schools' exchange activities. These are briefly described by David Houlton on pages 51–53. Note that these are not short 'visits', but joint activities over time. They also need well-prepared teachers to help correct the wrong or misleading information the children are likely to pass on if left entirely to themselves.

4   What is institutional racism and how does it operate?

This is the form of racism most white people find hardest to bring into conscious focus, partly because we are so much participants in it. We are involuntarily the beneficiaries and the agents of it. The individual and cultural elements come together in insitutional pressures which work in effect to the benefit of some more than others. As defined by David Wellman, it is action 'based on culturally sanctioned beliefs, that regardless of the intentions involved, defend the advantages that whites have because of the subordinated position of racial minorities.'[8]

As noted at many points throughout this book, this is the aspect of racism which moves beyond the emotive, psychological context of 'prejudiced attitudes' into the context of matters of political power, hierarchy and status. It is the form in which we are all involved in racism whether racially prejudiced or not in our personal relationships. But as we have also noted, it is the form which makes us most uncomfortable as we become aware of it. It often causes feelings of guilt or anger, which are born of the frustration that we were not ourselves responsible for events of the past, and yet cannot escape the fact that we live in a society on the benefits of past exploitation, rationalised by assumptions of black inferiority. Neither can we escape the cultural trap of our language, in which so may of those past rationalisations and attitudes remain embedded. As a result, many white people feel defensive or seek to evade recognising that it remains part of the black experience of British society to feel oppression and low status, which is expressed in many overt ways, but also in many subtle and indefinable ways. However, as the primary headmistress says in the film, such mixed emotions have to be experienced and lived through as part of the learning process. After her feelings of anger and of being threatened subsided, she felt more confident about adopting a strategy of action towards a multi-racial society, and a multi-cultural education within it, based on full equality of respect and opportunity, and without risk of tokenism, patronising assumptions, or confused conceptions.

Exercise in designing a subtly racist school system ($1\frac{1}{2}$ hours)

The aim
The aim is to allow participants to think out some of the elements of what is called 'institutional' racism and how this functions in the school system. Better understanding of the mechanisms which perpetuate disadvantage is a vital first step towards determining what action is needed (a) to combat them in the school and LEA itself, and (b) to equip the next generation to dismantle them in the wider society. And the exercise should help teachers discover how it is often an entirely unwitting combination of habitual assumptions, 'normal' behaviour and traditional procedures that support black disadvantage, rather than conscious and overt anti-black prejudice.

Institutional racism
The concept of institutional racism is a new idea to many people. The point is to move the group's thinking beyond questions simply of individual teachers' attitudes, and questions simply of multi-cultural exchange in schools, to thinking about institutional pressures, particularly in the exercise of power over decision-making in the school system.

Most Britons are proud of our democratic principles and traditions; however, the acid test of whether a democratic system is working properly is to ask 'Are the rights and interests of minority groups being fully protected in practice, as well as in theory?'. (If not, we have a form of tyranny by the majority over a permanent minority). National and local surveys demonstrate that large sections of black ethnic minorities (50 per cent of whom arrived 20–35 years ago; 40 per cent were born here) are still over-represented among the lowest groups according to the main social indicators: housing, employment and promotion opportunities, educational achievement, etc.[1] How and why is this? This exercise provides a 'scaffolding' for the group to bring into consideration, and to build its own meaning for the idea mentioned earlier, that even perhaps without conscious prejudice, 'white dominant' power and influence is wielded through institutions whose working unintentionally excludes black people from power, whose procedures function in ways which represent barriers to black people being able to affect their own 'life chances'.

The procedure
It is important for you to point out that each small (8/10) group is to design a subtly racist school system, rather than an obviously racist system on the apartheid model. The idea is to work out what kind of schooling would in practice preserve white majority advantage over a black minority in society, even though teachers were not personally colour prejudiced, racial discrimination was against the law, and LEA policies formally favoured equal opportunities for all in a multi-racial society. Ask one rapporteur in each group to set out the features of such a system in notes, perhaps on a large flip chart, as a visual aid for report-back. On a separate sheet another rapporteur could make notes of the explanations for why and how the features of the invented system would *in effect* work to maintain black disadvantage. Essentially the group will be thinking of 'apparently reasonable' practical barriers to the implementation of well intentioned, but still largely theoretical, non-racist policies. It is usual, but not necessary, to assume that the school includes a proportion of children of Afro-Caribbean and/or Asian background; groups can decide to invent either a primary or a secondary school. Emphasise that it is to be an exercise of *imagination*.

Stimulus Questions – that could help a group get started:

1 What *curriculum* would they teach? In what ways, if at all, would it be appropriate for education in a multi-cultural society?

2 What would be the school *language policy* on (a) bi-lingualism, (b) community languages, (c) mother-tongue teaching for English-

second language speakers, (d) E2L support. How much, if at all, would parents be directly asked to help in mother-tongue teaching, and under what conditions?

3 What would be the *staffing* policy, eg would there be ethnic minority staff? What would be their roles? What posts of special responsibility would there be? Who would get them and on what criteria?

4 What would be the *catering policy* for school meals, etc?

5 What kind of *assessment tests* would be used?

6 What would be the content and methods of *RE teaching*?

7 In *assemblies*, what festivals, etc would be recognised, and how would they be handled?

8 What 'pastoral' care would there by, and what means of *communication to parents*?

9 *Cultural evenings* – would there be any? If so, what would they involve?

10 How much, and what kind of *games, swimming and PE*? What would be the arrangements for these?

11 What priority would the school give, if any at all, to *In-service staff training and development* in (a) multi-cultural approaches in the curriculum; (b) teaching anti-racism; (c) improving cross-cultural communication skills in parent-teacher dialogue? What would be the arrangements for covering to send staff on LEA courses, or in organising school-based DIY staff meetings and workshops?

12 How would the school decide on *use of resources* from the LEA, eg staff allocated under Section 11 LGA; capitation; etc.

13 How would the school handle, if at all (a) racist incidents in the locality; (b) racist jokes or remarks among pupils in school; (c) racially prejudiced statements or arguments expressed by parents; (d) racist observations made in the staff room? Would such matters be left to individual responses, or would there be a whole-school policy? If the latter, what would it be?

14 How much encouragement and support would be given to English-speaking teachers to *learn languages*, such as Urdu, Punjabi, Bengali?

15 Would *checklists* on racism and sexism be used in relation to books and materials? If so, how?

16 *School uniform* policy? *Name* of school? Does it have a motto?

17 What sort of *headteacher*?

18 What emphasis on *authority v. democracy*; and on purely academic achievement in running of school?

19 What emphasis would be given to *the arts* in the curriculum and/or in after-school activities, and what kinds of music-making, drama, dance, painting and drawing would be resourced and encouraged?

The two most vital questions:

20 In each of the above, how would the issues be decided and by whom? In particular, would there be direct involvement of parents and community in the policy making – and, if so, how would this be organised and articulated?

21 In each of the above, if little or nothing is actually to happen, what reasoning or factors would be used to explain why?

Concepts to bring out into conscious focus in discussion of how subtle racism operates could include:

a ways of *marginalising* the interests of ethnic minorities;

b making *tokenist* gestures towards minority interest and cultures (see comments on statement 20, page 191) (i.e. 'paying lip service');

c acting on the basis of *stereotypes* in general, ie 'they all . . .' and negative stereotypes in particular – especially, perhaps, in terms of lower expectations of some groups of ethnic minority children;

d the effects of *omission* to modify, adapt, or change ways of thinking and doing things in school, despite the changing multi-cultural, multi-linguistic, multi-faith, and multi-racial character of the community the school is serving;

e making decisions on *patronising*, paternalist assumptions about others' cultural values – or, as some critics put it, 'white cultural imperialism' (The women in the group are usually well able to explain how this patronising element operates, and how it feels. Truly equal respect for other cultures requires great sensitivity and imagination, and a real willingness to listen and learn. For example, can one genuinely respect a culture for its Arts and social customs, while wholly ignoring its language?);

f hidden *assimilationist* assumptions in decisions about the use of resources in school, ie in effect treating black ethnic minority children only insofar as they are the same as white children (i.e. 'incorporation');

g *excluding minority groups from power* by using majority voting without special safeguards for minority interests, and the deployment of black staff on a basis of *responsibility without power*;

h *building in failure* – e.g. sending only individuals away on anti-racism training courses, with no report-back at school; no monitoring arrangements of the effects of policies; leaving whole-school issues to small working party groups, or ensuring such working parties fail to have much effect (i.e. 'sabotaging in advance the practical outcome of well-intentioned moves');

i *The rationalising* of failure to review attitudes and to modify procedures on a shared power basis, through the '*doing nothing*' syndrome, ie consideration of lack of resources, difficulties in spending time on working out priorities and where race issues come in them, 'not rocking the boat' or 'it's too difficult', etc. (i.e. 'recipes for paralysis'). Such rationalisings usually imply a failure to see that it is *all* children's needs that are at stake in tackling racism awareness in classrooms, staff room, and LEA administration.

Many people find some of these concepts a bit unfamiliar and difficult clearly to understand in abstract terms. This is partly because in a strongly 'white dominant' culture, white people have not needed personally to think about how black disadvantage is maintained, not being direct victims of it themselves. Thus your job in the exercise is to encourage each group member to contribute to thinking of practical features for an invented school system which would keep a black minority relatively socially disadvantaged and through this process to tease out the concepts (a)–(i), and any more the group can think of.

The sort of hidden assumptions that can lead individual 'well intentioned' teachers and educational administrators unwittingly to go along with those subtly racist practices of institutional racism can be explored through the next 'Assumptions' exercise. Once your groups (again ideally not more than 10 in each) have described their invented school in report-back, two crucial questions for discussion would be 'What are the differences between such an imagined school, and the school system we ourselves are currently operating?' and 'What did it feel like to be designing an institution with deliberately racist effects?'

'Anglo-Saxon attitudes' (Part 3)

At this stage, the rest of the film can serve as a valuable 'reinforcement' of the thinking and experience developed in the exercises and materials so far. Another widely used aid for understanding the nature of institutional racism is the tape/slide presentation *Recognising Racism*[12].

Also widely used are Salman Rushdie's Channel 4 talk *The New Empire in Britain*, available as off-print from *New Society*, 9 December 1982; and the ALTARF film (see page 56).

---

5 What are the unconscious assumptions that fuel the working of institutional racism?

This book has implied agenda questions for staff rooms and training courses throughout; there are also particular questions on the back cover, and pages 10, 159, 162. However, some teachers' inaction, if not indifference, in regard to racism and the harm it is creating for pupils, both black and white, is rationalised by a range of 'arguments', whose dependence on assumptions which hide factual ignorance, paternalist or assimilationist attitudes, harmful stereo-types, cultural ethnocentrism, and 'blaming the victim' of social injustice, may not be obvious at first.

Indeed, it is a feature of institutionalised racism that although individuals operating the institutions may have 'liberal' views, they justify no change by what appear on the surface to be reasonable and practical observations. The following statements have been reported as commonly heard by teachers attending workshops. Some are not in themselves necessarily racist; but all are remarks whose meaning we would need to check, as they could be symptomatic of the unconsidered assumptions that explain why teachers and others with discretion or power within our institutions, seek to evade the need for action and change to counteract the present 'status quo' of injustice to black people, evidenced in the facts of black disadvantage and the prevalence of varying degrees of colour prejudice in our society.[1] The exercise consists simply of handing out copies of the 57 statements to the group and inviting them to comment on the hidden assumptions. (Where a group wish to talk at length about the substantive issues raised in some of the statements, you might suggest that you go back to those issues after working through the rest of the list.) In effect, this exercise not only brings hidden assumptions into conscious focus – the pre-condition for anti-racist action – but it also gives practice in thinking through one's own replies as confidence-building preparation for those occasions when teachers meet objections to multi-cultural and anti-racist approaches.

Clearly, in any one group session, you will use only a selection of those most relevant to your situation; however, it is a list members of the group could take away to peruse for themselves, or to talk through more informally later. You might find it useful to distribute the list of statements for some personal reflection in advance of the group discussion. Alternatively the list could be used as the basis of role-play exercises in practicing discussing the school's objectives with sceptical parents, govenors, senior or junior staff colleagues, union/association members or representatives, even LEA advisers and inspectors.

ASSUMPTIONS EXERCISE: 57 VARIETIES

Can you identify (a) inadequate or wrong information, and (b) possible hidden assumptions which are racist in effect, behind these statements? What points would you make in replying to them?

1 'I'm not colour prejudiced, so there's no need for me to study the facts of black disadvantage.'

2 'I treat all the children the same – in our school we make no difference between children, black or white.'

3 'Our black pupils are a problem in this school – because they are very different, you know.'

4 'They don't speak English.' or 'They haven't got any language, you know'.

5 'I can't talk about attitudes towards racism with my colleagues – some of them would find it personally offensive, and raising such topics directly can be counter-productive.'

6 'Multi-cultural education is all about black children or, as we say now, ethnic minorities, isn't it?'

7 'Many immigrant children just can't perform so well – and that's not prejudice: our assessment tests, well tried since the '40s and '50s, prove it.'

8 End of term general essay exam question: Describe an English village.

9 'If the Asian children don't eat the curries we provide as an option at lunch, then it's their own fault if they are tired in the afternoons.'

10 'Some black groups, usually the Afro-Caribbeans, don't seem to have much opportunity or encouragement from their parents to get homework done on time.'

11 'Different social customs are all very interesting, but they are irrelevant to my curriculum.'

12 'More mother-tongue in school time would be fine – but while the Authority has such tight limits on resources it simply isn't practical.'

13 'Positive discrimination either means lowering standards or giving unfairly preferential treatment, or both.'

14 'We have to treat them as slow learners, at least while their English is so inadequate.'

15 'It simply makes sense to use extra resources offered because we have minority children in our school, on a school bus driver or an extra teacher of English or maths, or a swimming pool, or a new piano, or replacement slide projectors, etc, because not only the ethnic minority children benefit from such things, but everyone else does, too.'

16 'I favour black equal rights – I've made several suggestions of ways we can help them.'

17 'Little positive comes of ethnic minority community meetings because it is obvious they don't properly understand how our system works.'

18 'You can't expect teachers to adopt a multi-cultural approach until the Authority provides enough of the right materials.'

19 'The LEA's policy is really admirable – but it's only what I've been doing all the time.'

20 'We're very keen on multi-cultural approaches: for some years we have let them have Asian evenings at school, and we celebrate Diwali and Eid in assembly. Although there are only three children of Hong Kong parents, we had a special display on Chinese New Year.'

21 'People often find it hard to know whether black people want to be called 'black' or not.'

22 'You can't start being heavy about nationality jokes the kids make in the playground – after all, there have always been Irish and Taffy jokes, and all humour depends on stereotypes.'

23 'If there's an NF or BM meeting in the town, then to refer to it in school would be bringing politics into the classroom and children must be left to make up their own political opinions.'

24 'I find it hard to talk about racism freely and frankly when there are black people in the room.'

25 'We do now offer Asian languages in the secondary school – there are lunchtime lessons available for both Urdu and Punjabi speakers.'

26 'We give Asian languages full equal respect in our secondary school curriculum – Urdu and Bengali are taught up to 'O' level standard.'

27 'If Muslim, Sikh or Rastafarian parents send children to a Church of England primary school, then they must accept that their children should join in the Christian forms of worship followed in assembly.'

28 'I can't teach Muslim ways, because I can't sympathise with the way they regard and treat their women.'

29 'The Afro-Caribbean boys have so much natural ebullience compared to the Asians – that's why they're so difficult.'

30 'Many parents don't speak English well – but our school notes can be translated for them by their children, or by their friends and neighbours.'

31 'Our school is very democratic – the Head really does accept a majority vote. And we are continually disappointed that so few parents, especially the Asian parents, actually turn up to PTA meetings.'

32 'Multi-culturalism is all very well in theory – but there's little point in it while so many white parents really don't want their children to be eating Asian food, or doing projects about Africa, or discussing racial discrimination. They tell us that's not what they send their children to

school for. It's not our job to try to change their minds; and even if it were, there's simply no way you could persuade a lot of them anyway.'

33 'So our working party report says some of our schooling is racist: but they would say that, wouldn't they – it's the trendy lefty group who are on it.'

34 'We don't do multi-cultural education in our school because we have none of them.'

35 'We've done one thing properly – we used a racism checklist to get rid of all the old-fashioned racist books in school so that teachers can't use them unwittingly, and the children won't be exposed to stereotyped pictures and stories.'

36 'In our school we respect other cultures by looking at their social and artistic customs, and at their history and religion. You don't need to learn the language.'

37 'But the Asian parents tell us they don't want their children to be taught any language other than English. So isn't it patronising if we say they should want mother tongue teaching?'

38 'However desirable mother tongue, bi-lingual teaching might be, it is ridiculously impractical – we obviously couldn't learn all the 12 or 13 languages spoken by children in this school.'

39 'But there just aren't enough bi-lingual Asians qualifying to become nursery and primary school teachers. Muslim girls won't go away to college, for example.'

40 'I agree with equal rights – our job is simply to help black youngsters achieve better qualifications at school.'

41 'Racism is purely a class problem – white working class youngsters have all the same problems as black youngsters.'

42 'Racism is a capitalist tool – only when exploitative economic relations are overthrown will there be no racist oppression of black people.'

43 'The real problem is the racism in and between the black communities – what do we do about *that*?'

44 'You can't talk to their communities – who represents them? They're either split into too many factions, or they reject their official representatives as "Uncle Toms", or both.'

45 'You seem to be saying we must listen to the blacks and do everything they say.'

46 '"When in Rome, do as the Romans do." Doesn't this mean that it's *they* who have to adapt?'

47 'This is just another educational fashion or fad. Like primary school French, it'll have its day and then disappear.'

48 'Schools can't change society.'

49 'Racial attitudes come from parents – it would be unfair to set children against their own parents.'

50 'It's wrong to draw attention to skin colour differences – young children play together person to person, not black and white.'

51 'All immigrant groups expect a rough time at first – by the third generation they integrate and the problems disappear.'

52 'Aren't you chasing an impossible dream? Name me one successfully harmonious multi-racial society anywhere in the world.'

53 'There is a colour problem in this country – that's why I think we must help the blacks to help themselves more.'

54 'Isn't there a danger of over-emphasising the minorities' cultures?'

55 'Attacks on Asian British homes are appalling – but wouldn't the police be able to protect them better if they weren't all living together in a community of their own?'

56 'Most children's image of blacks comes from the media, so whatever we do in school is undermined by the "problem-oriented" negative imagery of blacks on TV – that's where the problem lies.'

57 'We don't need racism-awareness training because
   i) we have no problems in our school. Pupils and staff all get on together well.'
   or ii) we have no/few black children.'

Comments on the 57 statements
These are not 'correct answers': they are only some comments made by teachers in workshops that a group leader might find useful to feed in as a stimulus to a group, in working out their own view of a suitable reply in each case.

1 This fails to distinguish between prejudice and racism. The assumption that because we are not personally colour prejudiced there is no need to study the black experience of disadvantage in our society, nor to take any positive anti-racist actions, is in effect to go along with the status quo, to be party to the racist features in British society demonstrated in the evidence[1]. To take no action is to collude with institutional racism.

2 This could mean that a teacher is seeing children at best, only for what they have in common, or at worst, according to some self-reflecting 'ideal pupil' model (see page 156 ff). Either way, it is a failure to respect the blackness of black British children, and to recognise that their self-respect depends on a positive image of their differences. In fact, children are not all the same, nor are they simply individuals to be treated as such. They are individuals with various different group identifications – girl/boy, working class/middle class, black/white. Messages informing these group identifications are being beamed in to each child constantly

from 'the hidden curriculum' of their social lives. Because our society has inherited a culture which wrongly associates blackness with inferiority and negative images, schools need positively to support awareness and pride that 'Black is beautiful' – and that black children are part of the Black Consciousness – as much as they are already making white children feel it's good to be white.

3 Differences, such as they are, are not a problem – they are an enrichment. If any challenges or difficulties arise, a school does not have a 'pupil problem' because 'they are different'; if anything, it has a teacher problem – because of staff inability to adapt their approaches to take account of such differences.

4 This can indicate a negatively stereotypical attitude which children will pick up as a hidden curriculum message. The fact that some children are learning English as a second language could be put positively (as does Barbara Roberts, see page 17): 'We are proud of our potential bi- (or tri-) lingual children, ie they know, or are learning several languages.' (see chapter 12.)

5 This is often an evasion of responsibility. Initial apparent 'hardening of attitudes' does not necessarily mean that there will not be some positive long-term effects, even from a direct 'confronting' of racist views and attitudes. But part of fear 'of being offensive' or of producing 'counter-productive' results is often uncertainty, and a need for more information on the subject, and about ways to raise the issues effectively, which could be positively sought (see bottom of page 162). This chapter, and the film, are aids towards this.

6 Multi-cultural education is actually for and about *all* children; and 'Ethnic minority' does not always equal 'black' (see bottom of page 6 to middle of page 9).

7 You cannot draw cross-cultural comparisons from out-of-date assessment tests evolved in one culture, about culturally different groups of children. And why are children born in this country still often referred to as 'Immigrant children'? (see bottom of page 10 and pages 19–22).

8 Why only English? Could this not disadvantage any child with little experience of English rural life, and lose the wealth of different experience children with family backgrounds from overseas might bring?

9 This could be 'blaming the victim' for our failure to consult ethnic minority parents or community spokespeople about catering methods that will ensure their children can and do eat something nutritious at school dinner.

10 This could be to see some ethnic minority children in terms of a stereotype of a group too socially disadvantaged to be expected to do

well at school. The assumption that some children 'don't get parental support' or 'don't have opportunity to do homework', may be simply wrong (especially given the number of black 'Saturday' or 'supplementary' schools set up and run by Afro-Caribbean parents' groups), or be masking the fact that the syllabus is irrelevant, or that parents have not been invited to discuss the teachers' methods and how they may help.

11 This could be an excuse for not wanting to bother about bringing our teaching up to date in and for a multi-cultural, -lingual, -racial and -credal society.

12 As many schools have found, there is both expertise and willingness among the communities to give free help in doing this (see pages 13–15, 32–34, 131–142).

13 Positive discrimination or 'positive action' is designed simply to correct previous imbalance and injustice in equal opportunities. Discussion could turn on: Who decides what qualities and criteria are appropriate for a job? How is it decided what premium in multi-ethnic schools should be placed on 'role models' in the staff, and in all schools, on the value of a black perspective? Even if it were true that some black candidates are relatively inexperienced or have some particular difficulties, perhaps in communication skills, then this would be more a reason for arranging for appropriate training, to equip candidates to do the job well, rather than an excuse for not appointing them.

14 Failure to distinguish between 'inadequate English' and 'slow learning'.

15 Leaving use of resources allocated by LEAs for particular children's special needs to the discretion of each headteacher or head of department can mean that the resources are used towards assimilation (treating black children only in so far as they are the same as white), rather than to support particular learning needs and developments towards a pluralist curriculum.

16 Wanting to assist the achievement of black ethnic minority communities' equal rights in practice, but not wanting first to find out what such communities feel they need in their own terms, is, however charitable, a form of racial paternalism.

17 'They do not understand how our system works'!! Whose system? It is supposed to be a system for everyone and not something only a white person could explain. If anything, shouldn't No. 17 be 'We have made a bad job of working out a system'?

18 The assumption that multi-cultural education cannot be adopted because we lack the right resources and materials, or the right training, is a failure to see what this book has shown throughout, that it is actually only 'good teaching': it is the way available materials are used, and the attitudes brought to this, that are the crucial point. The community

itself can be the text book, and the home and social experience of the class itself the best 'audio visual aids' for understanding that this is a multi-cultural and multi-racial country in which we live. It is a dimension in all subjects and teaching practice, not a separate subject.

19 This might mask agreement only in theory with an LEA or school policy, without commitment to operate the policy in practice. This will be a major danger where teachers have not been personally involved in the research and decisions that go to the making of such policy.

20 This, of course, is tokenism; paternalism is also revealed in the words 'let them have'. It is valuable in discussion of tokenism to distinguish between good and essential 'first steps', as the beginning of a process of change, and 'tokenist moves', seen as sufficient, as an excuse for not moving further in the direction of change.

21 Since black people know whether they want to be called black or not, then who are the 'people' at the start of the statement? To speak habitually on the assumption that whites are 'just people', while the blacks are 'black people', is in effect to imply that blacks are 'not proper people'.

22 As children from Welsh and Irish backgrounds will confirm, such jokes can be hurtful. This also indicates a tendency in the teacher to a lack of sensitivity and to stereotypical thinking, which are inimical to the aim of education. By laughing at, or ignoring, racist jokes, we are supporting our own prejudices as well as legitimating those of others. (It could be useful here to listen again to the Moroccan girl, Suade, in the film.)

23 (See Martin Francis, page 54).

24 The inhibition of some white people if questions of racism arise when there are black people in the room could by a symptom of the disease of white racism – failure open-mindedly and frankly to learn about ourselves in terms of attitudes to blackness of skin and to the injustice of discrimination against blacks, with and through the contributions of others.

25 Perhaps justifiable as a 'first step', but the hidden curriculum message to children not in such classes is that such languages are less 'important' or 'valuable' (as confirmed by the Sikh schoolboy, Dilbagh, in the film) – a reflection of 'cultural imperialist' assumptions (see pages 133–135 and 138–139).

26 This could be racist disadvantaging of those with Asian mother tongues, if 'A' levels are only available in European languages (see page 138).

27 Would Jewish or Roman Catholic children be required to join in Protestant Christian worship?

28 You don't have to agree personally with something to be able to teach about it, and to teach in a way that is both respectful and 'sympathetic'

in reflecting the differences within other cultures. As a separate point, you may wish to note that it is a reinforcement of the negative stereotypes that lie behind prejudice to treat the history and heritage of countries in the so-called 'Third World' in a denigrating way, ie pointing out exotic or ugly practices, unbalanced either by appreciation of their good practices or by pointing out some of the ugly practices of the British as well.

29 Stereotypical assumptions about black children's behaviour can be seen in the view, for example, that they are most likely to be to blame for, or must have been the first to start, any quarrel; or, more subtly, in the belief that some ethnic groups are less deferential because of 'natural ebullience'.

30 This is a failure to see that when parents speak another language, notes and messages sent out from school only in English could act comparatively to disadvantage them.

31 Who sets the PTA meeting agenda? Does information to parents indicate that decision-making on how the school is to serve the children's needs depends on their advice and votes? Assumptions about 'majority rule' either in the staff room or PTA, can sometimes mask the importance of safeguarding the interests and needs of particular ethnic minority children.

32 It is part of being a non-racist, multi-cultural school to involve 'white' parents in developing the school's policies – to be prepared to explain convincingly to parents the school's educational objectives and what their children gain from a multi-cultural approach in preparation for living in a multi-racial society. (Staff could usefully practise such discussion in role-play.)

33 It is simply prejudice to dismiss *what* a group says because of *who* they are; and it is racist to seek excuses for continuing with school practices whose racist dimension has been brought to the staff's attention.

34 (See pages 7, 9, 57, 83–108.)

35 (See pages 37–44, especially 44.)

36 This is 'cultural imperialism' especially as 'we' expect those with 'other' cultures and languages to learn English as the essence of 'our' culture (see pages 131–132).

37 Not if those parents are not aware of the DES-backed research findings, which demonstrate that standard English is learned better when taught bi-lingually with the mother tongue (see pages 131–139).

38 At least some attempt to learn some of even one language spoken as a mother tongue, other than English, would demonstrate respect for other languages – the vital 'hidden curriculum' message to all the class (see pages 13–15, 136–139).

39 All the more reason for teachers to learn at least one of the languages of their school communities! (See page 122.)

40 No – our job is to re-educate attitudes of whites, whether now or for the future running of our institutions. The job is not to 'help blacks to achieve equal opportunities', it is to help whites – or preferably blacks and whites together – to remove the barriers currently operating against equal opportunities (see pages 171–173).

41 This demonstrates ignorance of the evidence of the additional disadvantage experienced by black youngsters, on top of disadvantages they may share with their white peers as working class, as women, as handicapped, etc.[1] Some local research into job take-ups is likely to give confirmation of this (see pages 8–9, 115–117, and the middle of page 162).

42 While they work for a revolution, which could prove a medium or long term task, left-wingers (no more than right-wingers) should not ignore injustice to blacks in the immediate short term, within the present economic system. In any event, the non-capitalist Soviet Union apparently continues to oppress its Jewish minorities.

43 If racism is prejudice plus power, then can there be racism – as opposed to prejudice – between black minorities in Britain? To the extent there is such prejudice, then that is for those communities to sort out. White people have no business to criticise it until we have dismantled prejudice and racism against black people. In other words, even if these statements were true, it is not a reason for evading our responsibility to tackle the racism of the white community.

44 This suggests that talking to black communities can happen only if they arrange themselves in ways and terms convenient to white people. White British society is split into many different ideological and social and interest groupings – why is it assumed that the black British communities should be any less so?

45 No – whites must be concerned to hold black people's respect, in any disagreement, for the reasons their ideas or proposals are turned down. The aim is for a dialogue of genuine equal respect. This is an essential condition of any attempt to run the school system in a non-racist way.

46 What a cultural impoverishment for the Romans! How much, in any case, have Britons abroad 'done as the Romans do'? Why expect others to do what we do not do, or find difficult to do? The point is made on page 174 that we are not 'Them' and 'Us', we are all a multi-cultural and multi-racial 'Us' in Britain.

47 Multi-cultural and indeed anti-racist teaching is not a new method or subject or educational theory. It is an up-dating, in response to major social transformations, of good teaching practice (see pages 8–9).

48 Perhaps not. But this is not a reason to evade our responsibility at least

to try and run our school as an anti-racist institution (see the middle of page 162). And schools *are* partly responsible for the attitudes of the future generation of adults.

49 This is why parental involvement is so important. Many are victims of mis-education in an earlier generation.

50 (See pages 17, 37–38, 50–55; and *Children and race – Ten years on* by David Milner, Ward Lock Educational.)

51 Leaving aside whether it has ever been right for immigrant groups 'to get a rough time', second and third generation blacks are different from previous children of immigrant parents, in that their blackness of skin remains an identifying feature whether or not they seek to 'integrate' or 'assimilate' themselves. This is why the evidence[1] of unchanging disadvantage for black '2nd and 3rd generations' is so significant.

52 Again, this should not be an excuse for inaction towards a more just multi-racial society; indeed, all the more reason for determination.

53 There is no such thing as a 'colour problem of blacks'; there is a problem of white racism and of dismantling the barriers to equal treatment and to mutual respect (see pages 37–38, and page 208).

54 This is to see multi-cultural education as only cultural enrichment. In any case, it could be useful to ask – how much would be left in a school, if everything of so called 'English' culture was taken out? This could put the question of 'over-emphasis' into perspective.

55 This may demonstrate ignorance of points about housing made by John Rex (see pages 27/28). It may also imply that the trouble arises because the British Asians are there in the first place, rather than because of white racism; or that the trouble is because of 'young hooligans', rather than because of schools' failure effectively to educate against 'mindless prejudice'. Either way is a case of blaming the victim: an evasion of one's own responsibilities.

56 All very true. So have we complained to the producers and editors in charge? And while doing that, are we teaching youngsters in what ways the media has not yet 'got its act together' in reflecting a multi-cultured and multi-racial society with due sensitivity?

57 i) Even if it were wholly true, we cannot be blind to reality in society 'outside school'.
ii) Racism awareness is about white attitudes in both children and adults, that, whether a school has black children or not, lie behind the facts of black disadvantage.

6   How well do whites listen to black people?

In a society blighted by white racism, black people cannot enter a dialogue on equal terms with whites about working jointly towards improving race relations unless those whites can show evidence both of their willingness to learn about the mechanisms of black disadvantaging and of their active determination to combat them – to 'dismantle structural racism'. Before making any new efforts to 'liaise' with black communities, white teachers may benefit from using the checklist, developed from Katz[9], which can be copied and given to any group for personal reflection at home (pages 196–7). You may feel it useful to accompany the checklist with the handout on 'unlearning racism' developed by Ricky Sherover-Marcuse (page 198).

One simple way of raising the question of white people's difficulty in 'hearing' black people's experience can be to ask a group what they remember of the black man who appeared before Lord Scarman at the beginning of the film. The same issue is raised, much more subtly, by the film sequence in *Anglo-Saxon attitudes* illustrating some debate in the Manchester school working party. A year after their report was completed, the working party are clearly concerned to find that despite three years of research, it is not leading to swift or far-reaching changes in teaching practice throughout the school. They are left with a fear that change is too slow 'to counter the tide of racism in society'. Since, as they say, it took the group three years to 'raise their consciousness', the logic is that working parties may not be a very effective way of seeking multi-cultural and anti-racist change in a school: it clearly needs to be organised as a whole staff involvement from the start.

It is interesting that many teacher groups do not see this point at first. In workshops, many have acknowledged that they simply regarded Corinne, the young black teacher, as 'too emotional', 'strident', 'unreasonable in her demands', 'not arguing effectively her own case', even as displaying an 'all too familiar chip on shoulder' attitude. However, other teachers see her as making clear points with commitment, which are (albeit unwittingly) patronisingly and systematically ignored. In discussing their own impressions of the sequence, members of your group might consider:

What points can they remember (a) the black teacher making? (b) the white teachers making? Do they recall more of (b) than (a)? If so, why?

What were Corinne's first words?

What was the response to that, for her, fundamental point?

Why was it completely ignored?

Why do the teachers repeat three times the argument 'if it has taken us three years, we can't blame the rest of the staff . . .'?

Do they think she hasn't heard it or understood it?

Does it serve as a way of not responding to the new points she has raised?

What happens when she starts to explain that 'white liberalism' is to her more dangerous than . . .?

Why was she not asked what she meant?

Is her 'manner' a) partly a symptom of being placed in a false position as 'token' b) partly frustration that there is little acknowledgement to the points she makes c) partly expressive of the fact that there is an emotional dimension to the subject of black children's achievements – and she knows that many black parents have passionate concern about this – but it is a dimension that white people in a 'professional' and institutional setting are embarrassed by, or at any rate, ill-prepared to recognise or acknowledge?

As will have become clear, one indication for a school in a 'multi-ethnic' area of its effort to be non-racist is the extent, both in quantity and quality, of its sharing of power over decision-making with all sections of the community it serves. It has to be admitted that communication difficulties can act as a block or disincentive to the dialogue this implies. White teachers often report that they are uncertain whether they are fully understanding, or are being fully understood by, some black parents, or community spokespeople. Here, an aid can be the film *Crosstalk* (see page 11) or the BBC documentary *Multi-Cultured Talk Swap*, which analyses unconscious cross-cultural communication difficulties which lead to failure of mutual understanding, in particular when white teachers and college staffs meet Asian-born parents or job candidates.

Combating racism – an individual checklist

As an indication of action you may have taken, tick the appropriate column:

YES	NO		
....	....	1	Do I actively seek out more information in an effort to improve my own awareness and understanding of racism (eg talking with others, reading, listening)?
....	....	2	Have I spent some time recently looking at my own attitudes and behaviour as they contribute to, or combat racism around me?
....	....	3	Have I examined my own use of terms or phrases that may be seen by others as degrading or hurtful?
....	....	4	Have I openly disagreed with a racist comment, joke or action among those around me?
....	....	5	Am I determined to take a positive stand, even at some possible risk, when the chance occurs?
....	....	6	Have I become increasingly aware of racist TV programmes, advertising, news broadcasts or press coverage? Have I complained to those in charge?

7 Do I accept that white British are trapped by their own culture and institutions, eg schools, homes, media, government, etc., even when they do not want to be racist?

8 Do I take steps to implement discussions with friends, colleagues, social clubs, or church groups?

9 Have I been investigating political candidates at all levels in terms of their stance and activity against racist government practices, and in terms of their will to secure fully effective implementation of equal opportunities policies?

10 Have I investigated curricula of local schools in terms of their treatment of the issue of racism (also text-books, assemblies, staff, etc.)?

11 Do I contribute to any organisation that actively confronts the problems of racism?

12 Do my buying habits support non-racist shops, companies or persons?

13 Is my school or place of employment a focus for my educational efforts in responding to racism?

14 In particular, have I sought to check whether decisions I'm involved in at work are sensitive enough to the rights and needs of all communities in our area and, where possible, do I share the decision-making with those communities?

15 Have I learnt to listen well, when and if black people raise questions of racial oppression in our society; and to address the questions they are raising?

16 Am I seeking to improve my ability to understand different communities' views as much in terms of their linguistic and cultural assumptions as in my own?

17 Is my union or association branch a focus for my anti-racist action?

18 In particular, is the NUT as a teachers' union right to call on its members to combat racism through their own example – because what I do is as important as what I say?

19 Am I seriously dissatisfied with my own level of activity in combating racism?

Some notes on unlearning racism

Racism is both institutional and attitudinal. Effective strategies against it must recognise this dual character. The *undoing* of institutional racism must be accompanied by the *unlearning* of racist attitudes and beliefs. Here are some *working* assumptions:

1   The systematic mistreatment of any group of people isolates and divides human beings from each other. This process is a hurt to all people. The division and isolation produced by racism is a hurt to people from all ethnic groups. The awareness that there is a division is itself a painful awareness.

2   Racism is not a genetic disease. No human being is born with racist attitudes and beliefs.

3   No young person aquires misinformation by her or his own free choice. Racist attitudes and beliefs are a mixture of misinformation and ignorance which has been imposed upon young people through a process of social conditioning.

4   Misinformation is harmful to all human beings. Misinformation about black people is harmful to all people. Having racist attitudes and beliefs is like having a clamp on one's mind. It distorts one's perception of reality.

5   No individual holds onto misinformation voluntarily. People hold onto racist beliefs and attitudes because this misinformation represents the best thinking they have been able to do, and because no-one has been able to help them out of this misinformation.

6   People change their minds about deeply held convictions under the following conditions: a) the new position is presented to them in a way which makes sense; b) they trust the person who is presenting the new position; c) they are not blamed for having had misinformation.

7   People hurt each other because they have been hurt themselves. In this society we have all experienced systematic mistreatment as young people – often through physical violence, but also through the invalidation of our intelligence, the disregard of our feelings, the discounting of our abilities.

As a result of these experiences we tend both to 'internalise' this mistreatment by accepting it as 'the way things are' and to externalise it by mistreating others. Part of the process of unlearning racism involves becoming aware how this cycle of mistreatment is perpetuated in day-to-day encounters and interactions.

8   As young people we have often witnessed despair and cynicism in the adults around us, and have often been made to feel powerless in the face of injustice.

9   There are times when we have failed to act, and times when we did not achieve as much as we wanted to in the struggle against racism. Unlearning racism also involves understanding those difficulties and learning how to overcome them, without blaming ourselves for having had those difficulties.

10   Racist conditioning need not be a permanent state of affairs. It can be examined, analysed and unlearned. Because misinformation is glued together with painful emotion and held in place by frozen memories of distressing experiences, the process of unlearning this misinformation must take place at an emotional as well as factual level.

11   A crucial part of unlearning racism is the recovery of accurate information about one's own ethnicity and cultural heritage. The process of recovering this will show that we all come from traditions in which we can take justified pride.

7 So what shall we do to combat racism?

The aim of racism awareness exercises is not simply to bring unwitting forms of racism into conscious awareness as a self-indulgent exercise for its own sake, nor simply to make more sense of what LEA policies on multi-cultural education and on equal opportunities mean. They can be justified only as a preparation for a better informed and effective active contribution to combating racism. Many schools have found that such action has to be a whole staff commitment, which in turn depends on each individual accepting responsibility for their own learning in this area of professional development; on a common understanding of the words used in policies; and on full involvement of all in the research, consultations, and decision-making on policy and how it is to be implemented. Any emotions engendered through racism awareness (e.g. defensiveness, guilt, depression) needs to be channelled into energy for action towards change in the social conditions affecting black people, and towards reversing any collusion with institutional racism. Such action will need to be collective (creating allies) as well as individual. So how can it be done?

Anti-racist strategies
The previous exercises are all simply to clear the way for this, the essential stage: what to do next?

a One might ask the group what areas they feel need practical follow-up; write these on the board, seek a consensus on groupings and priorities of these ideas, and then invite them to make up small groups to determine action. There would then be a report back from each group outlining its plans.

b Another way could be to distribute copies of a suitably-spaced page headed
'During the next two weeks; month; term; six months . . .'
At LEA level we should . . .
As a school we should . . .
In my dept. we should . . .
As teachers in class we should . . .
In union or association branches we should . . .
As an individual I shall . . .

Organisation of action could then be built on the result of that questionnaire.

c Tables one and two pages 201–3 are another useful basis for establishing action that is both committed and realistically effective. They give a checklist of factors which need to be present at school level. The tables are simply a collection of statements of the obvious, made by head teachers; but it can help to codify what we already know into a checklist.

They usefully emphasise the need for a many-pronged, multi-faceted strategy, and can assist with reflection and evaluation (have we done this?) (are we doing that?) as well as with preliminary planning. (The tables were compiled in this form by Robin Richardson, to contribute to in-service activities in Berkshire.) You could (a) ask your group, in 2's or 3's, to work through copies of the tables, sharing anecdotally their own experiences of successes (when the right hand column was operating) and of failures (when the left hand column was operating). Or (b) you could cut copies up, giving small groups the jumbled statements (without the headings) and a large piece of paper with glue. They then arrange or piece together the statements under headings they work out for themselves (e.g. one group might describe them as 'the DO's and DON'TS of curriculum development; another group might reveal the interactive, or mutually reinforcing, effects of the factors by arranging them into benign, or vicious, circles). Or (c) you could simply ask groups to improve the lists – what would they add or change?

Evaluation
It might be worth noting that immediate reactions are not necessarily the best guide in evaluating anti-racism training sessions. Many teachers need some time and personal reflection to 'digest' the ideas. A better test of effectiveness is whether the staff/group wish themselves to reconvene, eg six months later, to monitor progress and to share experiences or difficulties, or what they have learned in talking with black and white parents, pupils, and community spokespeople, as a basis for determining their further individual and collective steps of action.[15]

Monitoring would need to cover not just black representation (in the staffroom, in the LEA, in the union or association, in the PTA) and black pupils' achievement, but questions like: Should we find someone like Gus Horsepool to check whether our schooling is impinging on pupils' out-of-school attitudes and behaviour? Do our black pupils now have full confidence, both as individuals and through self help or political organisations, about ways of handling the forms of discrimination they are likely to run into? Do our white pupils, both as individuals and as future employers or future members of unions or political organisations, now have full confidence about tackling the discrimination they are likely to be party to (i.e. are they equipped to identify and expose institutional racism around them?) Have we found effective ways of 'demystifying' the media as a source of pupils' images of a multi-racial society? Perhaps the most crucial test must be whether black parents, in particular, have confidence in the staff, can sense the effects of transformation of the school into an anti-racist 'organism' and are fully involved in all decision-making.

history posters, the 'black and white' exercise and the 'designing a subtly racist school' exercise very useful for increasing understanding of the operation of racism.

4   A session in which the facilitators withdraw and the participants choose their own area to design anti-racist strategies in their own environment where they feel the need to effect change is the most vital part of the course. The feeling of a communal enterprise of joint action to bring about change leaves participants ready to go and become active campaigners against racism in their own schools or local authorities, drawing strength from mutual support and the increased understanding of institutional pressures which they have gained from the course.

Even though these residential workshops last a full two days, participants complained that this was not enough to work through their feelings and review available materials which they could use if setting up their own workshops. It was recognised that in addition to continuing evaluation and modification of the racism awareness programmes which we had designed there was a need for a more intensive and in-depth course of longer duration to train potential trainers and give them the confidence to work with other teachers on racism awareness locally. Such courses are now being planned for 1985.

From a follow-up meeting for participants held in June (1984) we learned there is a need for continuing support for members trying to implement anti-racist activity in their localities, where they can feel very isolated when dealing with the reality in their schools of teachers (and parents) who do not recognise the need for anti-racist understanding or action. We hope to set up a network of anti-racist campaigners through the Union to provide support for each other and exchange information about successful activities undertaken.

Although we feel that ideally local education authorities should be running their own in-service racism awareness courses for teachers, at present there exists a gap in provision and insufficient local expertise to facilitate courses. Until the demand can be met, the Union plans to continue racism awareness training as its contribution to beginning to dismantle the institutional racism of our education system, the power structures which operate to the disadvantage of black pupils and teachers, and the mis-education of white people about the potential contribution of black people to our society.

Note: to obtain copies of those workshop reports, or to borrow racism awareness materials, including the video *Anglo-Saxon attitudes*, as well as details of future workshops, apply to Shirley Darlington at NUT Head Office (see page 211).

Racism – a summary

For this book's final comment we turn to Brenda Thomson, who is seen in *Anglo-Saxon attitudes* and in *Teacher, examine thyself!* guiding the workshop for teachers she pioneered for Bradford LEA in 1980, and upon which much of this chapter has been based. She speaks from experience of teaching in Nigeria, and as a primary school E2L teacher in Bradford. She has also made a detailed study of the school system and its effects on British Asian children in particular, as a post-graduate at Bradford University. In July 1980 she wrote an article about racism awareness:

A West Indian mother put it this way:– 'The Whites have a problem and we are landed with it'. Racism in our society is that combination of ethnocentric prejudice that Whites have with the power to structure society on the basis of it, with Blacks in a subordinate position. In the seventeenth century, this white racism was a relatively comfortable way to deal with the insights of the Reformation concerning human dignity and yet take advantage of developing world trade. It is the institutionalised prejudice that could make black slavery and the colonisation of Africa and India 'laudable'. It is the white supremacy of imperialism that could support exploitative action in the colonies and call it 'civilisation' because the Blacks were perceived as inferior.

All that may seem like history now, but in fact structures of privilege are not dismantled easily. The racist structure of centuries remains, often unperceived by those for whom it is part of their social conditioning, and persisting as a rational means of 'keeping the peace' or of 'being fair'. It is the defence of white majority rights that could only have been established because of black minority subordination.

Blacks have to cope with the problem of racism. Whites, while their privilege is secure, do not have to, yet they are being damaged by it all the time, too. Racism was defined by a report from the U.S. Commission on Mental Health, as the top mental health problem in the States. In Britain, we who exported racism to America with the Pilgrim Fathers have been reluctant to accept that there could be racial prejudice in our fair and liberal society, let alone racial bias and racism. We are damaged though. We have been mis-educated with a false white-centredness. We teach our children that Columbus discovered America and in the same lesson describe the inhabitants of the country coming to greet him. We dodge the dilemma of matching the high ideals we hold of equality, humanity and fraternity with the documented facts of racial disadvantage by denying the endemic nature of racial inequality in our social structure and thus stunting both our ability to act towards equality of opportunity and our human dignity. A social structure is at once impersonal and yet empowered by persons. In Britain today, the racial group that has dominance in decision-making is white.

Racism awareness workshops

In the past, group experience as a learning technique towards better race relations has been of the inter-racial encounter group type. It has concentrated on affective approaches to racial harmony, extolling brotherly love. This does not confront the political component of racism. Further, partly because of this, the groups are likely to be exploiting the minority group members. The Blacks are asked to help the Whites to understand their situation.

Some information-based approaches have been used – the teaching of race relations history to counteract the miseducation; simulation games to give an understanding of the structure of inequality. In schools the current trend is towards a 'multi-cultural curriculum'. Leaving aside the problem of whether a curriculum can really be 'multi-cultural' in a school system that is essentially mono-lingual and that has a statutory Christian input, this has its problems. The multi-cultural curriculum tends to be implemented only in racially mixed schools while all schools would need it. In the hands of most teachers it focuses on minority culture, as with Black Studies, without a complementary focus on white culture. White culture is seen as the norm from which others deviate. It aims to develop a positive sense of identity in minority group children with an underlying assumption that whites do not need to develop one too. Thus, however well-meaning, in practice this too is racist. However, with a choice of either teaching racism by doing nothing since that is the status quo or actively teaching to combat it, the multi-cultural curriculum is a positive step forward. A racism awareness workshop will give the teacher of the multi-cultural curriculum a chance to face the racism in himself/herself and thus to be more effective in using the multi-cultural material in the classroom.

Each participant, enabled by a supportive group leader, builds on his/her own experiences. The aim is to develop attitude change that is affirmed by action. The participants use their newly acquired skills or knowledge as they move through each phase of the awareness process, thus reinforcing the attitude or behaviour change as it is developed. The supportive group is important. Care is taken to avoid a waste of energy in guilt feeling that may arise as awareness of the situation sharpens.

These workshops, incorporating some methods designed by Judy Katz in America[9], combine cognitive and affective learning approaches to enable individuals in a group to share experience with another in order to understand themselves and society better. The aim is that through facing racism they may take useful positive action to combat it. In my experience, a great benefit of these workshops has been the feeling of white group identity that has emerged and a willingness to accept responsibility to work together towards a racially just society[10].

Multi-cultural education

By the 1980's, educational practice has begun to attune itself to the multi-racial school and to consider the possibility of cultural pluralism in the curriculum. This may, in time, affect the assumptions that are mediated through the English language. It seems to me, however, that the 'multi-cultural curriculum', exciting and self-affirming though it may prove to the minority group child, and re-educative for the majority, would be of limited value taught by one who was unaware of its relevance in changing the assumptions of the present school situation. Further, it is of little worth in a racially unjust society unless seen as part of the whole programme of social change. In no way can we as adults teach children to transcend prejudices that we are not even aware of in ourselves, nor school them to live in the kind of racially harmonious society we have lamentably failed to provide ourselves. Hence my own basic emphasis is not so much on curriculum content as on an attitude of respect for those who learn, albeit demonstrated by offering every opportunity through the content of the curriculum for each to gain in dignity. Also, I have become acutely aware, both through study and action, that individual good intentions in the field of race relations are not enough. The subtle effects of institutionalised racism, seen as much in the absence as in the presence of things said and done, are constantly undermining individual effort.

White teachers are still often unaware of how, in playing however implicit or explicit a role in school decision making, in the use of finance, and in control of the curriculum, they are in effect acting to defend the privileged position of whites in our society.

The urgent need in schools would now seem not to be so much to help blacks towards equal opportunities as to stop hindering them.[11]

Reference and materials

There are now (1985) a large selection of books, journals, papers and teaching materials on multi-cultural and anti-racist approaches available at many Teachers' Centres. A selection was outlined in *Race Relations in the School Curriculum* by Gillian Klein in a November 1983 paper available from The Centre for Contemporary Studies, 202 New North Road, London N1 7BL (01-354 1535).

The DES lists many books in *Multi-Racial Education*, Library Booklist 29 (Feb 1984), Room 2/69 Elizabeth House, York Road, London SE1 7PH.

The Runnymede Trust (p 211) offers a reading list *Racism and Discrimination in Britain*.

(1) *Racial disadvantage in Britain* David Smith, Penguin Books, 1977 and *Black and White Britain* Heinemann, 1984.

(2) *Half a chance?* CRE Report, see page 211.

(3) *Racism and reaction* Dr Stuart Hall, in *Five Views of Multi-Racial Britain* available from the CRE, see page 211.
Asians in Britain Dr Bhikhu Parekh, in *Five Views of Multi-Racial Britain* CRE. Dr Parekh's public talk is available as a film for hire from Concord films, see page 211.

(4) *The nature of prejudice* G. W. Allport, Addison-Wesley n.e. 1979.

(5) *A History of Africa*, J. D. Fage, Hutchinson, 1978.
How Europe underdeveloped Africa, Walter Rodney, Bogle-L'Ouverture, 1972 (see page 71).
Black Mother: Africa and the Atlantic Slave Trade, Basil Davidson Penguin Books, n.e. 1980.
Universal History Essay by Geoffrey Barraclough in *Approaches to history* Ed. H. P. R. Finberg. Routledge and Keegan Paul, 1962.

(6) BCM-MONO-PFC, London W1N 3XX.

(7) *The English language is my enemy* Ossie Davis, 1967, reprinted in *Dragons Teeth*, January 1980. *Dragons Teeth* is the quarterly bulletin of the National Committee on Racism in Children's Books. For back copies and subscription: Ravi Jain, 46 High Street, Southall, Middx.

(8) *Portraits of white racism* D. T. Wellman Cambridge University Press, 1977.

(9) *White awareness: handbook for anti-racist training* Judy H. Katz University of Oklahoma Press, 1979. This book includes exercises and discussion points covering all aspects of racism awareness, many of which could be adopted for use in staffrooms or classrooms. This important book for teachers can be obtained in Britain from Housmans Bookshops, 5 Caledonian Road, London N1 (01-837 4473).

(10) The full version of that article *Racism Workshop* by Brenda Thomson was published in *Peace News*, 27 June 1980. That back copy and an article 'I am a white racist' in the pamphlet: *Taking racism personally* are available from Peace News, 8 Elm Avenue, Nottingham.

(11) The full article from which these last three paragraphs are taken, entitled *Racism Awareness Rules – Okay!* was published in *Dragon's Teeth*, March 1981.

(12) *Recognising Racism*, a filmstrip/slide and cassette presentation, setting out the concept of institutional racism, by Dr David Ruddell, is available from MDU, The Bordesley Centre, Stratford Road, Birmingham B11 1AR (021-772 5912). This is a 'British' version by a Birmingham teacher, of the filmstrip and cassette 'From Racism to Pluralism' by Patricia Bidol, available from Racism/Sexism Resource Center for Educators, 1841 Broadway, New York, NY10023.

(13) A black structuralist perspective on racism and its effects in the school system is given in the writings of Chris Mullard, eg *Racism in society and schools*, occasional paper no. 1, Centre for Multi-Cultural Education, University of London Institute of Education, and *Black kids in White schools: Multi-racial education in Britain*, a chapter in Race, migration and schooling ed John Tierney, Holt, Winston and Rhinehard, 1982.

(14) A contrasting 'liberal' perspective is set out in *Ideologies and Multi-Cultural Education*, by Robert Jeffcoate, in *Education and Cultural Pluralism* ed M. Craft (Falmer Press 1984); and in *Ethnic Minorities and Education* (Harper and Row, 1984).

(15) As an example of the start of such a process, see M. Zafar's account of the period 1982–4 at Layton Senior High School for Girls in *Making Waves*, an article in *Multicultural Teaching*, Autumn 1984 (journal available from Trentham Books, 30 Wenger Crescent, Trentham, Stoke-on-Trent, Staffs.).

(16) *Racism Awareness Programme Unit* The unit only runs courses for all-black groups and all-white groups separately. The objectives are:

a) To create awareness among participants of how institutional and personal racism operates in their lives and especially their work settings.
b) To work through this awareness towards identifying practices which counter racist collusion and combat racism.
c) To assist participants to find ways of incorporating such practices into their daily life.

RAPU, 5–5a Westminster Bridge Road, London SE1 7XW (01-261 9010)

(17) *Educational Opportunity in Multi-ethnic Britain*, article by Dr Bhikhu Parekh in *Ethnic Pluralism and Public Policy*, ed. Glaser and Young (Heinemann 1983).

(18) *Some reflections on the concept of Multi-cultural Education*, also by Dr Bhikhu Parekh, in *Multi-cultural Education: the interminable debate*, ed. G. Verma and F. Modgil (Falmer Press, 1985).

Some useful addresses

Commission for Racial Equality (CRE), 10–12 Allington Street, London SW1 5EH (01-828 7022). The Information Department can supply:

1 Fact sheets on racial disadvantage and booklets on ethnic minorities.
2 *Education Journal* for teachers, issued free once a term.
3 A catalogue of films both for teacher training and for use by teachers in multi-cultural schooling.
4 Information about local community relations, councils and ethnic minority organisations.
5 BBC TV's *Five views of multi-racial Britain* – the booklet on the sociology of race relations, which forms a companion volume to this project on multi-cultural education.

National Association of Multi-Racial Education (NAME), Gen Sec. Madeleine Blakeley, 71 Raglan Gdns, Oxley, Watford, Herts WD1 4LJ. Apart from organising conferences and workshops, NAME publishes a newsletter, a journal *Multi-racial education*, and can give information about its local branches.

The London NAME produce a twice termly newspaper *Issues in Race and Education* available from 11 Carleton Gdns, Brecknock Rd, London N19 5AQ.

Concord Films Council, 201 Felixstowe Road, Ipswich, Suffolk (0473 79300) has an important catalogue of films and video tapes on hire both for teacher training and for use in class in multi-cultural schooling.

Schools Publications Office, Thames TV, 149 Tottenham Court Road, London W1P 9LL. Can supply a booklet which accompanies the series 'Our People', widely used by teachers. The six films of Our People, graphically setting out the facts and the history of immigration to Britain, can be hired from Film Forum, 56 Brewer Street, London W1 (01-437 6487).

The Runnymede Trust, 37a Gray's Inn Road, London WC1 (01-404 5266). Send for the list of their research reports and pamphlets relevant to teachers. These include *Britain's black population* (1980), published by Heinemann Educational Books, 22 Bedford Square, London WC1.

NUT, Hamilton House, Mabledon Place, London WC1H 9BD, for statements of union policy, and for copies of *In Black and White*; *Mother Tongue teaching*; *Combating Racism* (advocates development of whole school policy); *Education for a Multi-cultural Society*; and Reports of NUT Racism Awareness Workshops.

ALTARF, Room 216, 38 Mount Pleasant, London WC1X 0AP (see p. 56).

Acknowledgment is due to the following:
FABER & FABER LTD for 'In a station of the Metro' by Ezra Pound;
LAURENCE POLLINGER LTD for extract from 'The red wheelbarrow' by William Carlos Williams from *The collected earlier poems*;
The extract from *Ten quick ways to analyze children's books for racism* is reprinted from *Guidelines for selecting bias-free textbooks and storybooks* by the Council on Interracial Books for Children 1841 Broadway, New York, NY 10023;
The poem 'Baus O' killing' is by Louise Bennett from *Jamaican Labrishe*.
The extract from *White awareness* by Judy H. Katz. Copyright © 1978 by the University of Oklahoma Press.

The photograph on the front cover
was specially taken for the BBC by CAMILLA JESSEL.